LECTURES

ON THE

BRITISH POETS.

BY

HENRY REED.

LATE PROFESSOR OF ENGLISH LITERATURE IN THE UNIVERSITY OF PENNSYLVANIA.

IN TWO VOLUMES.

VOL. II.

PHILADELPHIA:
J. B. LIPPINCOTT & CO.
1860.

STEREOTYPED BY L. JOHNSON & CO.
PHILADELPHIA.
COLLINS, PRINTER.

CONTENTS.

LECTURES ON ENGLISH POETRY.

LECTURE X.

BURNS, (WITH NOTICES OF JOHNSON'S LIVES OF THE POETS.)

LECTURE XI.

CONTEMPORARY LITERATURE.

LECTURE XII.

COLERIDGE.

LECTURE XIII.

SOUTHEY, (WITH NOTICE OF CHARLES LAMB.)

LECTURE XIV.

BYRON.

LECTURE XV.

WORDSWORTH.

MISCELLANEOUS ESSAYS ON ENGLISH POETRY.

ESSAY I.

ESSAY II.

LECTURES ON ENGLISH POETRY.

LECTURE X.

Burns.

(WITH NOTICES OF JOHNSON'S LIVES OF THE POETS.)

Monotony of Pope's verse—The revival of a truer spirit of Poetry—Chatterton—Merit of Cowper—Dr. Johnson's literary dictatorship—His "Lives of the Poets"—Sir Egerton Brydges's criticism on them—Cowper's judgment of them—Johnson's incapacity for poetical criticism—Johnson's judgments on Gray—"London"—"Vanity of Human Wishes"—Percy's "Reliques of Ancient English Poetry"—The character of this poetry—Robert Burns—His boyhood—Early trials—Mossgeil Farm—The freshness of his poetry—Its universality—Wordsworth's lines—The Mountain-Daisy—The Field-mouse—Cotter's Saturday Night—Tam O'Shanter—Mary Campbell—Morality of Burns's poetry—The bard's epitaph—Wordsworth's Lines to the Sons of Burns.

In my last lecture I was constrained to pass, somewhat too hastily, from the poetry of Pope to that of Cowper, thus bringing the earlier portion of the eighteenth century in too close contact with its later period. It has been my aim, throughout this course of lectures, to make it, as far as possible, comprehensive not only of the exposition of the individual poets selected, but of the progress of English poetry in its successive ages, as it has been modified by the influence of genius and the spirit of the times. I propose, therefore, in order not to deviate now from the plan as presented to my own mind at the outset, to endea vour to supply, in a very general way, the chasm in my last lecture between Pope and Cowper. Before proceeding to the chief subject of the present lecture, I wish to dispose in as short a space of some of the omitted subjects. The influence of Pope's poetry, or rather that school of poetry which began with Dryden and was completed by Pope, was unquestionably injurious on all the writers who came within its reach. It reduced poetry to mere versification, and thus, in the hands of pupils who were deficient in the natural powers of the masters, it became mechanical,—a thing of sound, and little else. Besides, the ear was habituated but to one fashion of sound; for Dryden and Pope had spent almost their whole effort upon one form of verse,—the rhyming couplet of the ten-syllable line. They had set English poetry to one tune in the position of its pauses and the balanced succession of the notes, so that every puny versifier could give, if not the same music, at least a very good echo of it. It became a kind of hand-organ operation, in which one hand could grind out the sounds nigh as well as another. Besides this levelling faculty, listening almost exclusively to one fashion of metrical sounds, the ear lost its power of receiving other metres. With the incessant, unrelieved tinkling of the heroic rhyming couplet, the sense of poetical music grew deaf to the richer and varied harmonies in which the elder poets had taken such delight and exhibited such manifold power both in the language and in themselves. The melody of Shakspeare's admirable dramatic blank verse, and the equally appropriate epic blank verse, and the variety of versifications in his smaller poems, ceased to be appreciated; and, when Pope is extolled as having brought verse to perfection, it is forgotten that there is a multitude of other metrical constructions besides that on which he relied. Indeed, when he departed from the one tune he played so sweetly, in other measures he failed egregiously; for, when attempting an unwonted lyrical strain in honour of St. Cecilia, to whom certainly his best music was due, the strain he uttered was one from which the saint herself could scarce have extracted melody; and in that much overrated ode, "The Dying Christian to his Soul," the sound of the verses is at once poor and inappropriate, falling greatly below the solemnity of the subject. But the imitators of Pope risked few such experiments, and followed their model in that species of verse in which he had been so successful that they were willing to consider it the chief and best of English measure, if not the only one worth cultivating. Prosperous as both Dryden and Pope had been in establishing each in his day, and though there have been critics who have praised that species of poetry as the highest order of poetry, it is a school in which not one poet of eminence has risen. In fact, it died with Pope; for, when carried to its legitimate results, it then became obvious how much nature had been sacrificed to art, and how, sooner or later, the heart of the nation craved that nature should be brought home to enjoy her own again. The truth was told in some lines by Dryden :—

> "There is music, uninformed by art,
> In those wild notes which, with a merry heart,
> The birds in unfrequented shades express,
> Who, better taught at home, yet please us less."

Giving to Pope all praise for skill as a versifier in one form of verse, I cannot but consider his metrical powers as greatly overrated, when I remember how limited they were in their application. Indeed, it seems to me conclusive of the sinking of English poetry during that period, that its music was monotonous. The Muse had given up many of her grandest and sweetest notes. Artificial poetical composition needs but a limited set of metres, like a musical instrument with its certain range of keys. But true poetry has its hundred, its unnumbered voices, like nature. The poet needs them all: each one in its true time is ready in his service. How narrow must the scope of poetry have grown when, as with the poets and critics of a considerable part of the eighteenth century, the high-wrought, one-toned verse of Pope attained such exaggerated and exclusive favour! It has not been so with the greatest of our poets; and it is indeed one proof of their greatness that there were perpetually rising, in their spirits, imaginations and thoughts and passions each naturally seeking and finding utterance in varied and appropriate measure. When calling quickly to my memory the vast variety of English metres, the compass of instrumental music seems an inadequate parallel to the many-toned voice of Poetry. I would find it rather in the multitudinous sounds of nature herself,—

"For terror, joy, or pity,
Vast is the compass and the swell of notes;
From the babe's first cry, to voice of regal city,
Rolling a solemn sea-like bass, that floats
Far as the woodlands, with the trill to blend
Of that shy songstress whose love-tale
Might tempt an angel to descend
While hovering o'er the moonlight-vale;
* * * * * *
The heavens, whose aspect makes our minds as still
As they themselves appear to be,

Innumerable voices fill
  With everlasting harmony;
The towering headlands, crowned with mist,
  Their feet among the billows, know
That Ocean is a mighty harmonist;
  Thy pinions, universal air,
Ever waving to and fro,
  Are delegates of harmony, and bear
Strains that support the seasons in their round:
Stern winter loves a dirge-like sound."

Turn to the pages of Pope or of his imitators: the sound comes like the melody from a well-tuned and well-touched musical instrument; but when you listen, with an ear well cultivated by the study of the metrical combination and flow of words, to the measured music that may be heard, either sensibly or imaginatively, from the pages of the greater poets, the sound comes with the touching and ever-varied harmony of nature,—at one time with the loud voice of the stormy wind, again with the soothing murmur of a breeze blowing through the tops of pine-trees; at one time with surges like ocean angry and enchafed, again like the ripples of a lake or river touching the sides of an anchored ship, or the gentle sounds of a running brook.

I notice this subject of versification because the merits of Pope in this department have been, I think, exaggerated in a manner injurious to English poetry, as superseding its noblest and most varied metres. A style of versification was introduced which fascinated the ear, because the tune, though soon monotonous, was not only smooth but marked. If the ear once content itself with this form, it is apt to neglect that cultivation which is essential for the enjoyment of the finest poetical melody in the language. It was a sign of the coming regeneration of English poetry when some appeared who sought other forms of verse than that one which Pope had bequeathed to his imitators. Simultaneous with this was a returning sense of what was due to nature,—an evident desire to quit the path which had been so artificially cut and beaten. Pope's immediate followers had pushed the system to its limits; and readers began at last to ask themselves whether something else was not wanted besides polished language, verse of an unrelieved smoothness, and a certain perpetually-recurring assortment of images, which had become so much the traditional property of the versifiers that a writer could set himself in the business, as any tradesman might supply himself with his stock in trade. People were growing weary of hearing nothing but cold mythological personifications. They scarcely ventured to say so; but, for all that, it was a relief to hear the sun called by his simple almanac-name instead of the loftier prescriptive title of Phœbus. The moon had been known only as Diana. Naiads were as plenty in every watercourse as fish. Dryads were as common as birds; and every west wind that blew, whether it was "the sweet south or the blustering northwester, was a gentle zephyr." The versifiers who took Pope for their model were like the artists who illustrated his poems by carrying the system out to all its consequences. In one of the early editions of his poems there is an engraving prefixed to the "Essay on Criticism," representing some venerable ancient introducing Pope, the little Queen Anne's poet, wrapped in a Roman toga, to the nine Muses, who are seated by the side of a kind of creek, clad in the usual amount of clothing deemed appropriate to the comfort of a Muse,—one of them with a foot in the water and looking up to the sky, and another seated on a small eminence and busy performing on the bass-viol. This was the taste of the times: poetry had set the fashion, and the arts followed in the train.

If Pope was followed by servile imitators, there also came after him poets who, with a truer fervour of inspiration, sought to unfetter the poetry of their country from the technicalities and the artifices which had been woven round it. They were obliged to toil against the influence of established authority and a dominant false taste. Thomson, and Gray, and Goldsmith, and Beattie, and Churchhill, and Collins, contributed to the revival of a truer spirit of poetry, and have left behind them poems which it is much easier for me to find space for in my good opinion than in my lectures. There was Chatterton, too truly

> "The marvellous boy,
> The sleepless soul that perished in his pride."

Hereditary insanity and the frenzy of a frustrated ambition tortured his young heart; and, after having baffled half the learning of Britain by his impostures, he ended his brief agony of life by poison.

The poets of the eighteenth century, especially its latter portion, deserved much for ridding English poetry of its cold formalities and pouring fresh life-blood into it. Especially was this the merit of him whom in the last lecture I presented to you in such a hurried, crowded comment,—the happy, unhappy—the cheerful, melancholy—Cowper.

These poets not only threw off the depressing weight of an artificial taste still remaining from the Anglo-

Gallian school of poetry, but there was an adverse authority, in the literary dictatorship of Dr. Johnson. This authority was exerted not only to the full extent of his colloquial influence, but made still more absolute and more lasting in a work to which I have alluded once or twice in the course of these lectures, and on which I must now dwell for a few minutes.

Let me preface what I have to say either directly or in illustration of Dr. Johnson with the remark that it applies to him solely as a critic of poetry. As the maker of the great Dictionary of our language, he is entitled to the most reverential gratitude of every student of English literature. He has written much excellent morality, and as a man he was kind in deeds while harsh in words. When the late Bishop White, visiting England in early life, was introduced to him, Dr. Johnson said to him, in allusion to the then recent Stamp Act difficulties, "Sir, if I had been prime minister I would have sent a frigate and levelled one of your principal cities." "But," added the bishop, in recording this remark, with the admirable discrimination of a gentle-hearted man, "I heard from him sentiments convincing me he would not have done as he said." The present examination has reference, however, to Dr. Johnson's words, his critical judgments. I have no ambition to stretch myself to the tiptoe height of my small stature to strike a blow at a lofty name. The reputation of Dr. Johnson, and the want of a better work on the subject, has given to his "Lives of the Poets" a circulation which has beyond all question been injurious to the cause of our imaginative literature. It was a luckless day for the poets when they fell into the hands of Samuel Johnson. This work, which it is absolutely necessary for me to notice, because it is the very book which is always resorted to as authority in the history and criticism of English poetry,—this work has an absurdity in the capital letters of its title-page:—"The Lives of the most Eminent English Poets;" and when we open it, to our astonishment, as has been well said, the first name we find is that of Cowley. What has become of the morning star of English poetry? where is the bright Elizabethan constellation? Or, if names be more acceptable than images, where is the ever-to-be-honoured Chaucer? Where is Spenser? Where Sydney? And, lastly, where is Shakspeare. These, and a multitude of others, not unworthy to be placed near them, their contemporaries and successors, we have *not.* But in their stead we have Roscommon, Stepney, and Phillips, and Walsh, and Smith, and Duke, and King, and Sprat, Halifax, Granville, Sheffield, Congreve, Broome, and other, reputed magnates, metrical writers utterly worthless and useless, except as instances to show what a small quantity of brains is necessary to procure a considerable stock of admiration, provided the aspirant will accommodate himself to the likings and fashions of the day. The truth is, that, amidst all the small deer that were herded together by Johnson as the most eminent English poets, Milton is the one solitary poet of high eminence. But the wrong does not stop here. Passing by the consideration that Johnson's registry excludes all but one of the greatest names, and includes all the little ones, or, at the least, abundance of them, the execution of the work is as wrong as the plan. It is full of false canons of criticism,—false, I do not hesitate to say as absolutely as Dr. Johnson could make an assertion,—false because at variance with the unimpeachable authority of the actual poetic inspirations of the great poets. Its incurable defect is an utter absence of imagination: it is a treatise on imaginative literature produced by an unimaginative intellect. Yet it acquired in its day an authority which none dared publicly to question, though there were minds well endowed with the elements of true poetic character which deeply felt what injury was done to the cause. That ardent enthusiast, full of the fervour of genius, Sir Egerton Brydges, who died only a few years ago, has recorded the impression the work made on his mind at the time of its publication. "The appearance of Johnson's Lives," are his words, "damped my spirits and froze the genial flowings of my soul: their captiousness, their hardness, their awkward humour, their affected raillery and capricious contempt, seemed like the burst of discordant sounds upon fairy dreams. If the splendour of Collins could not save him from such rudenesses, what, I thought, must inferior powers expect?" Another witness to a similar feeling, expressed, not after the lapse of years, but promptly, at the time, was Cowper. He revolted especially at Johnson's treatment of Milton, and expresses a meek man's warmest indignation at the critic's injustice. It is in one of the letters in that inimitable epistolary collection, the most natural and agreeable in our literature,—Cowper's Letters,—that he writes in these words, after noticing how he has smeared his canvass in the portraiture of Milton as a man:—"As a poet, Johnson has treated Milton with severity enough, and has plucked one or two of the most beautiful feathers out of his Muse's wings and trampled them under his great foot. I am convinced he has no ear for poetical numbers, or that it was stopped by prejudice against the harmony of

Milton's. Was there ever any thing so delightful as the music of 'Paradise Lost'? It is like that of a fine organ, has the fullest and the deepest tones of majesty, with all the softness and elegance of a Dorian flute,—variety without end, and never equalled. Yet the doctor has little or nothing to say upon this copious theme, but talks something about the unfitness of the English language for blank verse, and how apt it is, in the mouth of some readers, to degenerate into declamation. Oh, I could thrash his old jacket till I made his pension jingle in his pocket!" To this playful vengeance of the gentle Cowper, let me add the belief that Johnson's eulogy of the "Paradise Lost" bears the marks of having been extorted from him, chiefly, I presume, out of deference to Addison's celebrated critical papers on that poem in "The Spectator." He had no sympathy with the highest poetic genius that was contemporary with him. The fine powers of Gray, the elaborate finish of whose poetry, it might be thought, would have pleased him, were disparaged in a style disreputable to a candid critic. The high, aspiring imagination of the unfortunate Collins won no better treatment; and this is lamentable to think of, when we remember how his tender nature suffered for the want of sympathy, the fever of his visionary tremulous spirit turned in the anguish of disappointment to insanity, and his fitful career, closing in the succession of a moody melancholy, a few lucid intervals, and paroxysms of a maniac's violence, when his shrieks were heard in the most appalling manner echoing through the cloisters of Winchester Cathedral.

In all that was wrought by the pen of Dr. Johnson, or all that rolled from his tongue, there is no evidence of his having any apprehension of a high effort of a pure imagination, whether of the earlier great poets or his contemporaries. When he assumed the office of the great critic of English poetry, he ventured on a duty for which he was physically, intellectually, and morally unfit. Physically, because his shortsightedness amounted to a species of blindness, obliging him to hold communion with the visible world through the secondary medium of books. If I remember rightly, he was hard of hearing; he certainly was stone-deaf to the finest metres of English verse,—that sweet music which rises up to the imagination when reading poetry to our silent selves, catching the flow of the verse and beautiful sounds, though in silence as still as a midnight thought. Unless poetry beat stoutly and rattled loudly on the drum of Dr. Johnson's ear, he proclaimed there was no melody in it, as he said of blank verse (spirits of Shakspeare and Milton, what a thought!) that it was verse only to the eye. How far Dr. Johnson's education influenced his character it is not necessary to ask; but there was one of his teachers whose influence may have had some connection with the Johnsonian grandiloquence: this was a man that published a spelling-book and dedicated it to the Universe. Intellectually Dr. Johnson was disqualified for the guardianship of the memory of the poets, because, whatever were his powers of argumentation, no particle of imagination or fancy entered into his constitution. He was perpetually striving to disenchant poetry of all its magic, to strip it of the radiant vestments of its imaginative philosophy, "sky-robes spun out of Iris woof," and wrap it in the coarse, home-spun cloak of his logic. Morally, Johnson was unfit for the lofty task, without, of course, meaning to impeach the uprightness of his character or his piety. It has been said, with great truth, that, as the poet must write in the spirit of self-sacrifice, so the reader of poetry who would rightly feel and enjoy it must in like manner pass out of himself into it. He must forget himself and his own prejudices and predilections and associations, and give himself up to the work he is reading, and try to take his stand on the author's point of view. So that the obstacles which checks the spread of true, genial poetry—of such poetry as carries us out of the purlieus of our own habitual notions into fresh fields of the imagination—is still the spirit of selfishness,—man's unwillingness to abandon his old inveterate preconceptions. Now, taking this principle,—the truth of which must be felt by all,—can there be a moment's hesitation as to Johnson's moral unfitness for poetical criticism? If the principle hold good as to the reader of poetry, how much more as to him who sets himself up for a judge to guide and even command the reading of others! To forget himself and his own prejudices and predilections and associations, to take his stand on the author's point of view, were impossibilities for a nature constituted like Johnson's. It dwelt in the impenetrable centre of his own habitual notions,—in the thick fog of literary bigotry,—taking his stand in himself as the central point, and therefore, for the most part, beholding things in wrong proportions and in false lights. His poetic sympathies were few and contracted; and, instead of that catholic taste which is at once the true critic's power and his exceeding great reward, he was bitter and bigoted in his judgments and rugged in his feelings. What is the entire warp and woof of Boswell's curious biography of him but a tissue of unbroken dogmatism? Perhaps there never was a virtuous man with so much of selfishness. His appetite for argument was as voracious as his physical appetite. I will not say it was meat and drink to him, because his dogmatism was intermitted, and then only in the act of eating. Argumentative triumph was his ambition, his passion; and it would be edifying to observe into how many opinions, strange for a wise and good man, he was led by this overweening self-love, the adoration of his own opinions and tastes. It made him often the advocate even of shallow judgments magnified and mystified by swelling words, and sometimes of dangerous opinions; for instance, his absolute doctrine in these words:—"Contemplative piety, or the intercourse between God and the human soul, cannot be poetical," because, among other sophistical reasons, "the essence of poetry is invention;—such invention as, by producing something unexpected, surprises and delights. The topics of devotion are few." Contemplative piety cannot be poetical! the topics of devotion are few! Why, what in the world had become of the good man's Bible? Mark how Johnson's perpetual intrusion of his own personality, in some shape or other, made him censorious and scornful,—qualities fatal to all genial love of poetry. By it, and the added incense of flattery which his satellites were forever burning beneath his nostrils, the idea of self became an absorbing one. Look at the account of him in social life, seizing upon almost any opinion for the sake of opposition and disputation, with a dangerous recklessness of truth, as if it was a thing that could be safely so tampered with; insulting Garrick, ridiculing poor Goldsmith, treading upon Boswell as if he were, in rough sport, rubbing his huge foot upon a spaniel's back, and then, after monopolizing nearly all the talk to himself, with an inimitable self-complacency exclaiming, "What a fine conversation we have had!"—an exclamation which, considering the monstrous disproportion, was about as appropriate as if, on turning down the last leaf of one of the longest of these lectures, I were to say to you, "What a fine conversation we have had!"

Now, if an admirer of Dr. Johnson should be disposed to think that I have thrown off the bridle of my tongue, let it be remembered what authority his work on the poets has exercised. Let it be borne in mind how he has scattered his harsh and scornful judgments, pronouncing Milton's exquisite "Masque of Comus" a drama inelegantly splendid and tediously instructive; his sonnets, "the best only not bad;" "Lycidas," "vulgar and disgusting;" and undoing his reluctant eulogy of the "Paradise Lost" by declaring its perusal a duty rather than a pleasure, and that we retire harassed and overburdened, besides condemning its diction as harsh and barbarous, and waging perpetual war against what has been well styled eminently the English metre: how he could find in Milton's republicanism nothing but a selfish lawlessness; and how, after the lapse of more than a hundred years, he could venture to say of such a man as Milton, that, omitting public prayer, he omitted all. Let it be remembered, too, that the arch-critic could discover in Gray's fine odes nothing more than what he superciliously calls "a kind of strutting dignity,—a glittering accumulation of ungraceful ornaments, image magnified by affectation, and language laboured into harshness;" and that he dismissed the true poetry of the hapless Collins with the contemptuous opinion that it may sometimes extort praise when it gives little pleasure. These were judgments, too, coming from one who claimed to be himself a poet, esteeming the high-sounding declamation of his "London" and "Vanity of Human Wishes" as poetry, and priding himself upon his hundred lines a day. For all the wrong—unconscious wrong and wilful wrong—that Johnson has done the poets I might take a malicious vengeance in a retaliative censoriousness on some of his own poems. Indeed, I had written something of the sort; but some admirer of Johnson's might say that is ill-natured and has nothing to do with the matter. I think myself it would have something to do with it: but let it pass.

About the same time the "Lives of the Poets" was published, another work was also given to the world, which, though at first coldly received, and by Johnson treated with contempt, was destined to render good service to the cause of English literature. Percy's "Reliques of Ancient English Poetry" has been esteemed by high authorities as one of the chief agencies in reviving a genuine feeling for true poetry in the public mind. The traditionary minstrelsy, ancient ballads, and historical songs were collected, restored, and remodelled, and thus redeemed from their obscurity. It was a poetry which, to its own early generation, had ministered to an important public use by softening, and perhaps chastening, the rudeness of a martial and unlettered people. It was now to serve a widely-different purpose:—to help in restoring nature where it had been displaced by artifice, to give life again to what had grown cold, and to invigorate a poetry which was sickly from excessive refinement.

But this poetry, which Dr. Percy brought in his collection to the acquaintance of scholars and men of reading, had a life elsewhere. It was composed of winged words that had taken their flight from one generation to another. Its home was not so much in books as in floating tradition preserved by affectionate memory. It was a music in the air; for it might be heard sung by reapers in the field one harvest after another, by women lightening with its oft-repeated strains their household labours, by mothers singing over their children, or in some single chanting to a fireside group. It was a poetry dwelling chiefly in the North of Britain, secluded from Southern refinements. There was, for instance, a Scottish gardener's wife, who had an inexhaustible store of the ballads; some simple, solemn ditties, which when she chanted them could bring tears down an old man's cheeks, and others spirit-stirring, at sound of which the fire flashed in the dark eyes of her listening child. That deep dark-eyed Scottish bairn was Robert Burns. His ear was attuned in childhood to the old minstrelsy; the sounds sunk into his spirit to come forth again in after-years, his imagination giving them a more glorious poetry than they had ever echoed to before. The obligation of the poet to his other parent was careful religious instruction, which, if it did not furnish safeguards against sad excesses of his impetuous passions in after-life, at least saved him from ever sinking into the recklessness of a reprobate. He has recorded also a debt of his infant and boyish days to an old woman domesticated under the same humble roof, remarkable, he says, for her ignorance, credulity, and superstition, and having the largest collection in the country of tales and songs concerning devils, ghosts, fairies, brownies, witches, warlocks, spunkies, kelpies, elf-candles, dead-lights, wraiths, apparitions, cantrips, giants, enchanted towers, dragons, and other trumpery. "The household life of Burns's parents is represented in the imperishable portraiture of the 'Cotter's Saturday Night;' and the origin of those stanzas finely exhibits the continued presence of early salutary influences amid the tumultuous passions of the poet's heart." There was, he said, something peculiarly venerable to his thoughts in the phrase "Let us worship God," used by a decent, sober head of a family introducing family worship. That single simple sentiment, thus impressed in early life, was the germ which was expanded by his true poetic imagination into the admirable description above alluded to.

The adversity that befell the elder Burns weighed heavily on the poet's boyhood. In consequence of the father's misfortunes, there fell to the share of the boys more labour than was good for them,—the premature pressure which is too apt to force the young heart out of its true proportions. A good plain education led Burns to a course of reading which might shame many a one with better opportunities. But the poetic instinct in him was awakened, I imagine, less by what he saw on the pages of books than by the traditionary minstrelsy by which he was led along as by the music sung, up in the air, by the invisible Ariel. The earliest stirrings of his powers were rude rhymes half uttered when he was humming the tune, or, in Scottish phrase, crooning to himself, as he has described in one of the familiar poetical epistles he was fond of writing to his friends:—

"Amaist as soon as I could spell,
I to the crambo-jingle fell,
Tho' rude an' rough;
Yet crooning to a body's sell
Does weel enough."

The poetic fire was kindled by another fire; for the first of the long series of his love-stories dates in his fifteenth year, when the boy sought expression in verse for his devotion to his bonny partner in the harvest-field, where it was a Scottish custom to group the reapers in pairs, lad and lass. With one whose heart was like tinder, it was impulse enough to give speech to his imagination. The early trials of his strength were very speedily followed by the ambition of gaining for himself a name, and even more; and this shows how soon the consciousness of his might came to him,—the ambition of producing something to do honour to his country, his slighted country:—

"I mind it weel, in early date,
When I was beardless, young, and blate,
And first could thresh the barn,
Or haud a yokin' at the pleugh,
An' though forfoughten sair eneugh,
Yet unco proud to learn!
When first amang the yellow corn
A man I reckoned was,
An' wi' the lave ilk merry morn
Could rank my rig and lass.

"E'en then a wish, (I mind its power,)
A wish that to my latest hour
Shall strongly heave my breast,—
That I for poor auld Scotland's sake
Some usefu' plan or book could make,
Or sing a sang at least.

> The rough burr-thistle, spreading wide
> Amang the bearded bear,
> I turned the weedin'-heuk aside,
> An' spared the symbol dear."

Burn's first notoriety—his first becoming known, as he said, as a maker of rhymes—came in a way scarcely to have been expected, and less congenial with the spirit of true poetry than the simple effusions of his better feelings. The Church of Scotland was divided into two ecclesiastical parties, who were waging against each other a warfare of words the bitterness of which spread from the manse to the cottage; and, as Burns said, polemical divinity was putting the country half mad. In the midst of a general strife he was not one likely to remain unconcerned. How far he felt a real interest in the discussions of "Auld Light" and "New Light" it would be hard to say; but, be that as it may, it was a chance for him to feed his hungering after a name. He began his impetuous alliance in some of his free-spoken and irreverent productions, which were welcomed, as he described it, with a roar of applause. This was a welcome given—such was the heat of ecclesiastical factions—not only by laity, but by clergy, on the side the poet espoused. These audacious pieces wrought this effect to be noticed in tracing the progress of Burn's genius:—that they developed, and doubtless at the time increased, the nerve and force of his imaginative powers. The influence on the moral side of his genius was much more questionable. The excesses which Burns witnessed among men active in the national church of Scotland exaggerated his hatred of hypocrisy, and, at the same time, a recklessness of public opinion, a palliation of his own misdoings in the belief that the propriety was an assumed and superficial thing, as in the address to the "Unco Guid," or rigidly righteous:—

"O ye wha are sae guid yoursel,
  Sae pious and sae holy,
Ye've nought to do but mark and tell
  Your neebors' faults and folly!
Whose life is like a weel-gaun mill,
  Supplied wi' store o' water,
The heapet happer's ebbing still,
  And still the clap plays clatter."

Or in that better-known stanza,—

"Oh wad some power the giftie gie us
To see oursels as others see us!
It wad frae monie a blunder free us
    And foolish notion:
What airs in dress an' gait wad lea'e us
    And e'en devotion!"

Burns had an ambition to distinguish himself by his conversational powers,—oratory to groups of villagers: this made him a ready disputant in the polemics of the church. That soon passed; but he found another kind of intercourse,—unhappily, a live-long intercourse, with boon companions,—a freer field for his native wit.

"The star that rules my luckless lot
Has fated me the russet coat
And damned my fortune to the groat,
    But, in requit,
Has blessed me wi' a random shot
    O' country wit!"

Occasional intervals of absence from the homestead had early made Burns a looker-on in scenes of freer living than was known in the domains of peasant-life. The fondness for revelry had not yet begun to work its mischief upon him; and, while free from the sting of self-reproach and the misery of a dangerous indulgence, he was able to rouse the feeling of nationality on the subject of Scotch drink, and to give a poetic dignity to distilled liquors. The spirit of Pindar's first Olympic ode—the praise of water and the panegyric on the Sicilian ring—breathes in Burns's stanzas, giving as they do a dignity, a sublimity to strong drink, by a grand effort of imagination in associating it with the dying Highland soldier:—

"Bring a Scotsman frae his hill,
Clap in his cheek a highland gill,
Say such is Royal George's will,
And there's the foe!
He has nae thought but how to kill
Twa at a blow.

"Nae cauld, faint-hearted doubtings tease him.
Death comes; wi' fearless eye he sees him,
Wi' bluidy hand a welcome gies him;
And, when he fa's,
His latest draught o' breathing lea'es him
In faint huzzas.

"Sages their solemn e'en may steek,
An' raise a philosophic reek,
An' physically causes seek,
In clime and season.
But tell me Whisky's name in Greek,
I'll tell the reason."

It seems to have been reserved for Burns, in one of the genial moods of the better part of his life, to give a picture, at once humorous and elevated, of tipsyness :—

> "The clachan yill had made me canty,
> I was na fou, but just had plenty;
> I stachered whyles, but yet took tent aye
> To free the ditches;
> An' hillocks, stanes, and bushes kenned aye
> Frae ghaists and witches.
>
> "The rising moon began to glower
> The distant Cumnock hills out owre;
> To count her horns wi' a' my pow'r,
> I set mysel;
> But whether she had three or four,
> I could na tell."

The most propitious era of the poet's life was that portion of it spent at the Mossgeil Farm. The cottage, with its few acres, had been taken by the two brothers, with the dutiful and affectionate purpose of providing a shelter for their parents and the determination of earning their subsistence by manly labour. It was there made manifest that Scotland was in possession of a great national poet. The early inspirations of the Scottish Muse had been given to the indwellers of a palace,—the ancient King James Stuart; and, after poetry had declined with the decline of the national spirit, in consequence of the union of the two kingdoms of England and Scotland, after the lapse of centuries it was reanimated in the humble clay cottage of Mossgeil Farm. The poet's life was the outdoor-life of a labourer in the fields; he was in perpetual and quickly-sensitive communion with nature; and here especially was gained the glory of the peasant-poet of Scotland. The poetry of Burns was as indigenous as the thistle; it was a pure native growth, as different as possible from the trim, unnatural exotics which had been cultivated with hothouse temperature and method. The freshness of old Chaucer's genius seemed to be breathing again upon British poetry. The long-lost honours given by the chief of the early poets to the lowliest flower of the field, as I noticed in a former lecture, was now restored, when Burns suddenly checked his plough at the sight of the mountain-daisy looking up to him from the mid-furrows. It was a moment of genuine poetic inspiration; for, while actually holding the plough, his imagination fashioned itself into musical words:—

"Wee, modest, crimson-tippèd flower,
Thou's met me in an evil hour;
For I maun crush amang the stoure
Thy slender stem;
To spare thee now is past my power,
Thou bonnie gem.

"Alas! it's no' thy neebor sweet,
The bonnie Lark, companion meet,
Bending thee 'mang the dewy weet,
Wi' spreckled breast,
When upward-springing, blithe, to greet
The purpling East.

"Cauld blew the bitter-biting North
Upon thy early, humble birth;
Yet cheerfully thou glinted forth
Amid the storm,
Scarce reared above the parent-earth
Thy tender form.

"The flaunting flowers our gardens yield,
High sheltering woods and wa's maun shield;
But thou, beneath the random bield
O' clod or stane,
Adorns the histie stibble-field,
Unseen, alane.

"There, in thy scanty mantle clad,
Thy snawie bosom sunward spread,
Thou lifts thy unassuming head
In humble guise;
But now the share up-tears thy bed,
And low thou lies!

"Such is the fate of artless maid,
Sweet floweret of the rural shade!
By love's simplicity betrayed,
And guileless trust,
Till she, like thee, all soiled, is laid
Low i' the dust.

"Such is the fate of simple bard,
On life's rough ocean luckless starred:
Unskilful he to note the card
Of prudent lore,
Till billows rage, and gales blow hard,
And whelm him o'er.

"Such fate to suffering worth is given,
Who long with wants and woes has striven
By human pride or cunning driven
To misery's brink,
Till, wrenched of every stay but Heaven,
He, ruined, sink!

"Even thou who mourn'st the Daisy's fate,
That fate is thine,—no distant date;
Stern Ruin's ploughshare drives elate,
Full on thy bloom,
Till crushed beneath the furrow's weight
Shall be thy doom!"

Who can fail to feel that this was

> "Indeed a genuine birth,
> Of poetry:—a bursting forth
> Of genius from the dust?"

What a strain of truth and imagination, manly and tender-hearted! Compare Burns with Pope in descriptive poetry,—comparison in other departments would be ill-judged,—the grotto at Twickenham with the bleak Mossgeil mountain-side; and how redolent of nature is this little poem! It has the freshness and grateful odour that arises from the new furrows of a ploughed field. In that singular collection, the "Medical Remains of the great Lord Bacon," one of the fanciful prescriptions for the prolongation of life and the renewing of health was, in an early hour, after the sun is risen, to take an air from some high and open place with a ventilation of roses and fresh violets, and to stir the earth with infusion of wine and mint. Poetry in the eighteenth century seemed to need some such renovation; and, after her long confinement in the close air of an artificial system, the peasant-poet of Scotland ministered to her health. When Burns, in the rapt mood of inspiration, was standing with his hand on the plough, how little could he have dreamed that the music thus rising in his heart would wing its flight as far as the English language,—the spirit of every true Scotsman, whether in the centre of British India or at the farthest west of the wilds of America, kindling at the recollection of that one mountain-daisy! The criticism which more than any other delights me is that which may sometimes, though rarely, be discovered in the response made by the imagination of one poet to that of another. Some seven or eight years ago a great poet was travelling through that region of country which has earned even the title of The Land of Burns, and one of those itinerary records which the imagination of Wordsworth has scattered in every land he has visited is in these lines:—

"'There!' said a stripling, pointing with meet pride
Towards a low roof, with green trees half concealed,
'Is Mossgeil Farm, and that's the very field
Where Burns ploughed up the daisy.' Far and wide
A plain below stretched seaward; while, descried
Above sea-clouds, the Peaks of Arran rose
And, by that simple notice, the repose
Of earth, sky, sea, and air, was vivified
Beneath 'the random bield of clod or stone.'
Myriads of daisies have shone forth in flower
Near the lark's nest, and, in their natural hour,
Have passed away, less happy than the one
That by the unwilling ploughshare died to prove
The tender charm of poetry and love."

Another poem, composed under the same circumstances as the "Mountain-Daisy," was that on turning up, with the plough, the nest of a field-mouse. It is conceived in the same vein of imagination, and of feeling the association of the mishaps of his own life with that of the little creature:—

"I'm truly sorry man's dominion
Has broken nature's social union,
An' justifies that ill opinion
    Which makes thee startle
At me, thy poor earth-born companion
    An' fellow-mortal!"

The lesson of generosity, like mercy twice blessed,—to him that gives and him that takes,—is exquisitely told, when he bids the wee thief welcome to nibble at the corn:—

> "I'll get a blessing wi' the lave,
> And never miss't!"

"The Cotter's Saturday Night" was first recited to his brother as they walked together on a Sunday afternoon, a poem which, by its admirable soothing tone of reverence for holy things, a noble tribute to Scottish piety, has best served to shield the poet's memory from harsh judgments on his frailties. With Burns's quick apprehension, he was living a life which placed him in close communion with nature; and, though he delighted chiefly in portraying the stormy aspects of the elements, he did not overlook the minuter appearances worthy also of a poet's eye, as in that admirable piece of humorous imagination and vigorous thought, "The Brigs of Ayr," the couplet describing the formation of ice:—

> "The chilly frost, beneath the silver beam,
> Crept gently—crusting o'er the glittering stream."

And then the passage, rising to a higher strain of fancy, after the talk of the Auld Brig and the New is over:—

> "What further clishmaclaver might been said,
> What bloody wars, if sprites had blood to shed,
> No man can tell; but all before their sight
> A fairy train appeared in order bright;
> Adown the glittering stream they featly danced;
> Bright to the moon their various dresses glanced:
> They footed o'er the watery glass so neat,
> The infant ice scarce bent beneath their feet."

This fairy passage carries me in thought hastily to what Burns always thought, and rightly too, the best of all his productions, the matchless "Tam O'Shanter." Short as it is, it is a great poem, with merits unassailable by the most rigid criticism, and which the most enthusiastic cannot exaggerate. It is wonderful, especially for the power which harmonizes the terrific and the laughable,—a Shakspearian blending of tragedy and comedy. It was the work of a single day, composed by the river-side, where his wife found the bard crooning to himself, and soon, with strange and wild gestures, in a fit of ungovernable joy, bursting out loudly in one of the most animated passages. There is great dramatic power in the poem:—the spirited introduction of the hero; the first allusion to the bewitched spot he was to pass by; the forewarning of witchcraft in his wife's affectionate and cheerful predictions;—

"She prophesied that, late or soon,
Thou would be found deep drowned in Doon;
Or catched wi' warlocks in the mirk
By Alloway's auld haunted kirk."

The arch reference to lengthy conjugal counsels;—

"Ah, gentle dames! it gars me greet,
To think how mony counsels sweet,
How mony lengthened sage advices,
The husband frae the wife despises!"

The convivial exultation of the reprobate and his cronies, set forth in two lines, the most vivid that revelry was ever told in:—

"Kings may be blest, but Tam was glorious,
O'er a' the ills o' life victorious."

The transition from the careless, riotous enjoyment at the warm ingleside, by a different strain, giving one of the happiest imaginative illustrations in the range of poetry;—

"But pleasures are like poppies spread:
You seize the flower, its bloom is shed;
Or like the snow falls in the river,
A moment white,—then melts forever!"

Tam's midnight ride, and his approach to the haunted kirk, after passing several spots, each having its own peculiar awe in some deed of death likely to leave a ghost behind:—where a pedlar had been smothered in the snow; where a drunken traveller had broken his neck; where a murdered bairn was found by the hunters; and where some old woman had hung herself;—

"Nae man can tether time or tide.
The hour approaches Tam maun ride;
That hour of night's black arch the key-stane,
That dreary hour he mounts his beast in,
And sic a night he taks the road in
As ne'er poor sinner was abroad in.
The wind blew as 'twad blawn its last;
The rattling showers rose on the blast;
The speedy gleams the darkness swallowed,
Loud, deep, and lang, the thunder bellowed;
That night a child might understand
The deil had business on his hand.
Weel mounted on his gray mare Meg,
(A better never lifted leg,)
Tam skelpit on thro' dub and mire,
Despising wind, and rain, and fire,
Whiles holding fast his guid blue bonnet,
Whiles crooning o'er some auld Scots sonnet,

Whiles glowering round wi' prudent cares,
Lest bogles catch him unawares;
Kirk-Alloway was drawing nigh,
Where ghaists and houlets nightly cry."

"Heroic Tam," with a drunken heroism, rides on over the haunted ground, his ear beaten by wild, and, thus far, only natural, sounds, the waves of the Doon roaring with an angry flood, the tossing branches of the trees, and the incessant echoing of the thunders, when to his eye, dazzled by quick alternations of lightning and a mirk midnight,—

"Glimmering through the groaning trees,
Kirk-Alloway seemed in a bleeze;
Thro' ilka bore the beams were glancing,
And loud resounded mirth and dancing."

The scene that followed I shall not attempt either to quote or to describe:—witchcraft with all its intensity; what you feel inclined sometimes to laugh at, but, before you venture to do so, a shudder creeps over you at the mention of the Wicked One's horrid playthings; but that hideous image as appalling as any terror in Shakspeare's sorcery:—

"Coffins stood round, like open presses,
That shaw'd the dead in their last dresses;
And, by some devilish cantrip slight,
Each in its cauld hand held a light."

The hideousness of the supernatural scene is aggravated by the introduction of one human being mingling in the spectral revelry,—a woman who had dealings in witchcraft. The scene suddenly changes; for, when Tam's silent amazement gave way to an impudent exclamation of applause at the agility of the beldame dancer,—

"In an instant all was dark,
And scarcely had he Maggie rallied
When out the hellish legion sallied."

The chase by the witches, and Tam's very narrow escape across the running stream with the loss of his gray mare's tail, bring the poem to an appropriate ending. It won an immediate popularity, for it was circulated among the Scottish cottages, and one peasant did not meet another without one or both indulging in quotations. This had been the case also with Burns's earlier poems. Allan Cunningham mentions the fact of his father's having procured the volume from a Cameronian clergyman, with this remarkable admonition:—"Keep it out of the way of your children, John, lest ye catch them, as I caught mine, reading it on the Sabbath." One very remarkable evidence of the popularity of "Tam O'Shanter" is the fact that it made the churchyard of Alloway's old haunted kirk quite a fashionable burial-place; for the neighbouring gentry began to vie with humbler worth and noteless industry, in finding in its little area room for their last resting-place.

I do not attempt to trace the course of Burns's personal story closely, as it is connected with his poetic career, as in the affecting incident of his love for Mary Campbell, and his pathetic lament over her as his "Highland Mary." On every leading event his poetic heart spake from its fulness, as when what he called a bitter blast of misfortune's cold "nor'west" was near driving him from his native land, and he wrote, in obvious allusion to himself, the stanzas "On a Scottish Bard gone to the West Indies:"—

"Auld cantie Kyle may weepers wear,
An' stain them wi' the saut, saut tear;
'Twill mak' her poor auld heart, I fear,
In flinders flee;
He was her laureate monie a year
That's owre the sea.

"He ne'er was gien to great misguiding
Yet coin his pouches wad na bide in;
Wi' him it ne'er was under hiding;
He dealt it free;
The Muse was a' that he took pride in
That's owre the sea.

"Jamaica bodies, use him weel,
An' hap him in a cozie biel:
Ye'll find him ay a dainty chiel,
And fu o' glee;
He wad na wranged the vera deil
That's owre the sea."

The introduction of Burns to Edinburgh society, and his intercourse with it, were hurtful to the moral growth of his genius. It brought him into a closer contact with life, presenting the inequality of human condition, especially amid aristocratic institutions. His own sense of independence, and of his own intrinsic intellectual worth, was strong enough to make him realize social inequality, but not strong enough to raise him above it to a magnanimous contentment:—

"See yonder poor, o'erlaboured wight,
So abject, mean, and vile,
Who begs a brother of the earth
To give him leave to toil.

"If I'm designed yon lordling's slave
By nature's law designed,

Why was an independent wish
E'er planted in my mind?"

Kindly as the peasant-poet was received in Edinburgh, he detected that often in that kindness there was condescension; and, with a sensibility as tremblingly exquisite as his sense was strong, he suspected, as has been remarked by one of his biographers, "that the professional metaphysicians who applauded his rapturous bursts surveyed them, in reality, with something of the same feeling which attends a skilful surgeon's inspection of a curious specimen of morbid anatomy." "I doubt," said Burns himself, in a private record, "whether one man may pour out his bosom, his every thought and floating fancy, his very inmost soul, with unreserving confidence, to another, without hazard of losing part of that respect which man deserves from man, or, from the unavoidable imperfections attending human nature, of one day repenting his confidence." Happy would it have been could Burns have held his spirit at the elevation which he reaches in another strain:—

"It's no in titles nor in rank;
It's no in wealth like Lon'on bank,
To purchase peace and rest;
It's no in makin' muckle mair;
It's no in books, it's no in lear,
To make us truly blest.
* * * * *
"Think ye that sic as you and I,
Wha drudge and drive thro' wet an' dry,
Wi' never-ceasing toil,—
Think ye, are we less blest than they
Wha scarcely tent us in their way,
As hardly worth their while?"

Happier still would it have been could he have realized one of his purest aspirations :—

"To make a happy fireside clime
  For weans and wife,
That's the true pathos and sublime
  Of human life."

The question as to the morality of Burns's poetry may be reduced to a simple statement. That he, in his way of life, departed widely from paths which his conscience vainly persuaded him to, in opposition to ungovernable passions, cannot and ought not to be concealed. He never debased himself to a sottish intemperance, but sought convivial excitement, and the worst relief from morbid bodily affections brought on by premature distress. He has uttered a touching appeal for charitable judgments :—

"Gently scan your brother man,
  Still gentler sister woman;
Though they may gang a kennin' wrang!
  To step aside is human:
One point must still be greatly dark,—
  The moving why they do it:
And just as lamely can ye mark
  How far perhaps they rue it.

"Who made the heart, 'tis He alone
  Decidedly can try us;
He knows each chord—its various tone,
  Each spring—its various bias:
Then at the balance let's be mute;
  We never can adjust it:
What's done we partly may compute,
  But know not what's resisted."

His poetry has been charged—falsely, it seems to me—with a contempt or affectation of prudence, decency, and regularity, and an admiration of thoughtlessness, oddity, and vehement sensibility; in short, with a belief in the dispensing power of genius in all matters of morality. Burns had too much masculine good sense ever to fall into that wretched fallacy. He never so deceived himself. Wild words, indeed, often broke from him; and once, in well-known lines, most wrongly, perhaps somewhat impiously, he pleaded that the light which led astray was light from heaven. But he has written enough of self-condemnation, self-reproach, to show he did not think so. Who can doubt this on reading that sincere and solemn avowal in the stanzas he styled "The Bard's Epitaph?"—as touching a confession as ever was composed:—

"Is there a whim-inspired fool,
Owre fast for thought, owre hot for rule,
Owre blate to seek, owre proud to snool?
Let him draw near,
And owre this grassy heap sing dool,
And drap a tear.

"Is there a bard of rustic song,
Who, noteless, steals the crowds among,
That weekly this area throng?
Oh, pass not by!
But, with a frater-feeling strong,
Here heave a sigh.

"Is there a man whose judgment clear
Can others teach the course to steer,
Yet runs himself life's mad career
Wild as the wave?
Here pause, and, through the starting tear,
Survey this grave.

"The poor inhabitant below
Was quick to learn and wise to know,
And keenly felt the friendly glow
And softer flame;
But thoughtless follies laid him low,
And stained his name.

"Reader, attend: whether thy soul
Soars fancy's flights beyond the pole,
Or darkling grubs this earthly hole
In low pursuit;
Know, prudent, cautious self-control
Is wisdom's root."

That grave for which this epitaph in fancy was meant has been visited by those who perhaps deemed the poor inhabitant below to have been no better than a miserable drunkard, by others who wrongly condemned him for having perverted his great endowment to the vindication of moral lawlessness. It has been, too, visited phrenologically. The phrenologists, as Allan Cunningham sarcastically describes the affair, disinterred the skull, applied their compasses, and satisfied themselves that Burns had capacity equal to the composition of "Tam O'Shanter," "The Cotter's Saturday Night," and "Mary in Heaven." "Oh for an hour of Burns for these men's sakes!" exclaims a kindred spirit: "were there a witch of Endor in Scotland, it would be an act of comparative piety in her to bring up his spirit: to stigmatize them in verses that would burn forever would be a gratification for which he might think it worth while to be thus brought again upon earth." All mankind have heard of the malediction which Shakspeare utters from his monument, and of the dread which came upon the boors of Stratford-upon-Avon as they presumed to gaze upon his dust. No such fears, however, fell upon the craniologists of Dumfries. The clock struck one as they touched the dread relic: they tried their hats upon the head and found them all too little, and, having made a mould, they deposited the skull in a leaden box, carefully lined with the softest materials, and returned it once more to the hallowed ground.

The grave has been visited by those who brought a better power and a better purpose,—a poet and his sister. He has described their finding it in a corner of the churchyard; and, looking at it with melancholy and painful reflections, they repeated to each other his own verses beginning—

"Is there a man whose judgment clear?"

He, taking the music of that epitaph, has given what is at once the best tribute to the dead and the best warning to the living. I know of no fitter close for this lecture than Wordsworth's lines "To the Sons of Burns, after visiting their father's grave."

"'Mid crowded obelisks and urns,
I sought the untimely grave of Burns:
Sons of the Bard, my heart still mourns
With sorrow true;
And more would grieve, but that it turns
Trembling to you!

"Through twilight shades of good and ill
Ye now are panting up life's hill;
And more than common strength and skill
Must ye display
If ye would give the better will
Its lawful sway.

"Hath nature strung your nerves to bear
Intemperance with less harm, beware!

But if the poet's wit ye share,—
Like him can speed
The social hour,—of tenfold care
There will be need.

"For honest men delight will take
To spare your failings for his sake;
Will flatter you,—and fool and rake
Your steps pursue,
And of your father's name will make
A snare for you.

"Far from their noisy haunts retire,
And add your voices to the quire
That sanctify the cottage fire
With service meet:
There seek the genius of your sire;
His spirit greet.

"Or where, 'mid 'lonely heights and hows,'
He paid to nature tuneful vows,
Or wiped his honourable brows
Bedewed with toil,
While reapers strove, or busy ploughs
Upturned the soil.

"His judgment with benignant ray
Shall guide, his fancy cheer, your way;
But ne'er to a seductive lay
Let faith be given,
Nor deem that 'light which leads astray
Is light from heaven.'

"Let no mean hope your souls enslave;
Be independent, generous, brave:
Your father such example gave,
And such revere;
But be admonished by his grave,
And think and fear!'

LECTURE XI.

Contemporary Literature.

The present age not an unpoetical one — Five names worthy of distinction — Samuel Rogers — The "Pleasures of Memory" — Rogers's "Italy"—Galileo and Milton — Moore's Songs — Irish patriotism—The true question respecting poetical composition—Lamb's lines on the "Old Familiar Faces"—Scott's career of authorship—Scott the second in rank of Scottish poets—His childhood at Sandy Knowe—His early reading—His interview with Burns—Influence of the Story of the Rebellion of 1745 on his genius—His love of natural scenery—The minstrelsy of the Scottish border—Hallam's remark on the Scottish ballads — Story of Christie's Will—"The Lay of the Last Minstrel"—Scott's merit as a poet——Influence of the French Revolution on his mind—"Marmion"—"The Lady of the Lake"—Decline of his poetical powers—"Bonny Dundee"—"Battle of Otterburne"—His pilgrimage to Italy.

THIS course of lectures, so kindly and patiently followed by you, has now brought us to the limit of the poets of a past generation. The lives of those two true poets who were last considered reached the closing years of the last century,—the death of Burns having taken place in the year 1796, and that of Cowper in 1800. The mind naturally draws a boundary-line which separates them from the poets of the present century and our own times. The remaining lectures will be appropriated to some of our contemporaries who have devoted their genius to the cultivation of that vast and noble field of English literature we have been travelling over.

It is quite an habitual opinion to characterize the generation of the nineteenth century as unpoetical; and in many respects, it must be confessed, the censure is well directed. But when the philosophic critic of some future age shall seek to judge us, the judgment will be a different one. We are apt to form our estimate with minds diverted to the countless agencies visibly at work around us,—to the various manifestations of the busy, bustling, superficial temper of the times, which leads men to seek the unsure and brief support of mere expedients, instead of the constancy and security of abiding principles. There are perpetually obtruded on our notice some traits of the times, showing the race occupied rather with the world of sense than with strenuous efforts of thought or high aspirations of imagination. But these—the more obvious characteristics—are temporary; they pass away, and in their place remain those which are more durable. When some future literary historian shall come to write the character of his ancestry in the early portion of the nineteenth century, he will seek for evidences of that character, not in such things as from time to time flash upon us, awakening some admiration or amazement, but in the surviving literature of the generation, and especially in the imaginative department of it, which, gaining a wider and more permanent command of the sympathies, has therefore a more lasting life. It endures from age to age, and to it men of other times are apt to look as the mirror of the generation to which that literature belonged. It is a somewhat vain and perhaps presumptuous thing to attempt to gain futurity for a point of imaginative vision, and thus anticipate the judgment of posterity. As far as we may indulge in such speculation, we may fancy some eye, as yet unborn, conning what is now the fair page of some fresh book, but then turned into the "sere and yellow leaf;" and if it should chance to be a page on which is inscribed some shallow piece of pride in the superiority of the age,—some ostentation of the incomparable advancement of physical science or the mechanic arts, or of universal education and the march of mind, or some loud boasting of political regeneration,—it might prompt the compassionate smile at such ebullitions of inordinate and short-sighted vanity; short-sighted, because these are matters in which, great as may be the achievements of one generation, they are usually outstripped and set aside by those of a succeeding generation. From such manifestations of our character we might be pronounced a sensuous, unimaginative generation,—self-centered, self-seeking, self-satisfied, prone to divorce the present from both past and future, breaking covenant with the mighty dead by irreverent violation of time-honoured institutions and usages, as being, according to the phrase, behind the times, and not looking with prophetic eye to days that are to come. But the chief evidence of the character of an age is sought in its literature; and, contemplating that of our times, the writer of some distant day will find that there flourished during the early period of the nineteenth century a numerous company of poets, and among them not a few truly inspired, who would do honour to any age. Indeed, unimaginative and unpoetic as we are, too often, in the habit of considering the generation of our own times, if we measure both the amount and merit and variety of the poetry which has been produced within the last thirty or forty years, this age, in the annals of English poetry, is surpassed only by the golden age of Queen Elizabeth, with which, indeed, it may not inappropriately be compared.

The list of successful poets in our times is, in truth, a registry which contrasts finely with the poverty of several former periods; and, on approaching what may be called our contemporaries' poetry, I have found a necessity of making some selection from a numerous company of poets who would all be entitled to consideration in a more extended course. I have, therefore, chosen five names as worthy of chief distinction, hoping to be able occasionally to present some incidental notices of those to whom more space would, under other circumstances, be due. The choice names—chosen not without reflection, and with regard to their eminence and their influence—are the names of Scott, Coleridge, Southey, Byron, and Wordsworth. The ranks of the poets of the nineteenth century have been already thinned by death. Of the five names just repeated but two survive, and only one in the unimpaired possession of his genius. That one has witnessed the passing away of his brother bards, in quick succession too, within the last few years,—a speedy action of death, not lost upon the thoughtful imagination of the survivor:—

"Like clouds which rake the mountain summit,
Or waves that own no curbing hand,
How fast has brother followed brother
From sunshine to the sunless land!

"Yet I, whose lids from infant slumbers
Were earlier raised, remain to hear
A timid voice, that asks, in whispers,
Who next will drop and disappear?"

Byron, and Scott, and Coleridge, and Crabbe, and the Ettrick Shepherd, as he is called, to escape the unpoetic name of James Hogg,—and Mrs. Hemans, each having filled a space in the literature of this century, are in their graves. The survivors, not a few in number, are for the most part mute in song as the dead; but, to appreciate the extent of living poetic power, it is only necessary to recall the names of Rogers, and Campbell, and Moore, and Milman, and Southey, and Wordsworth, to say nothing of some others of good repute.

It is a noticeable fact that among the poets of our days the one who first gained an honourable award of reputation, the first and oldest of them all, is still among the living, "a worthy and a prosperous gentleman,"—the poet Samuel Rogers. He came into public notice as the author of the "Pleasures of Memory," which appeared during the last century; and he is now living in cheerful and esteemed old age, after a life of purity and affluent elegance, on the verge of eighty years. He stands truly the patriarch of the poets of the nineteenth century; and, as such, honour should first be done to him before I pass on to the chief subjects of this and the succeeding lectures.

Rogers's first poem was produced at a time most propitious to the acquisition of a general popularity. It was a period of poetical dearth. The career of Burns as well as of Cowper were wellnigh over when this poem upon the pleasurable emotions of memory was cordially and widely welcomed to supply a void in the public mind.

It was on a theme of universal interest and of ready comprehension, and abounding in a succession of pleasing pictures, rather than presenting any lofty efforts of imagination; and, therefore, it is not surprising that it should have won, under such circumstances, a widespread favour. At the present day, or even somewhat later than the publication of the "Pleasures of Memory," I do not think it could have secured so favourable a reception. There has since been so much of the stronger inspiration that the avenue to a poetic reputation is by no means so open to entrance. Indeed, this is shown by the state of popular opinion respecting some of Rogers's later poems. His "Italy," for example, seems to me to show a far more vigorous and cultivated imagination,—to be, in a word, a greatly superior poem to his first poem; but Rogers's name became first known as the Poet of Memory, and as such will it be preserved. Passages of genuine poetry are scattered through his "Italy," giving it a higher value than is perhaps recognised. It is a descriptive poem, finely enriched, as descriptive poetry should be, with moral associations, in the present case arising chiefly from historical and biographical allusions. The interesting visit of the young Milton, a traveller in Italy, to the aged Galileo, is thus introduced and fitly touched:—

"Nearer we hail
Thy sunny slope, Arcetri, sung of old
For its green wine,—dearer to me, to most,
As dwelt on by that great astronomer,

Seven years a prisoner at the city-gate,
Let in but in his grave-clothes. Sacred be
His cottage; (justly was it called the jewel!)
Sacred the vineyard where, while yet his sight
Glimmered, at blush of dawn he dressed his vines,
Chanting aloud, in gaiety of heart,
Some verse of Ariosto. There, unseen,
In manly beauty, Milton stood before him,
Gazing with reverent awe,—Milton his guest,
Just then come forth, all life and enterprise;
He in his old age and extremity,
Blind, at noonday exploring with his staff;
His eyes upturned as to the golden sun,
His eyeballs idly rolling. Little then
Did Galileo think whom he bade welcome;
That in his hand he held the hand of one
Who could requite him,—who would spread his name
O'er lands and seas,—great as himself, nay, greater:
Milton as little that in him he saw,
As in a glass, what he himself should be,
Destined so soon to fall on evil days
And evil tongues,—so soon, alas! to live
In darkness, and with dangers compassed round
And solitude."

[There is a break in the manuscript here, which I have found it impossible to repair. Diligent search has been made for the missing matter, but without success.—Ed.]

In the last lecture I had occasion to make some remarks on the subject of lyrical poetry, and its demand for a highly-musical versification and a variety of rhythm. The remarks were connected with the higher department of lyrical composition,—the Ode,—but now lead me to mention slightly the numerous contributions of a living poet to another department of lyrical poetry. No English writer, that I am aware of, has produced so many songs as Moore. Familiar, too, by musical accompaniments, they have gained a wide popularity by the alliance of many a sweet voice that has sung them. But, as a matter of poetry and not of music, a good song is an exceedingly rare production. In the whole extent of English poetry the number is quite small. Moore, prolific song-writer as he has been, has written much fewer of decided merit than would be supposed, considering the success they have had. When you come, for instance, to read over his "Irish Melodies," you find too much elaboration, too much of art,—strains of overwrought and artificially-stimulated fancy. They want the simplicity, the natural impulse and emotion, the bird-like utterance, which characterize the song of the true lyrical poet. The musical accompaniments of Moore's songs have served not only to give them their due effect, but also to conceal their faults. This is perceived when they are simply read. But, at the same time, the poet's merit is considerable in the variety of his versification, and many of his songs display his skill in developing the compass of English metres. The following stanzas are much simpler in style than Moore's usual strain, and a more peculiar measure than he often uses. With something of his bright fancy, they are not devoid of a pleasing plaintiveness:—

"Bright be thy dreams! May all thy weeping
Turn into smiles while thou art sleeping!
Those by sea or death removed,
Friends who in thy spring-time knew thee,
All thou'st ever prized or loved,
In dreams come smiling to thee!
There may the child whose love lay deepest,
Dearest of all, come while thou sleepest;

Still be the same,—no charm forgot,
Nothing lost that life had given;
Or, if changed, but changed to what
Thou'lt find her yet in heaven!

There is much more of the true poetic fire in some of Moore's national than in his amatory lyrics. They glow with a very impetuous fervour of patriotism,—Irish patriotism, of which it has been said, half in jest and half in earnest, that it is something very like British treason. Be that as it may, when his theme is poor, misruled, poverty-stricken Ireland, there is the air and tone more of reality in his effusions. They come more from the heart, as seems to be the case with these energetic lines:—

"Oh, where's the slave so lowly,
Condemned to chains unholy,
Who, could he burst
His bonds at first,
Would pine beneath them slowly?
What soul, whose wrongs degrade it,
Would wait till time decayed it,
When thus its wing
At once may spring
To the throne of Him who made it?
Farewell, Erin! farewell, all
Who live to weep our fall!

"Less dear the laurel growing
Alive, untouched, and blowing,
Than that whose braid
Is plucked to shade?
The brows with victory glowing
We tread the land that bore us;
Her green flag glitters o'er us;

The friends we've tried
Are by our side,
And the foe we hate before us!
Farewell, Erin! farewell, all
Who live to weep our fall!"

Let me take this opportunity to remark that Moore's poetry may well serve to illustrate the difference between true natural feeling and that bright and often delusive reflection of it which our language supplies a very apt term to describe,—sentimentality. It is a counterfeit resemblance of sentiment, and very current in poetry. There are few points on which it is more important for the reader to be able to discriminate between the reality and the shadow, especially as they are often separated by almost imperceptible lines. Moore, for instance, has written a great number of very pretty things; but the reader must have a low estimate of the art who supposes that it is merely pretty things which constitute good poetry. Often the fancy is touched, and it will be thought the heart is touched too, when in truth its pulses may be beating all the while as sluggishly as ever. The gentle and even pulsations of sentimentality are very often mistaken for the strong stirrings of the feelings; and, if that confusion were done away with, it is wonderful how much false and sickly poetry would be done away at the same time. The reader of poetry is often exposed to this imposition; for there are writers whose delight it is to dally with the feelings, as if they were mere playthings, to be tricked out in the finery of pretty words and figures and affectations; whereas a genuine emotion is a strong and simple utterance from the very depths of the poet's heart, arrayed, it may be, but not encumbered, by the glory which his imagination gives to it. There are a great many verses in the literature of all nations in which the display of sentiment is considerable, but it is all on the surface. It is the thin soil of sentimentality, fit only to sustain the growth of a few slight flowers. We should be prepared, therefore, to ask ourselves the question respecting poetical composition, "Is there real feeling here?" We should seek to satisfy ourselves that the poet truly and imaginatively experienced the emotion for which he asks our sympathy, and that it is not mere affectation and exaggeration. Nor is it always easy to discriminate; for sentimentality is not so much an absolute mockery of real sentiment as it is sentiment dressed up in fine clothes. Besides, it is to be borne in mind that a powerful emotion, when joined with a strong imagination, will grasp at thoughts and images which might be judged too remote, but which it makes its own. This is one of the most natural and legitimate functions of the poetic faculty, and which reconciles the highest acts of the imagination with the most sincere and deepest feeling. This is, I believe, a kind of mystery to some persons who are inclined to doubt the possibility of a man's feeling strongly what he expresses in verse, as if poetry were universally an empty shadow,—an unreal imitation of real emotions. So very often it is; and this makes it necessary to distinguish. It is a matter of very serious misapprehension in the reading of poetry; and, as the materials for illustration are at hand, let me briefly exemplify. Those lines of Charles Lamb on the "Old Familiar Faces," which I have this evening repeated, express a feeling which has, I presume, been experienced by every one who is now listening to me,—that painfully hollow sense of destitution when there comes across us the memory of faces familiar to some former period of life; the craving after the departed; the missing of something which had been a portion of our very selves, incorporated in our existence. Several of the stanzas go on to mention the memory of what has been and never more will be. This is told in language as simple as possible, — just such words as the feeling would express itself in, finding natural utterance in earnest conversation, being only distinguished by a metrical construction of equal simplicity. But suddenly, as the feeling is dwelt upon, the imagination expands, and, as the shadowy recollections of childhood—memories of the old familiar faces—throng around him, the mourner feels the spectre-like haunting of the scenes of childhood, and his loneliness makes the earth a very desert:—

"Ghost-like I paced round the haunts of my childhood,
Earth seemed a desert I was bound to traverse,
Seeking to find the old familiar faces."

This strikes me as a genuine burst of true imaginative emotion. No one can for a moment doubt the perfect sincerity of the poet's feelings. By the side of it let me place a piece of fanciful, sentimental poetry,—a fair specimen of that sort,—turning on much the same memory of departed youth and gladness. It is one of Moore's melodies,—well-known verses, and so familiar, no doubt, to the ears of many of you in connection with their musical accompaniment, that they may sound rather oddly under the rude handling of criticism:—

"Oft in the stilly night,
Ere slumber's chain has bound me,

Fond memory brings the light
   Of other days around me:—
      The smiles, the tears
      Of boyhood's years,
   The words of love then spoken;
      The eyes that shone,
      Now dimmed and gone,
   The cheerful hearts, now broken.
Thus, in the stilly night,
   Ere slumber's chain has bound me,
Sad memory brings the light
   Of other days around me.

"When I remember all
   The friends, so linked together,
I've seen around me fall,
   Like leaves in wintry weather,
      I feel like one
      Who treads alone
   Some banquet-hall deserted,
      Whose lights are fled,
      Whose garlands dead,
   And all but he departed.
Thus, in the stilly night,
   Ere slumber's chain has bound me,
Sad memory brings the light
   Of other days around me."

In passing to the consideration of the chief name to be presented in this lecture, let it be remembered that that brilliant chapter in English literature, the Waverley Novels, is not comprehended within the scope of the present course. That Scott's principal fame will rest upon them I entertain no doubt; but we have at present to deal only with the character of his poems. Scott's career of authorship was probably the most amazing that has ever been witnessed in any country, whether we consider it with reference to its almost inexhaustible fertility, its substantial remuneration, or its wide-spread popularity and the innocent gratification afforded to an incalculable number of readers. His poems form comparatively but a small proportion of all his productions. The rapid and brilliant popularity of Scott's poetry has been eclipsed by his imaginative prose, and thus people have often allowed themselves to judge of that poetry carelessly, disregarding it as a thing gone by and superseded. That is hardly fair; for poetry which had won a general admiration by no unworthy arts is entitled to a more deliberate judgment to know both the grounds of that popularity and the causes of its decline. Turning, then, away from the Waverley Novels as from a subject unconnected with this course of lectures, interesting as a general criticism of them might be, I must confine myself to the consideration of the character of Walter Scott as a poet.

In my last lecture I had occasion to allude to the influence of the traditionary minstrelsy in the development of Burns: it was an influence still more strikingly manifested upon the character of Scott, the second in rank of the Scottish poets. The succession had been quickly followed; for it was in the very year of Burns's death that Scott's first attempt in verse was published. His first attempts were not successful, for they were made in a track not truly congenial for the development of his powers. His first impulse was taken, not from the indigenous poetry of his own land, but from the ballads of German poets,—a foreign literature which acquired a short-lived popularity in the closing years of the last century. Imitation of the German ballad-poetry was not the true direction of the young poet's genius, which was destined to receive an impulse more effectual because more Scottish. The study of the ballads of some of the German poets was a mere matter of fashion among the literary circles of Edinburgh society; and Scott, quick in his apprehensions, was naturally affected by it for a season.

A much more abiding influence had begun earlier, and is to be traced back to a very early period of his life. In his second year, by a sudden paralysis, Waltes Scott was a cripple for life, the unformed strength of the tottering infant having then been stricken by a malady of old age. Among various remedies, he was sent from Edinburgh to dwell for a time in the open air of a neighbouring farm, where the regimen which invigorated his sickly frame wrought manifestly on his genius. It was at Sandy Knowe that his education began, his first teacher an illiterate shepherd, and the infant-school the rough ground of a Scottish sheepfold. When the old man went forth to watch the flocks as they browsed upon the hills, the child was carried along; and Scott long after said it was his delight to roll about upon the grass all the day long in the midst of the flock, and that the fellowship he thus formed with the sheep and lambs had impressed his mind with a degree of affectionate feeling towards them which lasted through life. Such, with his earliest consciousness of existence, was the beginning of his education,—the shepherd and the shepherd's dog and the flock his daily companions. But, more than this, he was thus placed in familiar intercourse with nature herself; and no one can divine how it is that the material world around us exercises its influence upon the spiritual world within us. It is no overstrained fancy to say that the senses of the little child began even then to be tributary to his imagination and his moral being. For what an image of the poet's childhood is presented in the tradition illustrative of such influences, which tells of his having been one day forgotten among the knolls in a thunder-storm, and being found lying on his back, clapping his hands at the lightning, and crying out "Bonny! bonny!" at every flash!

Another part of his education consisted of the old songs and tales familiar to his daily companions as the lore appropriate to the spot itself; for the summit overhanging the farm-house commanded the prospect of a district of which it was said every field had its battle and every rivulet its song. With these the child became familiar, thus, no doubt, acquiring much before he could read. But, besides his communings with the outward world, and with the minstrelsy with which, it may be almost said without exaggeration, the air was filled, there is one reminiscence which shows that his mind must early have dwelt with some earnestness on the pages of books. A lady writes to Mr. Lockhart that she distinctly remembers a sickly boy sitting at the gate of the house of one of his relatives, with his attendant, when a poor mendicant approached, old and woe-begone, to claim alms. When the man was retiring, the servant remarked to Walter that he ought to be thankful to Providence for having placed him above the want and misery he had been contemplating. The child looked up with a half-wistful, half-incredulous expression, and said, "*Homer was a beggar.*" "How do you know that?" said the other. "Why, don't you remember," answered he,—

> "'Seven *Roman* cities strove for Homer dead,
> Through which the living Homer begged his bread'?"

The lady smiled at the "*Roman* cities;" but already

> "Each blank in faithless memory void
> The poet's glowing thoughts supplied."

This is a small matter, and so, in one sense, are all things respecting children; but there seems to us a ray of true genius in such thinking of so mere a child,—the finding in beggary an association between the idea of Homer and the mendicant, and then by a process of imagination investing the Scotch pauper with somewhat of the dignity of the prince of bards.

With Scott, the influence of tuition—that which is often exclusively styled education—bore an unusually small proportion to the self-education on which his genius chiefly relied. This was, perhaps, in some measure of necessity the case, for the ordinary school-process, at first delayed by his bodily infirmity, was interrupted by the general feebleness of his health. The boy, however, had acquired an impetuous love for reading, and the bent of his intellect was shown by the mastery he gained over the region of imaginative literature. While yet a mere stripling, he had peopled his mind with the old romances, the legendary poetry, the "Arabian Nights," and the loftier visions of the English poets. All this was undirected; and it was only a turn for historical pursuits, which never forsook him, that he conceived saved his mind from utter dissipation. Still, the boy's appetite for works of imagination, fierce as it was, was too healthy to feed on trashy fictions. His spirit, taking its first impulse from the Border-song, then roved at will through the fantastic realms of Oriental fiction, the gorgeous gallery of the

"Fairy Queen," the spheres of the "Paradise Lost," and the world revealed upon the pages of Shakspeare.

An interesting evidence of the extent of Scott's early reading, comprehensive not only of the chief English poets, but of many of inferior rank, may be noticed in his reminiscence of his one interview, if it may be so called, with his great predecessor Burns. When the peasant-poet, then in the full flush of his fame, paid his first visit to Edinburgh, Walter Scott was a lad of about fifteen years of age, and was present, on one occasion, when Burns was entertained in the most accomplished society of the Scottish metropolis. There chanced to be shown a print representing a soldier lying dead on the snow, his dog sitting on the one side, and on the other his widow with a child in her arms; underneath these lines:—

"Cold on Canadian hills or Minden's plain,
Perhaps that parent wept her soldier slain,
Bent o'er her babe, her eye dissolved in dew.
The big drops, mingling with the milk he drew,
Gave the sad presage of his future years,
The child of misery baptized in tears."

Burns was much affected by the print, and asked whose the lines were. It chanced that nobody remembered, except young Walter Scott, that they occurred in a scarcely-known poem by Langhorne. He modestly whispered the information to a friend, who mentioned it to Burns. The kind look with which it was acknowledged was a pleasurable recollection for Scott many a year after.

Scott's poetical character was not only greatly fashioned by the influence of the traditionary minstrelsy, but it was impregnated by an intense nationality; and this may also be traced to a very early period of his consciousness. During his residence at the farm-house, besides the border-legends, the mingled fact and fiction of a remote age, the child's thoughts were made familiar with the nearer story of the sufferings of his countrymen some thirty years before, in the Rebellion of 1745. The vengeance which triumphant England wreaked upon Scotland was freshly remembered by many; and, as the child listened to the narratives of the atrocities which fastened on the victor the horrid title of the "Butcher Cumberland," there sprang from his childish sympathy a deep affection for his injured country. The smouldering fires of Scottish resentment had burst forth in two wide-spread rebellions in support of the banished family of Stuart, and the power of England over the prostrate cause of the Pretender was maintained by the bloody penalties which followed the victory at Culloden. The Duke of Cumberland, hardened in the trade of war, carried English vengeance into every sphere of life: the cottage-hearths were wet with slaughter, and the sounds that went up from the glens of Scotland were the shrieks and the death-moans of famishing women and children. In the language of Smollett's fine lyric, uttered at the time,—

"When the rage of battle ceased,
The victor's soul was not appeased:
The naked and forlorn must feel
Devouring flames and conquering steel!
No strains but those of sorrow flow,
And nought is heard but sounds of woe;
Whilst the pale phantoms of the slain
Glide nightly o'er the silent plain."

Now, it was in this history that the infant spirit of

Walter Scott was nursed; and it is no marvel that thus was kindled in his breast a fervid Scottish feeling, that went out only with the flame of life. It entered into his childish games, as described in one of the poetical epistles prefaced to "Marmion:"—

"While, stretched at length upon the floor,
Again I fought each battle o'er;
Pebbles and shells in order laid
The mimic ranks of war displayed;
And onward still the Scottish Lion bore,
And still the scattered Southron fled before."

From his childhood Walter Scott was trained to be in all his heart a Scotchman. There was much the same feeling as kindled the early aspirations of Burns:—

"E'en then a wish, (I mind its power,)
A wish that to my latest hour
Shall strongly heave my breast,—
That I for poor auld Scotland's sake
Some usefu' plan or book could make,
Or sing a sang at least."

Walter Scott's poetry is full of this spirit of nationality, —a mixture of national pride and that peculiar feeling, the filial piety of her children for "poor auld Scotland."

Scott's love of natural scenery, especially when associated with historic incidents, had its origin, no doubt, when he was residing in childhood at the farm-house amid the romantic localities at Sandy Knowe. A part of his boyhood was spent in another romantic neighbourhood, within sight of the meeting of two superb rivers,—the Tweed and Teviot, both renowned in song,—the ruins of an ancient abbey, and the more distant vestiges of Roxburgh Castle. "To this period," he writes, "I can trace distinctly the awaking of that delightful feeling for the beauties of natural objects which has never since deserted me. The romantic feelings predominating in my mind naturally rested upon and associated themselves with these grand features of the landscape around me, and the historical incidents or traditional legends connected with many of them gave to my admiration a sort of intense impression of reverence which at times made my heart feel too big for my bosom. From this time the love of natural beauty, more especially when combined with ancient ruins or remains of our fathers' piety or splendour, became with me an insatiable passion, which, if circumstances had permitted, I would willingly have gratified by travelling over half the globe."

Such were the dawnings of the genius of the last and greatest of the border minstrels. It had long been Scott's delight to gather, wherever he could glean them, the traditions and fragments of the ancient ballads of his own land. These researches, carried on without any definite ulterior object, were storing his imagination with the wealth he was at a future day to pay back a thousand-fold increased. One of his companions in excursions through the region of the Border describes the process well in saying, "He was making himself all the time, but didna ken, may be, what he was about, till years had passed. At first he thought of little, I dare say, but the queerness and the fun." The accumulation of these relics at length led to the conception of the minstrelsy of the Scottish border, and that work decided Scott's whole career: it was the impulse which moved his genius; it made him a poet; it made him the magician of the Waverley Novels. While engaged in the task—no task, but a delight—of editing the legendary ballads, he gathered about him the materials on which his imagination was to dwell during a career of authorship as astonishing as any the world has known. One of the critics of the day prophetically said that the minstrelsy contained the elements of a hundred romances; and afterwards, at the time when Waverley was a new book and the authorship was a mystery, Professor Wilson exclaimed, "I wonder what all these people are perplexing themselves with: have they forgotten the prose of the minstrelsy?" No one acquainted with that ancient poetry, now accessible in various collections, can fail to appreciate the influence it must have exercised in the development of Scott's powers,—a point on which we may avail ourselves of the opinion of one of the calmest and most philosophical critics of the age. Mr. Hallam, in his recent invaluable work on the literature of Europe, remarks:—"The Scottish ballads of an historical or legendary character, especially the former, are ardently poetical: the nameless minstrel is often inspired with an Homeric power of rapid narration, bold description, lively or pathetic touches of sentiment. They are familiar to us through several publications, and chiefly through the minstrelsy of the Scottish border, by one whose genius those indigenous lays had first excited, and whose own writings, when the whole civilized world did homage to his name, never ceased to bear the indelible impress of the associations that had thus been generated."

Scott's first purely-original ballads were much more in the vein of German than of Scottish poetry, being highly coloured with the supernatural. The compilation of the minstrelsy brought him home to his true path. It was not a work of mere compilation and collection; for the imperfect traditions often required remodelling and renovation,—a process of great delicacy and difficulty. It demanded original imaginative power, combined with a modest subordination to the tone of the ancient song. This was an admirable school for the training of such talent as Scott was gifted with. It even encouraged a bolder and more vivid strain of composition than he would have ventured on in his early avowedly original writings; for, assuming the position of the ancient minstrel, he spoke with an ancient freedom and fervour. Many of the ballads were completed by him where lines or stanzas were wanting, but the skill with which Scott adopted the style and spirit of an earlier age is especially shown in one which may be considered almost entirely as a modern imitation from his pen, for he speaks of it as not being of unmixed antiquity, but written from the remnant of a few stanzas current upon the border in a corrupted state. The exploit which forms the subject of it has been told also in Scott's agreeable prose. In the reign of Charles I., when the moss-trooping practices were not entirely discontinued, a borderer called Christie's Will was taken on some marauding party and imprisoned in the Tolbooth of Jedburgh. The Earl of Traquair, hearing of it, inquired the cause of his confinement; to which Will replied he was imprisoned for stealing two *tethers*. On being more closely questioned, he acknowledged an omission in his first confession,—the fact of there having been a delicate colt at the end of each tether. The joke amused the earl and gained the prisoner's release. Some time after, a lawsuit came on in which it was known that the opinion of the presiding judge was unfavourable to Lord Traquair's interests.

The point to be gained, therefore, was to keep the judge out of the way; and the earl had recourse to Christie's Will, who at once offered his services to kidnap Lord Durie, the obnoxious justiciary. This was accomplished by Will's suddenly seizing the judge from his horse while riding on the sands of Leith, muffling him in a large cloak, and then escaping into a secluded quarter, where he deposited his weary and terrified burden in an old castle in Annandale. During his confinement in the vault of the castle the only sounds he heard were a shepherd calling his dog and an old woman talking to her cat,—sounds he mistook for the invocations of spirits. The judge's horse being found, it was concluded the rider had been thrown into the sea; his friends went into mourning, and a successor was appointed on the bench. Lord Traquair gained his lawsuit, and Christie's Will was ordered to set the judge at liberty. This was effected in a manner equally mysterious, so that the judge and his friends were fully persuaded that he had been spirited away by witchcraft. Scott, taking these facts and the very imperfect fragments of the lost ballad, has given one of the most successful of the modern imitations:—

"Traquair has ridden up Chapelhope,
  And sae has he down by the Grey Mare's Tail,
He never stinted the light gallop
  Until he speered for Christie's Will.

"Now Christie's Will peeped frae the tower,
  And out at the shot-hole keeked he;
'And ever unlucky,' quo' he, 'is the hour
  That the warden comes to speer for me!'

"'Good Christie's Will, now have nae fear!
Nae harm, good Will, shall hap to thee;
I saved thy life at the Jeddart air,
At the Jeddart air frae the justice tree.

"'Bethink how ye sware, by the salt and the bread,
By the lightning, the wind, and the rain,
That, if ever of Christie's Will I had need,
He would pay me my service again.'

"'Gramercy, my lord,' quo' Christie's Will,
'Gramercy, my lord, for your grace to me!
When I turn my cheek and claw my neck
I think of Traquair and the Jeddart tree.'

"And he has opened the fair tower-gate
To Traquair and a' his companie;
The spule o' the deer on the board he has set,
The fattest that ran on the Hutton Lee.

"'Now, wherefore sit ye sad, my lord?
And wherefore sit ye mournfullie?
And why eat ye not of the venison I shot
At the dead of night on Hutton Lee?'

"'O weel may I stint of feast and sport,
And in my mind be vexéd sair;
A vote of the cankered Session Court
Of land and living will make me bare.

"'But if auld Durie to heaven were flown,
Or if auld Durie to hell were gane,
Or . . . . if he could be but ten days stoun,
My bonny braid lands would still be my ain.'

"'O, mony a time, my lord,' he said,
'I've stown the horse frae the sleeping loon;
But for you I'll steal a beast as braid,
For I'll steal Lord Durie frae Edinburgh town.

"'O, mony a time, my lord,' he said,
'I've stown a kiss frae a sleeping wench;
But for you I'll do as kittle a deed,
For I'll steal an auld lurdane aff the bench.'

"And Christie's Will is to Edinburgh gane;
At the Borough Muir then entered he;
And, as he passed the gallow-stane,
He crossed his brow and he bent his knee.

"He lighted at Lord Durie's door,
And there he knocked most manfullie;
And up and spake Lord Durie sae stour,
'What tidings, thou stalward groom, to me?'

"'The fairest lady in Teviotdale
Has sent, maist reverent sir, for thee;
She pleas at the session for her land, a'haill,
And fain she wad plead her cause to thee.'

"'But how can I to that lady ride
With saving of my dignitie?'
'O, a curch and mantle ye may wear,
And in my cloak ye sall muffled be.'

"Wi' curch on head and cloak ower face,
He mounted the judge on a palfrey fyne;
He rode away, a right round pace,
And Christie's Will held the bridle-reyn.

"The Lothian edge they were not o'er,
When they heard bugles bauldly ring,
And, hunting over Middleton Moor,
They met, I ween, our noble king.

"When Willie looked upon our king,
I wot, a frighted man was he!
But ever auld Durie was startled mair,
For tyning of his dignitie.

"The king he crossed himself, I wis,
When as the pair came riding bye
An uglier crone and a sturdier loon,
I think, were never seen with eye.

"Willie has hied to the tower of Greæme,
He took auld Durie on his back;
He shot him down to the dungeon deep,
Which garred his auld banes gie mony a crack.

"For nineteen days and nineteen nights,
Of sun, or moon, or midnight stern,
Auld Durie never saw a blink,
The lodging was sae dark and dern.

"He thought the warlocks o' the rosy cross
Had fanged him in their nets sae fast;
Or that the gypsies' glamoured gang
Had lair'd his learning at the last.

"'Hey! Batty lad! far yaud! far yaud!'
These were the morning sounds heard he;
And ever 'Alack!' auld Durie cried;
'The deil is hounding his tykes on me!'

"And whiles a voice on Baudrons cried,
With sounds uncouth and sharp and hie
'I have tar-barrelled mony a witch,
But now, I think, they'll clear scores wi' me!'

"The king has caused a bill be wrote,
And he has set it on the Tron :—
'He that will bring Lord Durie back
Shall have five hundred merks and one.'

"Traquair has written a privie letter,
And he has sealed it wi' his seal :—
'Ye may let the auld brock out o' the poke;
The land's my ain, and a's gane weel.'

"O, Will has mounted his bonny black,
And to the tower of Greæme did trudge;
And once again, on his sturdy back,
Has he hente up the weary judge.

"He brought him to the council stairs,
And there full loudly shouted he,
'Gie me my guerdon, my sovereign liege,
And take ye back your auld Durie!'"

From the minstrelsy of the border naturally grew the "Lay of the Last Minstrel,"—the first of Scott's important poems, with which his career of prolific and prosperous authorship began. It is a poem which was due, like "Cowper's Task," to a woman's suggestion. I am very much disposed to rank it first in merit as well as time of Scott's poetical productions. Certainly it at once presented the prominent traits of his character as a poet. "The Lay of the Last Minstrel," "Marmion," and the "Lady of the Lake," all won a speedy and wide popularity. There was an animation about them which gave to all readers delight; but after a while it began to be discovered that it was a pleasure not to be sustained at its first elevation: the poems did not bear that repeated and repeated reperusal which the highest order of poetry always admits of. Then people were begging back the fame they had given with such open hand.

This makes it necessary to judge more carefully of the real character of Scott's poetry. Certainly it has no pretensions to be classed with the greatest productions of the art. Admirable as were his powers, he did not possess that sage and meditative imagination—the rare endowment of "the vision and the faculty divine"—which alone constitutes the inspiration of the greatest poets. But, having taken the true measure of his own strength, that which he attempted he achieved; and his poems have set him beyond the reach of rivalry as the descriptive bard of a period of history and legend rich in adventure and romance. They are full of the martial spirit which was a predominant passion with him; and to no one could be more aptly appropriated the lines of a bard of ancient Greece,—

> "If the glory of their days,
> Their strength of arm, their steely war,
> Be the chosen theme of praise,
> Let any score a leap for me afar;
> And he shall see
> With what a lightsome knee
> My bounding sinew springs:
> The mighty eagle beats his wings,
> And, lo! he is beyond the sea."

The character of Walter Scott's poetry admits of a very specific and express statement. Its chief merit lies in its power of description and narrative. Beyond this it does not pass into the region of the deep passions of human nature. He is the descriptive poet of the manners and society of some former ages. Numerous passages of the most vivid description might be cited. One may be mentioned,—as fine a piece of descriptive poetry of its kind as could be found in the whole range of poetry:—the night-ride of William of Deloraine to Melrose Abbey, in the "Lay of the Last Minstrel." It is something of a risk to break the continued flow of the passage; but I must venture one or two fragments of it:—

"Unchallenged thence, pass'd Deloraine
To ancient Riddel's fair domain,
Where Aill, from mountains freed,
Down from the lakes did raving come,
Each wave was crested with tawny foam
Like the mane of a chestnut steed.
In vain; no torrent deep or broad
Might bar the bold moss-trooper's road;
At the first plunge the horse sunk low,
And the water broke o'er the saddle-bow;
Above the foaming tide, I ween,
Scarce half the charger's neck was seen,
For he was barded from counter to tail,
And the rider was armed complete in mail;
Never heavier man and horse
Stemmed a midnight torrent's force.
The warrior's very plume, I say,
Was daggled by the dashing spray;
Yet, through good heart and our Ladye's grace
At length he gained the landing-place."

The midnight opening of the grave of the wizard, Michael Scott, is given with fine effect:—

"Full many a scutcheon and banner riven
Shook to the cold night-wind of heaven
Around the screenèd altar's pale;
And there the dying lamps did burn
Before thy low and lonely urn,
O gallant chief of Otterburne,
And thine, dark Knight of Liddesdale!
O, fading honours of the dead
O, high ambition lowly laid!

* * * *

An iron bar the warrior took,
And the monk made a sign with his withered hand
The grave's huge portal to expand.
With beating heart to the task he went;
His sinewy frame, o'er the gravestone bent,

With bar of iron heaved amain,
Till the toil-drops fell from his brow like rain.
It was by dint of passing strength
That he moved the massy stone at length.
I would you had been there to see
How the light broke forth so gloriously,
Streamed upward to the chancel roof,
And, through the galleries, far aloof,

* * * *

And, issuing from the tomb,
Showed the monk's cowl and visage pale,
Danced on the dark-browed warrior's mail
And kissed his waving plume.
Before their eyes the wizard lay
As if he had not been dead a day.

* * * *

Now, speed thee what thou hast to do,
'Or, warrior, we may dearly rue;
For those thou mayest not look upon
Are gathering fast round the yawning stone!'
Then Deloraine, in terror, took
From the cold hand the mighty book,
With iron clasped and with iron bound;
He thought, as he took it, the dead man frowned:
But the glare of the sepulchral light
Perchance had dazzled the warrior's sight."

The escape of the soldier from the supernatural spot into the fresh morning air fitly closes the description:—

"The knight breathed free in the morning wind,
And strove his hardihood to find.
He was glad when he passed the tombstones grey
Which girdled round the fair Abbaye!

* * * *

Full fain was he when the dawn of day
Began to brighten Cheviot grey;
He joyed to see the cheerful light,
And he said Ave Mary as well as he might."

Scott's second poem showed another influence at work upon his mind. Although just entering manhood when Europe was startled by the outbreak of the French Revolution, he appears not to have been much affected by that great convulsion. With the times that succeeded it was widely different.

The mighty military genius of Bonaparte was sweeping in every direction with the swiftness of a destroying wind. In every quarter of Europe—to borrow a figurative illustration from a usage in times of danger in ancient Greece—might be seen on the walls of the towns the signal of torches waved in tumultuous consternation. It is an interesting fact in Scott's history that his authorship began when the military fervour was at its height. Napoleon's meditated invasion of Great Britain was stirring the latent energies of the nation. Among his own countrymen Scott saw the ancient martial spirit of their ancestors—the decline of which he had mourned over—reanimated, and, like the spectre of the elder Hamlet, bursting its cerements and starting from the tomb in arms. Edinburgh was converted into a camp; citizens of all classes wore the military dress, and upwards of ten thousand volunteers were constantly under arms, and beacon-fires were kept in readiness along the coast and through the mountains. In all this Scott took a large and active part. The zeal with which he shared in the military movements of his countrymen suggested to him afterwards that spirited chapter at the close of "The Antiquary," describing the false alarm from the mistaken firing of one of the beacons. The notes added to that fine novel, after the lapse of many years, still manifest the same deep feeling in recording some interesting recollections of that agitating period :—

"Through the border counties the alarm spread with rapidity; and on no occasion, when that country was the scene of perpetual and unceasing war, was the summons to arms more rapidly obeyed. In Berwickshire, Roxburghshire, and Selkirkshire, the volunteers and militia got under arms with a degree of rapidity and alacrity which, considering the distance individuals lived from each other, had something in it very surprising: they poured to the alarm-posts on the sea-coast in a state so well armed and so completely appointed, with baggage, provisions, &c., as was accounted by the best military judges to render them fit for instant and effectual service. . . . . Two members of the Selkirkshire yeomanry chanced to be absent from their homes and in Edinburgh on private business, when that corps made a remarkable march. The lately-married wife of one of these gentlemen, and the widowed mother of the other, sent the arms, uniforms, and chargers of the two troopers, that they might join their companions at Dalkeith. The author was very much struck by the answer made to him by the last-mentioned lady, when he paid her some compliment on the readiness which she showed in equipping her son with the means of meeting danger, when she might have left him a fair excuse for remaining absent. 'Sir,' she replied, with the spirit of a Roman matron, 'none can know better than you that my son is the only prop by which, since his father's death, our family is supported. But I would rather see him dead on that hearth than hear he had been a horse's length behind his companions in the defence of his king and country.'

The writer mentions what was immediately under his own eye and within his own knowledge; but the spirit was universal, wherever the alarm reached, both in Scotland and England."*

This was the period of the composition of "Marmion." Many of the most energetic descriptions were conceived while he was in quarters with the cavalry; and it was his delight, while composing, to walk his powerful steed up and down upon the Porto Bello sands, within the beating of the surge, and now and then plunging in his spurs, to go off as at the charge, with the spray dashing about him. This was the hot enthusiasm of a soldier-poet; and the fruit of it was the most stirring description of a battle that ever was realized by a poet's imagination to the imagination of his reader. The passage is too well known for me to quote from; but observe the admirable representation in these four or five lines of the approach of the Scottish army:—

"Nor martial shout nor minstrel tone
 Announced their march: their tread alone,
 At times one warning trumpet blown,
  At times a stifled hum,
 Told England, from his mountain-throne
  King James did rushing come!"

But the single stroke of description which, more than any other, shows Scott's mastery in this department of poetry, is that vivid appeal to the imagination in the first intimation of Marmion's fate. As a matter of fact, nothing is told of him; as a matter of imagination, every thing is told in the lines,—

* Notes to "The Antiquary."

"Fast as shaft can fly,
Bloodshot his eyes, his nostrils spread,
The loose rein dangling from his head,
Housing and saddle bloody red,
Lord Marmion's steed rushed by."

In noticing the martial tone of Scott's poetry, I am reminded of a tribute paid to one of his poems which is one of the finest acknowledgments on record to the power of verse. When the "Lady of the Lake" was published, Scott's friend, Captain Adam Ferguson, was serving in the Peninsular War. When a copy of the poem reached him, he was posted on a point of ground somewhere on the lines of Torres Vedras, exposed to the enemy's artillery. "The men were ordered to lie prostrate on the ground. While they kept that attitude, the captain, kneeling at their head, read aloud the description of the battle in the sixth canto, and the listening soldiers interrupting him only by a joyous huzza whenever the French shot struck the banks close above them."

Was ever poem recited under such circumstances?—enough of danger for pleasurable excitement, with enough of security for attention.

What a subject for the painter,—for Wilkie, for instance, a friend both of Scott and Ferguson, familiar, too, as he chances to be, both with Scottish character and Spanish landscape. The Highlanders, not unused to a minstrelsy, grouping around the reader, interchanging looks of sympathy and delight; the sturdy soldier casting off a tear, half angry at his inability to check the proverbial sympathy of a mountaineer at the mention of his distant home, the hills and the lakes of Scotland brought before him by the poet's question,—

"Where shall he find, in foreign land,
So lone a lake, so sweet a strand?"

Some one, perhaps, waving his arm at the same time with a half-uttered huzza, as the shot from the enemy's battery scatter the broken branches of the olive-tree over the group; others, more impetuous, starting from their recumbent posture as the array of Scottish standards is called up by these lines :—

"Is it the thunder's solemn sound
That mutters deep and dread?
Or echoes from the groaning ground
The warrior's measured tread?
Is it the lightning's quivering glance
That on the thicket streams?
Or do they flash on spear and lance
The sun's retiring beams?
I see the dagger-crest of Mar,
I see the Moray's silver star
Wave o'er the cloud of Saxon war
That up the lake comes winding far.
To hero bound for battle-strife,
Or bard of martial lay,
'Twere worth ten years of peaceful life,—
A glance at that array!"

After the "Lady of the Lake," Scott found his popularity waning, and perhaps his poetic resources exhausted; for he was not a man to recognise a poet's solemn responsibility of cultivating his imagination by laborious meditation. The power he had employed with such brilliant success never left him. He was the minstrel still, even in his later years, when calamities weighed heavily upon him. On one occasion, amid his commercial difficulties, he chanced to be reading the historical account of Claverhouse, Viscount Dundee's, leaving Edinburgh, in 1688, and making a last and dying effort to rally the Highlanders in support of the house of Stuart. It inspired the animated stanzas of "Bonny Dundee." "I know not," he wrote in his diary, "what could have induced me to take a frisk so uncommon of late as to write verses. I suppose the same impulse that makes the birds sing after the storm is blown over."

"To the Lords of Convention 'twas Claver'se who spoke :—
'Ere the king's crown shall fall, there are crowns to be broke;
So let each cavalier who loves honour and me,
Come follow the bonnet of bonny Dundee!'
Come, fill up my cup; come, fill up my can;
Come, saddle your horses and call up your men;
Come, open the west port and let me gang free,
And it's room for the bonnets of bonny Dundee!

"Dundee he is mounted and rides up the street,
The bells are rung backwards, the drums they are beat
But the provost, douce man, said 'Just e'en let him be;
The gude town is well quit of that deil of Dundee!'
Come, fill up my cup, &c.

"As he rode down the sanctified bends of the Bow,
Ilk carline was flying and shaking her pow;
But the young plants of grace they looked couthie and slee,
Thinking 'Luck to thy bonnet, thou bonny Dundee!'
Come, fill up my cup, &c.

"With sour-featured Whigs the Grass-market was crammed,
As if half the West had set tryst to be hanged;
There was spite in each look, there was fear in each ee,
As they watched for the bonnets of bonny Dundee!
Come, fill up my cup, &c.

"The cowls of Kilmarnock had spits and had spears,
And lang-hafted gullies to kill cavaliers;
But they shrunk to close heads, and the causeway was free
At the toss of the bonnet of bonny Dundee!
Come, fill up my cup, &c.

"He spurred to the foot of the proud castle-rock,
And with the gay Gordon he gallantly spoke:—
'Let Mons Meg and her marrows speak twa words or three,
For the love of the bonnet of bonny Dundee!'
Come, fill up my cup, &c.

"The Gordon demands of him which way he goes:
'Where'er shall direct me the shade of Montrose!
Your Grace in short space shall hear tidings of me,
Or that low lies the bonnet of bonny Dundee!
Come, fill up my cup, &c.

"'There are hills beyond Pentland, and lands beyond Forth;
If there's lords in the Lowlands, there's chiefs in the North:
There are wild Dunnies wassals three thousand times three
Will cry '*hoigh*' for the bonnets of bonny Dundee!
Come, fill up my cup, &c.

"'There's brass on the target of barkened bull-hide;
There's steel in the scabbard that dangles beside;
The brass shall be burnished, the steel shall flash free,
At a toss of the bonnet of bonny Dundee!
Come, fill up my cup, &c.

"'Away to the hills, to the caves, to the rocks,
Ere I own a usurper I'll couch with the fox:
And tremble, false Whigs, in the midst of your glee:
You have not seen the last of my bonnet and me!'
Come, fill up my cup, &c.

"He waved his proud hand, and the trumpets were blown,
The kettle-drums clashed, and the horsemen rode on,

Till on Ravelston's cliffs and on Clermiston's lee
Died away the wild war-notes of bonny Dundee!
 Come, fill up my cup; come, fill up my can
 Come, saddle the horses; come, call up the men;
 Come, open your gates, and let me go free,
 For it's up with the bonnet of bonny Dundee!"

It is curious to observe how, when beneath their enormous load Scott's mind began to fail, his memory clung to the ancient minstrelsy, although it lost its hold of some of his own compositions. On hearing the verses from "The Pirate," set to music,—

"Farewell! farewell! The voice you hear
 Has left its last soft tone with you;
Its next must join the seaward cheer
 And shout among the shouting crew!"—

he said, "Capital words! Whose are they? Byron's, I suppose." But, on visiting the ruined castle of Douglas, he repeated his favourite of the old ballads,—"The Battle of Otterburne;" and the closing stanza left him in tears:—

"'My wound is deep; I fain would sleep;
 Take thou the vanguard of the three,
And hide me beneath the bracken-bush
 That grows on yonder lily lee.'
This deed was done at the Otterburne
 About the dawning of the day:
Earl Douglas was buried by the bracken-bush,
 And the Percy led captive away."

A more striking proof of the tenacity to the strains which had been familiarized to his ear in childhood occurred on his hopeless pilgrimage to Italy. There were pointed out to him the Lake of Avernus, the Temple of Apollo, the Lucrine Lake, Baiæ, Misenum, and the surrounding monuments: and what was the reply? The fragment of a Jacobite ditty. "I found," says his companion, "that something in the place had inspired recollections of his own beloved country and the Stuarts; for he immediately repeated, with a grave tone and with great emphasis,—

'Up the craggy mountain and down the mossy glen,
We canna gang a milking for Charlie and his men.'

I could not help smiling at this strange commentary on my dissertation on the Lake of Avernus."

There are many traits of Scott's character as a man, —especially in his calamitous years,—many as a writer, the notice of which does not belong to this course of lectures. It is, however, not inappropriate that the existence of the last and the greatest of the Border Minstrels closed in the centre of that region which his genius has peopled with spiritual creations, and not far away from that spot where his young imagination was early fed with the traditions of Scottish song.

LECTURE XII.

Coleridge.

Advantage of connecting critical with historical considerations—Spenser and his age—Spirit of the French Revolution—Contrast between the American and the French Revolutions—Its influence over thought and action—Coleridge's "France"—Nature of lyrical poetry—Early developments of Coleridge's genius—His philosophy—His critical papers—His consciousness of his own poetical endowment—His boyhood at Christ's Church Hospital—Monody on Chatterton—His love of nature—Ode on Dejection—Translations of Schiller's tragedies—"The Ancient Mariner"—"Christabel"—Its metrical beauty—His epitaph.

In tracing the progress of English poetry from its early eras, I have sought in this course of lectures so to connect critical with historical considerations as to give, I trust, some assistance in forming an idea of the intellectual and moral altitude of each of the illustrious poets whose characters we have been contemplating. This has been attempted under a conviction that it was part of the duty which is resting upon me; for I regarded the process as wellnigh essential to a true appreciation of the genius of the poets. How, for instance, could there be a just, or at least an adequate, sense of the glory of that matchless allegory, "The Fairy Queen," if the student were not drawn to some knowledge of the age in which

Spenser flourished?—if I may apply such a word to a life closing early and in neglect and sorrow. Extraneous as history is to literature, it is the framework which is important to give due effect to the portraiture of men who have earned distinction in the annals of letters. It is thus that the proportions and colours are better realized. Fancy, for one moment, some one perusing the wonderful poem just alluded to,—that majestic fragment of Spenser's imagination; fancy it read with some confused and false notion that it was a production of the times of Charles II.,—that detested and opprobrious period of English history, which all the language of loathing I could heap upon it was not strong enough to stigmatize: and what a feeling of incongruity would come over the reader as he found himself following the spotless moral poet through the limitless land of Fairy! The poet, thus ignorantly misplaced, would seem as if he had alighted upon the wrong planet. But when you appropriate Spenser to his own age,—that thoughtful and adventurous age, philosophical and chivalrous, of whose representative men it might be said, as it was said of one of them, that they were so contemplative you could not believe them active, and so active you could not believe them contemplative:—place the poet, I say, in that age, and how true, how natural, is his position, and what a light is reflected on the character of his inspirations! Or, again, how almost inexplicable would be the production of the "Paradise Lost" in a generation unworthy of it, did we not consider the mighty ordeal through which Milton's mind had been passing in the times of the Commonwealth and the Protectorate! and how inadequately would the reader judge of the poetry of Pope, did he not remember the characteristics of those times, an age peculiarly of wits and freethinkers! Poetic inspiration is, indeed, one light, for it is light derived from heaven; but, like the starlight, it has its many magnitudes, its various phases in the cloudless ether or in the haze of the horizon

"The stars pre-eminent in magnitude,
And they that from the zenith dart their beams,
Visible though they be to half the earth,
Though half a sphere be conscious of their brightness,
Are yet of no diviner origin,
No purer essence, than the one that burns
Like an untended watch-fire on the ridge
Of some dark mountain, or than those which seem
Humbly to hang, like twinkling winter lamps,
Among the branches of the leafless trees:
All are the undying offspring of one Sire."

It has been my aim to show the poetry of each age shining in its own region of time and its own atmosphere; but, on bringing the course down to what may be considered contemporary literature, there is less occasion for historical illustration. One influence, however, requires to be noticed. I refer to the general agitation of Europe consequent to the French Revolution. The closing years of the last century were years of change. Things which had endured for ages were perishing, not by slow gradations of decay, but by quick and unlooked-for violence. Time-honoured institutions were not suffered to attain the limit of their natural existence and then to sink under the gradual accumulation of years, but were swiftly swept away by a new force. The clenched hand of prescriptive tyranny was forced to quit its grasp; and, more than that, if it had been the fond traditional belief of other generations that

> "Not all the water in the rough rude sea
> Can wash the balm from an anointed king,"—

it was found that the outpoured blood from the severed neck of an anointed king could wash the balm from off his brow. The people in one of the central monarchies of Europe had suddenly started up, and, casting away respect to gray-haired prerogative, boldly questioned the authority of the power which so long had trampled on them. Men began to ask why the bounties of heaven should be accumulated, reserved, and wasted for the bloated and ingrate luxury of the few, while the many were pining, hungry and heart-stricken. The sympathies of Christendom were enlisted: the pulse of other nations began to beat quicker. The French Revolution assumed the aspect of a general European revolution. Ancient opinions and rules of life were abandoned, and new modes of thought and feeling began to predominate. The political revolution became an intellectual and moral one; for so entire was the subversion of old institutions, that in reconstructing society men were of necessity led to speculate on its very elements and on the principles and destiny of human nature,—speculations which, from a revolutionary forsaking of the old paths, unhappily fostered a self-sufficient and faithless philosophy. And here let me notice where seems to me to lie the important difference between the French Revolution and the great British and American Revolutions, besides the difference in the genius and temperament of the two nations. In the latter the struggle was to vindicate and secure old principles; to guard the Constitution; not to manufacture new schemes of government; to save the good old cause, as it was styled. In the American Revolution, for instance, the war was in truth a mighty constitutional dispute. It was a question of law; and the claim of our fathers was simply for old British rights,—rights as ancient as the Great Charter; and it was this that made them so strong, so consistent, so indomitable. They were seeking nothing new—at first, not even independence, which was not aspired to till it became an indispensable means for the security of their end,—civic freedom. Indeed, the mother-country had thrust her children away from her, and, ridding herself of a parent's responsibility, had given them many of the privileges of manhood. When afterwards she wished to call them back again to her lap, they were too stout to come there, and they claimed to be British *men*, entitled to ancient British rights. The Revolution was characterized by the composure of men acting with a consciousness of having the right with them. How free from all excess and licentiousness! how pure, in the memory of after-times, alike from reproach and regret! It was a strife actuated and impregnated with a spirit of magnanimity,—a sense of duty and law—of religious responsibility. I speak of the American Revolution only for the sake of the contrast with that of France, which was much more stimulant to the minds of men, and, consequently, to literature. The French Revolution was no contest of the Constitution or of law, for both were swept away, and every thing was to be remodelled,—in fact, made anew. New creeds of liberty were taught, new doctrines of the rights of man; the human heart was anatomized; Christianity, with its blessed day of sanctity and rest, sacred from the creation, was banished to make way for a sensual, brutalizing philosophy, with its tenth-day Sabbaths and its idolatry of human reason. Theories of ecclesiastical, political, and social regeneration were propagated with apostolic zeal to all lands,—doctrines which cast a cloud on the glittering spire of every village church, which made the husbandman tremble in the tenure of his little property of a few acres,—a patrimony, perhaps, and an ancient homestead from one generation after another,—and which struck dismay where the domestic virtues were grouped at the once secure and happy fireside. It was a commotion of the very primal elements of society. The scene was a new one—suddenly a new one—in the drama of civilization: the power of strange rights was thrust into the hands of men; the weight of strange duties was harnessed on their backs. Ancient landmarks covered with the moss of a long tract of years were torn up; and thus it became necessary alike for those who hailed and those who abhorred the change to acquaint themselves with the power, the will, and the destiny of man. The guidance of principles, drawn not from any customary or conventional authority of constitution or law, but from the depths of human nature, was needed. Men, long accustomed to float on the placid waters of a river within sight and reach of safe and smiling shores, found themselves suddenly driven out upon a stormy and shoreless sea; and in their peril some were earnestly gazing for a beacon-light from the lost shore, some were idly gazing at the flashing fires which crest the dark billows of the deep, and a few were looking upward hopefully for a heaven-lit ray from some star in the clouded sky. To express myself less imaginatively, the agitation of the

French Revolution forced men, whether the political and social changes were congenial to them or not, into deeper moods of thought and further-reaching sentiments. Absolute authority had lost its sufficiency. With so widespread a spirit of freedom, too often miserably degenerating into licentiousness, superficial precepts, whether in government, philosophy, or literature, were not enough. The influence, either direct or indirect, of that convulsion was far extended over all departments of thought and action. No such agency is to be attributed to the American Revolution, which was achieved so much less tumultously, so much more happily—more lastingly. There was no such turmoil, such heaving of the very earth by the agitation of the deep-seated elements of government and of society. It was comparatively a tranquil process, for it was a revolution that always kept the law on its side. Observe the different effect of the two revolutions upon a mind like Burke's. When the British colonial contest arose, it called from him his statesmanly speeches on taxation and conciliation; but these were only parliamentary arguments upon questions of the Constitution and law and policy. When the French Revolution came on, a discussion more profound was demanded; and Burke, feeling that the crisis called for something more than even a statesman's argument, gave to the world his celebrated "Reflections," which are the expression of philosophy scanning the fundamental principles of political society, the texture of social life, and the universal elements of human nature.

I have dwelt on this subject much more than I intended, and more perhaps than even the discursive character of lectures will quite justify, because I have been often impressed with the thought that there are few topics of more vital interest to the American mind than to understand and appreciate the essential differences between the American and French Revolutions. There is a moral gulf between them as wide as the Atlantic, as might be shown on a fitting occasion. My present purpose, however, is with the Revolution of France, and with it an account of its influence on European literature, and especially on English poetry. I have been reminded of this influence on approaching the poetry of Samuel Taylor Coleridge. Upon his genius it was powerful; for, hoping impetuously of human nature, he was an enthusiast in the cause of freedom. It was by the intense interest and impassioned zeal thus inspired that his powers were chiefly called into action. In dedicating some of his poems to his brother, he recalls the time

> "When with joy of hope thou gav'st thine ear
> To my wild firstling lays. Since then my song
> Hath sounded deeper notes, such as beseem
> Or that sad wisdom folly leaves behind,
> Or such as, tuned to these tumultuous times,
> Cope with the tempest's swell!
> These various strains,
> Which I have framed in many a various mood,
> Accept, my brother! and, (for some perchance
> Will strike discordant on thy milder mind,)
> If aught of error or intemperate truth
> Should meet thine ear, think thou that riper age
> Will calm it down, and let thy love forgive it!"

Coleridge's enthusiasm in the promise of the French Revolution was in no way hurtful to the moral tone of his genius. Miserably as the hope was frustrated, when tyranny and cruelty were busy in disguise and the word "revolution" began to acquire a fearful meaning, the poet's spirit repudiated the adulterous cause, but cherished with as strong a fervour the love of freedom. These feelings form the theme of one of his odes,—that entitled "France," which is said to have been pronounced by Shelley the finest English ode of modern times. This opinion is rather too strong a one; but certainly the finest specimens of the higher order of English lyrical poetry have been produced by the poets of our own times. I know of none to be mentioned in the same range of the same department of poetry, unless it be Milton's "Ode on the Nativity," and some of the odes of Collins and Gray. Under the title of lyrical poetry are included the song, the ballad, the elegy, the hymn, and, above all, the ode, which especially calls for the poet's power and his temperament, with the best mastery over the metrical music of the language and knowledge of the subtle laws of harmony. It was lyrical poetry which, as the name indicates, was once considered that species of verse composed with an adaptation to musical accompaniments. It was well said by Charles Lamb that Milton almost requires a solemn service of music to be played before you enter upon him. But he brings his music, to which who listens had need bring docile thoughts and purged ears. The observation has recurred to my mind in turning to the subject of lyrical poetry; for it seems to me, that, in reading any great ode, something of the preparation that music gives to the imagination and feelings is wanted to set us in right tune, as it were, for the articulate cadences. There is no more varied metrical construction than that which the true lyrical poets adopts as the fit expression for the ebb and flow of the imaginative passion. This ode of Coleridge's embodies in a true poetic shape the best emotions inspired by those momentous years of European history. The lofty opening invocation of the elements, the first flush of enthusiasm for the French cause, the sorrow for England's adversity to it, the clinging to the cause in spite of the first misgivings, the recantation and the plea for forgivenness when the cause proved an unworthy one, France assailing freedom in her ancient mountain-home of Switzerland, and the fine close of the ode, closing, as it began, by rising above the strife of nations and the falsehood of mankind to the tokens of liberty in the elements, the "guide of homeless winds and playmate of the waves,"—all these passages go far to sustain the high eulogy pronounced by Shelley.

"Ye clouds! that far above me float and pause,
Whose pathless march no mortal may control!
Ye ocean waves! that, wheresoe'er ye roll,
Yield homage only to eternal laws!
Ye woods! that listen to the night-birds' singing,
Midway the smooth and perilous slope reclined,
Save when your own imperious branches, swinging,
Have made a solemn music of the wind!
Where, like a man beloved of God,
Through glooms which never woodman trod,
  How oft, pursuing fancies holy,
My moonlight way o'er flowering weeds I wound,
  Inspired beyond the guess of folly
By each rude shape and wild unconquerable sound!
O ye loud waves! and O ye forests high!
And O ye clouds that far above me soared!
Thou rising sun! Thou blue rejoicing sky!
Yea, every thing that is and will be free!
Bear witness for me, wheresoe'er ye be,
With what deep worship I have still adored
  The spirit of divinest Liberty.

"When France in wrath her giant limbs upreared,
And with that oath, which smote air, earth, and sea,
Stamped her strong foot, and said she would be free,
Bear witness for me how I hoped and feared,
With what a joy my lofty gratulation
Unawed I sang, amid a slavish band;
And when, to whelm the disenchanted nation,
Like fiends embattled by a wizard's wand,
The monarchs marched in evil day,
And Britain joined the dire array,
Though dear her shores and circling ocean,
Though many friendships, many youthful loves,
Had swoln the patriot emotion
And flung a magic light o'er all her hills and groves,
Yet still my voice, unaltered, sang defeat
To all that braved the tyrant-quelling lance,
And shame too long delayed and vain retreat!
For ne'er, O Liberty, with partial aim
I dimmed thy light, or damped thy holy flame,
But blessed the pæans of delivered France,
And hung my head, and wept, at Britain's name.

"'And what,' I said, 'though Blasphemy's loud scream
With that sweet music of deliverance strove?
Though all the fierce and drunken passions wove
A dance more wild than e'er was maniac's dream?
Ye storms, that round the dawning east assembled,
The sun was rising, though he hid his light!'
And when, to soothe my soul, that hoped and trembled,
The dissonance ceased, and all seemed calm and bright,—
When France her front deep-scarred and gory
Concealed with clustering wreaths of glory,—
When, insupportably advancing,
Her arm made mockery of the warrior's tramp,—
While, timid looks of fury glancing,
Domestic treason, crushed beneath her fatal stamp,
Writhed like a wounded dragon in his gore,—
Then I reproached my fears that would not flee;
'And soon,' I said, 'shall Wisdom teach her lore

In the low huts of them that toil and groan,
And, conquering by her happiness alone,
Shall France compel the nations to be free,
Till Love and Joy look round and call the earth their own.'

"Forgive me, Freedom! Oh, forgive those dreams!
I hear thy voice; I hear thy loud lament
From bleak Helvetia's icy cavern sent;
I hear thy groans upon her blood-stained streams.
Heroes that for your peaceful country perished,
And ye that fleeing spot your mountain-snows
With bleeding wounds, forgive me, that I cherished
One thought that ever blessed your cruel foes!
To scatter rage and traitorous guilt
Where Peace her jealous home had built;
A patriot race to disinherit
Of all that made their stormy wilds so dear,
And with inexpiable spirit
To taint the bloodless freedom of the mountaineer.
O France, that mockest heaven, adulterous, blind,
And patriot only in pernicious toils,
Are these thy boasts, Champion of human kind?—
To mix with Kings in the low lust of sway,
Yell in the hunt and share the murderous prey?
To insult the shrine of Liberty with spoils
From freemen torn? to tempt and to betray?

"The sensual and the dark rebel in vain,
Slaves by their own compulsion! In mad game
They burst their manacles, and wear the name
Of Freedom graven on a heavier chain!
O Liberty! With profitless endeavour
Have I pursued thee many a weary hour;
But thou nor swellest the victor's strain, nor ever
Didst breathe thy soul in forms of human power,
Alike from all, howe'er they praise thee,
(Not prayer, nor boastful name delays thee,)
Alike from Priestcraft's harpy minions
And factious Blasphemy's obscener slaves
Thou speedest on thy subtle pinions,
The guide of homeless winds and playmates of the waves.

"And there I felt thee! on that sea-cliff's verge
Whose pines, scarce travelled by the breeze above,
Had made one murmur with the distant surge!
Yes! while I stood and gazed, my temples bare,
And shot my being through earth, sea, and air,
Possessing all things with intensest love,
O Liberty, my spirit felt thee there."

In considering the literary influences of the French Revolution, and the expression of feelings awakened at the time, I have passed over the earlier development of Coleridge's genius. If ever mortal could be said to have been endowed supereminently with genius as distinguished from talents, it was that frail though pure and tender-hearted, aspiring, wayward being, the poet, the philosopher, Coleridge. He is one of the poets who, like Milton and Cowper and Southey, are honourably known also by their prose writings. Indeed, it will probably be to the philosophical works of Coleridge that a deeper gratitude will be due than to his poetry, while whatever popular fame may attach to his memory will be the acquisition of his poems. One spirit, indeed, pervades all his productions; one intellectual character is stamped upon them all, only modified by the subjects. The great moral element of his genius was a perpetual thirsting after truth,—ideal truth. The most striking traits of his intellectual character are imaginative powers of wonderful originality combined with habits of profound meditation. These powers were unhappily under the government of only an undisciplined will, and the movements of his mind were fitful, wayward, and incomplete. His wisdom is scattered in fragments, in recollections of his eloquent discourse, and often in notes written on the margins of books; and from these various quarters it has been gleaned by the dutiful and affectionate hands of his disciples. His life was afflicted with almost life-long disease, the wretchedness of which first drove him to a remedy which soon multiplied manyfold his burdens, a suicidal use of opium,—a long-continued habit, at last, however, conquered; and it has been said by those who best knew him that his long and passionate struggles and final victory over this infirmity are among the brightest as well as most interesting traits of the moral and religious being of this humble, this exalted Christian. In his personal career he enjoyed as little of worldly prosperity as he possessed little of worldly wisdom; but it resembled poor Cowper's course of life in this:—that one kind friend was raised up after another affectionately to shelter and cherish a man who, with all his grasp of intellect, with all his tenderness of feeling, was sadly unfitted for many of the responsibilities of life. When he placed himself, in the almost-despairing hope of breaking his opium habits, under the care of a physician, being received an inmate in his family, this connection, beginning in little more than a professional visit, lasted for near twenty years,—in fact, during the remainder of his life; for he spent the rest of his years under the roof of his magnanimous friend, his medical adviser. The great purpose to which he conceived that the faculties of his mind were dedicated was his philosophy, an end always in his view, and in his hopes always reached after but never attained,—the reconciliation of philosophy with Christian religion. It was one of his last regrets that his life and strength were not spared to him to complete his philosophy. "For," said he, "as God hears me, the originating, continuing, and sustaining wish and design in my heart was to exalt the glory of his name; and, which is the same thing in other words, to promote the improvement of mankind." It is not for me now, even if I possessed the ability, to dwell upon the philosophical writings of Coleridge; and I pass from them, therefore, with this one remark:—that when I recall the many passages adorned with rich and verdant imagery, their enthusiastic, and, as it were, triumphant, eloquence, mighty not only in self-communion and a profound reverence for God's written word, but in the long-sustained flow of his sonorous sentences, and all consecrated to the cause of Christianity, thoughts and images and words come across the spirit, not as if from one man, but rather like the waving of the palm-branches and the many-toned voice of an adoring multitude.

The prose writings of Coleridge which are more appropriate for me to allude to before resuming the consideration of his poetical character are his critical papers. I know of no English writer who has given his thoughts to the criticism of imaginative literature, combining so much ability to the task. It is in the spirit of poetry that poetry must be criticized; the might of imagination and its laws are best realized and expounded by imagination itself: indeed, the perfect enjoyment of poetry arises only where there is an active sympathy between the imagination of the poet and the reader. It is the dearth of imaginative energy that makes so much of criticism mere lifeless disquisition. When the poets fall into the guardianship of some unimaginative, fancyless critic, he sets them before you like so many caged birds, their eyes dimmed with the loss of their native freedom, and wings drooping or beating against their bars, or even like the stuffed dead forms in glass cases, instead of pointing to the imagination of the poet resting on some lofty perch that nature gives, or "soaring the air," winging its flight athwart the blue sky, "as full of gladness and as free of heaven," and thus a portion of the poet's own vision is caught, and, the beholder's

"Senses gradually wrapt
In a half sleep, he'll dream of better worlds,
And dreaming hear thee still, O singing lark,
That singest like an angel in the clouds."

To the arduous work of poetical criticism Coleridge brought a mind at once poetical and philosophical,—all the original instincts of poetry, creative power with an exquisite sense of the rhythm of language, and deep reflection on the principles of the art. The best criticism on Shakspeare is that which Coleridge has left; for he "had," as has been well said, "for understanding the great dramatist the two powers which are scarcely less mighty in our intellectual than in our moral and spiritual life,—faith and love:—a boundless faith in Shakspeare's truth, and a love for him akin to that with which philosophers study the works of nature, shrinking from no labour for the sake of getting at a satisfactory solution, and always distrusting themselves until they have found one, in a firm confidence that wisdom will infallibly be justified of her children." There is a passage of his prose—a very high-wrought piece of fancy—in which Coleridge expresses his modest consciousness of his own poetical endowment, and his reverential homage to those whose imagination he contemplated as bearing them on higher and longer-sustained flights. It is a singularly imaginative piece of prose composition, and very characteristic of the author:—

"I have too clearly before me the idea of a poet's genius to deem myself other than a very humble poet; but, in the very possession of the idea, I know myself so far a poet as to feel assured that I can understand and interpret a poem in the spirit of poetry and with a poet's spirit. Like the ostrich, I cannot fly; yet I have wings that give me the feeling of flight, and, as I sweep along the plain, can look up towards the bird of Jove, and can follow him and say, 'Sovereign of the air, who descendest on thy nest in the cleft of the inaccessible rock, who makest the mountain-pinnacle thy perch and halting-place, and, scanning with steady eye the orb of glory right above thee, imprintest thy lordly talons in the stainless snows that shoot back and scatter round his glittering shafts, I pay thee homage. Thou art my king. I give honour due to the vulture, the falcon, and all thy noble baronage; and no less to the lowly bird, the skylark, whom thou permittest to visit thy court and chant her matin song within its cloudy curtains: yea, the linnet, the thrush, the swallow, are my brethren. But still I am a bird, though but a bird of the earth. Monarch of our kind, I am a bird even as thou; and I have shed plumes which have added beauty to the beautiful and grace to terror, waving over the maiden's brow and on the helmed head of the warrior chief; and majesty to grief, drooping o'er the car of death!"

The juvenile poems of Coleridge were remarkably prophetic of his future powers. In fact, his whole character was typified in his youth: the child was indeed the father of the man. The wild imagination, the mastery over metrical melody, the thoughtfulness, the magic powers of discourse, all were there. His schoolmate and life-long friend, Charles Lamb, recalling the days spent many years before in that famous London school, the noble foundation of good King Edward VI., thus apostrophizes the "inspired charity-boy." "Samuel Taylor Coleridge, Logician, Metaphysician, Bard:—how often have I seen the casual passer through the cloisters stand still, entranced with admiration to hear thee unfold in thy deep and sweet intonations the mysteries of Iamblicus or Plotinus, or reciting Homer in his Greek, or Pindar, while the walls of the old Grey-Friars' echoed to the accents of the *inspired charity-boy.*" The day-dreams that filled so large a portion of the visionary Coleridge's existence,—they too began in early life. The story is told of him when quite a child, going down the Strand, (a crowded London thoroughfare,) he was very earnestly thrusting his hands out, so as to come in contact with a person walking before him, who seized him and accused him of an attempt to pick his pocket. The little dreamer sobbed out his protestations of innocence, and, to the astonishment of the bystanders, explained how he thought himself Leander swimming across the Hellespont.

I may cite an instance of the early force of Coleridge's imagination from his monody on the death of Chatterton. The wondrous career of that young poet, and the melancholy close of it by suicide in boyhood, were then fresh recollections. Nature had beautifully endowed him, and the world by a wicked harshness extinguished all light in a spirit already darkened with somewhat of the gloom of hereditary insanity. This earth was no home for him; and it is a fine stroke of imagination when Coleridge associates the chance knell from any distant steeple with the mother-voice of nature calling back the young and earth-hapless poet.

"Oh, what a wonder seems the fear of death,
Seeing how gladly we all sink to sleep,
Babes, children, youths, and men,
Night following night, for threescore years and ten.
But doubly strange where life is but a breath
To sigh and pant with up Want's rugged steep.
* * * * *
"Lo! by the grave I stand of one for whom
A prodigal nature and a niggard doom
(*That* all bestowing, *this* withholding all)
Made each chance knell, from distant spire or dome,
Sound like a seeking mother's anxious call:—
Return, poor child! home, weary truant, home!"

When Coleridge's genius was developing itself, he avowed a high admiration and gratitude to a poet somewhat his senior, though still surviving him,—one whose reputation has never been a general one, the poet Bowles,—perhaps chiefly known by his controversy with Lord Byron on the subject of the poetry of Pope. Coleridge's admiration of Bowles's poems is not to be accounted for by any of that intensity of imagination which was eminently his own characteristic, but because he found in them something more real, more true and manly, than in most of the poetry then in fashion,—a combination of natural thoughts with natural diction. I can digress from my main subject no longer than to give one short specimen of Bowles's poetry,—what strikes me as a well-told recollection of childhood, and what all who have experienced it will recognise as truly recording the impression made on the imagination on the occasion of a first approach to the ocean:—

"I was a child when first I heard the sound
Of the Great Sea. 'Twas night, and, journeying far,
We were belated on our road, 'mid scenes
New and unknown,—a mother and her child,
Now first in this wide world a wanderer.
My father came, the pastor of the church
That crowns the high hill-crest above the sea;—
When, as the wheels went slow and the still night
Came down, a low, uncertain sound was heard,
Not like the wind. 'Listen!' my mother said,
'It is the sea! Listen! it is the sea!'
My head was resting on her lap; I woke;
I heard the sound, and closer prest her side.
Much of the sea, in tearful wonderment,
I oft had heard, and of the shipwrecked man
Who sees, on some lone isle, day after day,
The sun sink o'er the solitude of waves,
Like *Crusoe;* and the tears would start afresh,
Whene'er my mother kissed my hair and told
The story of that desolate wild man,
And how the talking bird, when he returned,
After long absence, to his forlorn cave,
Spoke as in tones of human sympathy,
'Poor Robin Crusoe.'
Thoughts like these arose
When first I heard at night the distant sound,
Old ocean, of thy everlasting voice!"

There are no passages of Coleridge's poetry in which the peculiar traits of his genius are more distinct than those of a descriptive cast. He shared that which belongs to all poetic minds,—a genuine and unaffected love of nature. In the lines of one of his poems,—

"I know
That nature ne'er deserts the wise and pure.
No plot so narrow, be but nature there,
No waste so vacant, but may well employ

Each faculty of sense, and keep the heart
Awake to love and beauty!"

But the predominant habit of his genius was self-communion, *in*-looking rather than *out*-looking, so wrapt in meditation as perhaps often to preclude that open submissive susceptibility to impressions from the outward world of sense. This, however, led him finely to proclaim that great tenet of the poetic creed, that the influences of inanimate nature are dependent on the shaping faculty of imagination:—

"That outward forms the loftiest still receive
Their finer influences from the life within."

Unhappily, Coleridge did not steadily possess that genial mood of imagination by which the poet's song

"Should make all nature lovelier, and itself
Be loved like nature."

He tells of this very unhappiness—this morbid torpor of the imagination—in some of the stanzas in his ode on "Dejection:"—

"A grief without a pang, void, dark, and drear,
A stifled, drowsy, unimpassioned grief,
Which finds no natural outlet, no relief
In word, or sigh, or tear.
O lady, in this wan and heartless mood,
To other thoughts by yonder throstle wooed,
All this long eve, so balmy and serene,
Have I been gazing on the western sky
And its peculiar tint of yellow green.
And still I gaze; and with how blank an eye!
And those thin clouds above, in flakes and bars,
That give away their motion to the stars;

Those stars, that glide behind them or between,
Now sparkling, now bedimmed, but always seen;
Yon crescent moon, as fixed as if it grew
In its own cloudless, starless lake of blue:
I see them all so excellently fair;
I see, not feel, how beautiful they are.

"My genial spirits fail;
And what can these avail
To lift the smothering weight from off my breast?
It were a vain endeavour,
Though I should gaze forever
On that green light that lingers in the west.
I may not hope from outward forms to win
The passion and the life, whose fountains are within."

In another strain of the same ode the important imaginative truth is set forth:—

"From the soul itself must issue forth
A light, a glory, a fair luminous cloud
Enveloping the earth.
And from the soul itself must there be sent
A sweet and potent voice of its own birth,
Of all sweet sounds the life and element."

When Coleridge's poetry gives forth

"This light, this glory, this fair, luminous mist,
This beautiful and beauty-making power,"—

the purport of his descriptions is to discover "religious musings in the forms of nature." "Let me," he exclaims in an admirable passage of his prose, "digress for a few moments from the written word to another book, likewise a revelation of God,—the great book of his servant nature. That in its obvious sense and literal interpretation it declares the being and attributes of the Almighty Father none but the fool in heart has ever dared gainsay. But it has been the music of gentle and pious minds in all ages; it is the poetry of all human nature, to read it likewise in a figurative sense, and to find therein correspondencies and symbols of the spiritual world." This disposition to consider the perishable material world as the shadow of an eternal spiritual reality is sublimely expressed in one of his poems, with an allusion perhaps to Plato's hypothesis of the cave wherein we are placed with our backs to the light and behold reflections in its arch:—

> "What is freedom but the unfettered use
> Of all the powers which God for use had given?
> But chiefly this, him first, him last to view
> Through meaner powers and secondary things
> Effulgent, as through clouds that veil his blaze
> For all that meets the bodily sense I deem
> Symbolical, one mighty alphabet
> For infant minds; and we in the low world
> Placed with our backs to bright reality,
> That we may learn with young unwounded ken
> The substance from its shadow."

I pass by Coleridge's dramatic poems and his remarkable translations of Schiller's tragedies—remarkable as perhaps the only versions of which it was ever said that the translation was even superior to the original—and proceed to the two poems which are most characteristic of the poet's genius, and on which his poetic fame chiefly rests,—"The Ancient Mariner" and "Christabel." These extraordinary poems—neither of them of any great length —are the highest proofs of the originality of Coleridge's imagination. Their origin is traced by him to some conversations with Wordsworth, turning, as he describes them, on the two cardinal points of poetry,—the power of exciting the sympathy of a reader by a faithful adherence to the truth of nature, and the power of giving the interest of novelty by the modifying colour of imagination. The sudden charm which accidents of light and shade, which moonlight or sunset diffused over a known and familiar landscape, appeared to represent the practicability of combining both. These are the poetry of nature. The thought suggested itself that a series of poems might be composed of two sorts. In the one, subjects were to be chosen from ordinary life, in the other, the incidents and agents were to be supernatural; and the excellence aimed at was to consist in interesting the affections by the dramatic truth of such emotions as would naturally accompany such situations, supposing them real. The supernatural fell to the share of Coleridge; and his endeavour, he tells us, was to transfer from our inward nature a human interest and a semblance of truth sufficient to procure for the shadows of imagination that willing suspension of disbelief for the moment which constitutes poetic faith. This has been accomplished with wonderful skill. Both the poems are essentially, absolutely, imaginative. They are pure originals. They are extraordinary manifestations of the magic power of imagination in blending together the natural and supernatural,—spectral creations with emotions of common humanity. They are the work of a wild and wondrous witchery. The veil is rent asunder which separates the mortal bodily life from the ghostly immaterial life of phantoms,—the world of sense from the world of spirit. The argument of the

"Ancient Mariner" was originally set forth in these few words:—how a ship, having first sailed to the equator, was then driven by storms to the cold country towards the South Pole; how the ancient mariner cruelly and in contempt of the laws of hospitality killed a sea-bird; and how he was followed by many and strange judgments, and in what manner he came back to his own country.

> "It is an ancient mariner;
>   And he stoppeth one of three:—
> 'By thy long gray beard and glittering eye,
>   Now, wherefore stopp'st thou me?'"

It is a wedding guest that he holds by the fascination of his eye. The seafaring man's escape from supernatural dangers has left him the victim of a mysterious and woeful agony, to be calmed only by travelling from land to land and recounting his fearful adventures:—

> "Since then, at an uncertain hour
>   That agony returns,
> And till my ghastly tale is told
>   This heart within me burns.
> I pass, like night, from land to land;
>   I have strange power of speech.
> That moment that his face I see
> I know the man that must hear me:
>   To him my tale I teach."

This narrative opens with the ship passing out from the placid atmosphere of actual life, losing sight of the church-steeple, of the highlands, and of the light-house. Quickly struck by the storm-blast, it is borne far away to the south and entangled among islands of ice and the accumulated snow of the polar latitudes. In the desperate danger there comes an albatross, that huge bird of the Southern seas: it is hailed as a bird of good omen, and a way is found to steer the ship through the ice. The bird follows, alighting on mast or shroud and fed by the grateful crew, but in a wicked and luckless moment is killed by the ancient mariner. His shipmates become parties to his guilt, for, with a fickle superstition, they ascribe their ill-luck to the bird, and justify the wanton death of one of God's mute creatures. The mysterious vengeance begins with the misery of a dead calm beneath a torrid sky:—

"The fair breeze blew; the white foam flew
The furrow followed free:
We were the first that ever burst
Into that silent sea.

"Down dropped the breeze; the sails dropped down;
'Twas sad as sad could be:
And we did speak only to break
The silence of the sea!

"All in a hot and copper sky
The bloody sun at noon
Right up above the mast did stand,
No bigger than the moon.

"Day after day, day after day,
We stuck: nor breath, nor motion:—
As idle as a painted ship
Upon a painted ocean.

"Water, water, everywhere,
And all the boards did shrink;
Water, water, everywhere,
Nor any drop to drink."

The ship lies becalmed a weary time, and the crew have

dark assurances in their dreams that invisible fiends are pursuing and plaguing them. At length, afar off, between them and the sun, there is beheld a something in the sky, seen at first as a little speck, then a mist, and then the strange skeleton-shape of a spectral bark. As it nears them, hideous figures are discerned upon the deck and frightful voices and noises are sounding across the waters of the sluggish sea. It vanishes; but death has struck the crew of the becalmed ship, and the ancient mariner alone is left in the central solitude of a motionless ocean, with dismal hauntings of remorse and the memory of supernatural terrors, and with the open-eyed dead lying in groups around his feet:—

"The stars were dim, and thick the night;
The steersman's face by his lamp gleamed white;

* * * * *

"One after one, by the star-dogged moon,
Too quick for groan or sigh,
Each turned his face with a ghastly pang
And cursed me with his eye!

* * * * *

"Alone, alone,—all, all alone,—
Alone on a wide, wide sea;
And never a saint took pity on
My soul in agony!

"The many men, so beautiful!
And they all dead did lie;
And a thousand thousand slimy things
Lived on; and so did I!

"I looked upon the rotting sea,
And drew my eyes away;
I looked upon the rotting deck,
And there the dead men lay!

"I looked to heaven, and tried to pray,
But, or ever a prayer had gusht,
A wicked whisper came, and made
My heart as dry as dust!

"I closed my lids and kept them close,
And the balls like pulses beat;
For the sky and the sea, and the sea and the sky,
Lay like a load on my weary eye,
And the dead were at my feet.

"The cold sweat melted from their limbs,
Nor rot nor reek did they;
The look with which they looked on me
Had never passed away.

"An orphan's curse would drag to hell
A spirit from on high;
But, oh! more horrible than that
Is the curse in a dead man's eye.
Seven days, seven nights, I saw that curse,
And yet I could not die!"

In his loneliness and wretchedness and perpetual wakefulness, the ancient mariner's heart, touched by a skyey influence, yearneth towards the tranquil motions of the heavenly bodies:—

"The moving moon went up the sky,
And nowhere did abide
Softly she was going up,
And a star or two beside."

He looks beyond the enchanted shadow of the ship, and beholds the bright creatures of the deep; and, as the wanton murder of the bird had brought the mysterious affliction upon himself and his companions, the spell begins to break when there springs in his heart a sudden sympathy with the happiness of the animals floating in his sight; and when from his lips breaks a blessing upon them,—

"O happy living things! no tongue
Their beauty might declare.
A spring of love gushed from my heart,
And I blessed them unaware.
Sure my kind saint took pity on me,
And I blessed them unaware:

"The selfsame moment I could pray!"

The utterance of prayer brings to the mariner's wasted spirit the blessing of sleep, rain upon the parched planks of the ship, and the help of a troop of angelic spirits, which, incarnated in the dead bodies of the crew, man the ship. Wild commotions and strange sights fill the sky and the elements, and soft spiritual music and voices soothe the lone human being into a trance. When that is abated, the penance is renewed for a brief space; but the curse is at last expiated:—

"I woke, and we were sailing on
As in a gentle weather:
'Twas night, calm night; the moon was high:
The dead men stood together!

"All stood together on the deck
For a charnel-dungeon fitter;
All fixed on me their stony eyes,
That in the moon did glitter.

"The pang, the curse, with which they died,
Had never passed away:
I could not draw my eyes from theirs,
Nor turn them up to pray.

"And now this spell was snapt: once more
I viewed the ocean green,
And looked far forth, yet little saw
Of what had else been seen.

"Like one that on a lonesome road
Doth walk in fear and dread,
And, having once turned round, walks on
And turns no more his head;
Because he knows a frightful fiend
Doth close behind him tread.

"But soon there breathed a wind on me,
Nor sound nor motion made:
Its path was not upon the sea,
In ripple or in shade.

"It raised my hair; it fanned my cheek
Like a meadow-gale of spring:
It mingled strangely with my fears;
Yet it felt like a welcoming.

"Swiftly, swiftly flew the ship;
Yet she sailed softly too.
Sweetly, sweetly blew the breeze;
On me alone it blew."

The wild voyage, haunted by fiends and blessed by good angels, is drawing to a close. There dawns upon the mariner's eye the light-house top, the hill, and the church,—happy visions of his native land! At the same time he looks to the lifeless bodies which had risen up to do the service of the ship, and, lo! the angelic spirits are leaving them, and the last guardian act is the waving of their seraph-hands across the waters of the calm harbour-bay, as signals to the pilot and to the hermit who dwells in the wood on the seashore, thus giving the mariner over to the care of his fellow human beings :—

"Each corse lay flat, lifeless and flat;
And, by the holy rood!
A man all light, a seraph-man,
On every corse there stood.

"This seraph-band, each waved his hand:
It was a heavenly sight;
They stood as signals to the land,
Each one a lovely light.

"This seraph-band, each waved his hand:
No voice did they impart,—
No voice; but, oh! the silence sank
Like music on my heart."

The poem of "Christabel" is a more pleasing production than the "Ancient Mariner." There is less wildness of imagination, though quite as high an effect of it. It has more of human interest, presenting, however, the same remarkable combination of the natural and supernatural. It is a story of witchcraft, but not the witchcraft of ugly hags like the weird-sisters in Macbeth, but the magic power of a beautiful sorceress. It is a story of the alliance of the strength of goodness and prayer with the guardianship of the sainted dead, potent against the demoniac power of evil. The heroine, Christabel, is as lovely a creation as ever poet's imagination formed. Orphaned of her mother, the pride and sole prop of her aged father, the betrothed of a knightly lover,—gentle, innocent, pious, and beautiful, —she is the fairest victim witchcraft ever struck at. It must also be noticed that the poem is one of the most remarkable specimens of versification in the language, and shows Coleridge's great powers in that important branch of his art. To the eye it has the appearance of very irregular verse; to the ear and to the feelings no such effect is produced, for the variations it presents accord with some transitions of the imagery or the passion, and the rhythm throughout may be said to be faultless. The poem was recognised as a perfect specimen of musical versification by Sir Walter Scott and Lord Byron, and imitated by them both. It was the acknowledged model of metre of the "Lay of the Last Minstrel."

The scene of "Christabel" is laid in an ancient baronial castle, at midnight, when the only sounds are the hootings of the owls and the howling of the old mastiff, answering the striking of the clock:—

"Is the night chilly and dark?
The night is chilly, but not dark;
The thin gray cloud is spread on high;
It covers but not hides the sky.
The moon is behind, and at the full,
And yet she looks both small and dull;
The night is chill, the cloud is gray;
'Tis a month before the month of May,
And the spring comes slowly up this way.

"The lovely lady, Christabel,
Whom her father loves so well,
What makes her in the wood so late,
A furlong from the castle-gate?
She had dreams all yesternight
Of her own betrothéd knight,
And she in the midnight wood will pray
For the weal of her lover that's far away.

"She stole along; she nothing spoke;
The sighs she heaved were soft and low,

And naught was green upon the oak
But moss and rarest misletoe:
She kneels beneath the huge oak-tree,
And in silence prayeth she.
The lady sprang up suddenly,
The lovely lady, Christabel;
It moaned as near as near can be,
And what it is she cannot tell;
On the other side it seems to be
Of the huge, broad-breasted old oak-tree.

"The night is chill, the forest bare:
Is it the wind that moaneth bleak?
There is not wind enough in the air
To move away the ringlet-curl
From the lovely lady's cheek;
There is not wind enough to twirl
The one red leaf, the last of its clan,
That dances as often as dance it can,
Hanging so light, and hanging so high,
On the topmost twig that looks up at the sky

"Hush, beating heart of Christabel!
Jesu, Maria, shield her well.
She folded her arms beneath her cloak,
And stole to the other side of the oak:
What sees she there?"

While the innocent Christabel is thinking her prayers from the depths of her pure and loving heart, the witch is close by, in the shape of a woman richly clad and exceedingly beautiful. She asks for pity on her distress, telling that her name is Geraldine, and giving a deceitful story. The tender heart of Christabel is touched, and she bids the witch welcome to share her couch with her. The supernatural thickens as they enter into the castle, and the victim is getting entangled in the meshes of sorcery. According to the popular superstition, the witch sinks, as if in sudden pain, at the threshold, and is lifted over by Christabel, who devoutly proposes a thanksgiving for their safety; but the evil spirit eludes it:—

> "'Alas, alas!' said Geraldine;
> 'I cannot speak for weariness.'"

As they move along, the sleeping mastiff utters an angry moan, and the dying embers on the hearth dart forth a tongue of flame, while a beautiful relief is given to the supernatural by an impulse of simple nature, in Christabel's tender thoughtfulness for her aged parent:—

> "They passed the hall, that echoes still
> Pass as lightly as you will!
> The brands were flat; the brands were dying,
> Amid their own white ashes lying:
> But when the lady passed, there came
> A tongue of light, a fit of flame,
> And Christabel saw the lady's eye,
> And nothing else saw she thereby,
> Save the boss of the shield of Sir Leoline tall,
> Which hung in a murky old niche in the wall.
> 'Oh, softly tread,' said Christabel;
> 'My father seldom sleepeth well.'"

Christabel speaks, too, of her departed mother, when, lo! at her child's fond and innocent wish, echoed mysteriously by the witch, the guardian spirit of the mother is at hand, invisible except to the spectral sight of the sorceress; and a conflict ensues between the good and evil spirits:—

> "'O mother dear! that thou wert here!'
> 'I would,' said Geraldine, 'she were!'
> But soon with altered voice said she,
> 'Off, wandering mother! Peak and pine!

I have power to bid thee flee.'
Alas! what ails poor Geraldine?
Why stares she with unsettled eye?
Can she the bodiless dead espy?
And why with hollow voice cries she,
'Off, woman! off! this hour is mine,
Though thou her guardian spirit be;
Off, woman! off! 'tis given to me!'

"Then Christabel knelt by the lady's side,
And raised to heaven her eyes so blue,
'Alas!' said she, 'this ghastly ride,
Dear lady! it hath wildered you.'
The lady wiped her moist, cold brow,
And faintly said, ''Tis over now!'"

The power of witchcraft goes on increasing. Geraldine's silken robe falls; and, beautiful and stately lady as she shone before, there is now disclosed to the heart-stricken Christabel an untold sight of some hidden, hideous deformity, some superhuman stump, such as could only belong to a witch's body. The poor maiden sinks into a trance, and her power of speech is sealed up by the incantation that is uttered over her by the demon drawing close to her side: —

"In the touch of this bosom there worketh a spell
Which is lord of thy utterance, Christabel."

I cannot trace the story of the poem without too much impairing the effect, and shall therefore only notice one or two passages in the remainder of it. The most striking of these is the apostrophe to the friends, and the sublimest image of a broken friendship to be found in the whole range of poetry:—

"Alas, they had been friends in youth;
But whispering tongues can poison truth,

And constancy lives in realms above,
And life is thorny, and youth is vain:
And to be wroth with one we love
Doth work like madness in the brain.
And thus it chanced, as I divine,
With Roland and Sir Leoline.
Each spake words of high disdain
And insult to his heart's best brother;
They parted, ne'er to meet again!
But never either found another
To free the hollow heart from paining.
They stood aloof, the scars remaining,
Like cliffs which had been rent asunder;
A dreary sea now flows between.
But neither heat, nor frost, nor thunder,
Shall wholly do away, I ween,
The marks of that which once hath been."

The admirable skill in the versification of the poem, and its exact adaptation to the spirit of different passages, may be shown by observing, in contrast with any of the passages I have recited, the sound of the spirited lines containing the command given by the knight to one of his retainers:—

"Bard Bracy, bard Bracy! your horses are fleet;
Ye must ride up the hall, your music so sweet,
More loud than your horses' echoing feet!
And loud and loud to Lord Roland call,
'Thy daughter is safe in Langdale Hall!
Thy beautiful daughter is safe and free:
Sir Leoline greets thee thus through me.
He bids thee come without delay,
With all thy numerous array,
And take thy lovely daughter home;
And he will meet thee on the way,
With all his numerous array,
White with their panting palfreys' foam.'"

The bard then narrates a dream which had distressed

his sleep, in which he had seen a beautiful bird—the pet dove of the castle—fascinated in the forest by a serpent, and fluttering and writhing in its toils. The dream needs no interpretation for either Geraldine or the spell-bound Christabel. When the witch hears it, she stealthily turns a look of withering fascination on her mute victim. The shrinking up of her eyes, and the large dilating of them when she assumes an air of innocence, are given with great power, as well as the effect on Christabel, who passively imitates the serpent-look that had appalled her:—

"A snake's small eye blinks dull and shy,
And the lady's eyes they shrunk in her head;
Each shrunk up to a serpent's eye,
And with somewhat of malice and more of dread.
At Christabel she looked askance:
One moment—and the sight was fled!
But Christabel in dizzy trance,
Stumbling on the unsteady ground,
Shuddered aloud with a hissing sound;
And Geraldine again turned round,
And, like a thing that sought relief,
Full of wonder and full of grief,
She rolled her large bright eyes divine
Wildly on Sir Leoline.

"The maid, alas! her thoughts are gone;
She nothing sees,—no sight but one!
The maid devoid of guile and sin,
I know not how, in fearful wise,
So deeply had she drunken in
That look, those shrunken serpent eyes,
That all her features were resigned
To this sole image in her mind;
And passively did imitate
That look of dull and treacherous hate!
And thus she stood in dizzy trance,
Still picturing that look askance,

With forced unconscious sympathy,
Full before her father's view,—
As far as such a look could be
In eyes so innocent and blue!
And when the trance was o'er, the maid
Paused a while, and inly prayed;
Then, falling at the baron's feet,—
'By my mother's soul do I entreat
That thou this woman send away!'
She said: and more she could not say
For what she knew she could not tell,
O'ermastered by the mighty spell."

It is that description of the serpent-look of the witch's eyes which, on being read in a company at Lord Byron's, is said to have caused Shelley to faint.

The poem of "Christabel" is a fragment. It was so left by the poet. Other writers have aspired to complete it, but their imitations have proved adventures as vain as presumptuous. Coleridge himself meditated its completion; but, like other of his poems, it was a work of to-morrow—and to-morrow—and to-morrow. And his petty pace of life crept away without it.

In my lecture on Burns, I quoted to you the stanzas which the peasant-poet in fancy appropriated as the epitaph for his own tomb. It was an admonition to the living, and a touching plea for a little charity to the memory of the poor inhabitant below. The deeply-meditative imagination of Coleridge was busy too in taking the measure of an unmade grave, and dictated his own epitaph. His mind had roamed through the vast regions of human learning, and trod the highest places of speculative philosophy; his imagination had taken the boldest and most limitless flights; but this late effusion of his genius—probably his last verses—has its best beauty in its simplicity and its perfect Christian humility. The initials will be recognised as his customary designation of his name :—

"Stop, Christian passer-by! Stop, child of God,
And read with gentle breast. Beneath this sod
A poet lies, or that which once seemed he.
Oh, lift one thought in prayer for S. T. C.,
That he who many a year, with toil of breath,
Found death in life, may here find life in death!
Mercy for praise—to be forgiven for fame—
He asked and hoped, through Christ. Do thou the same."

LECTURE XIII.

Southey.

(WITH NOTICE OF CHARLES LAMB.)

Charles Lamb, the friend of Coleridge and Southey — "The Old Familiar Faces"—"Elia"—Robert Southey—Character of his prose —His complete poetical works—His mental derangement—Personal interest of his poems — Satirical power — "Wat Tyler"— "Joan of Arc"— The product of imagination is often truth — "Madoc"—"Roderic"—"Thalaba"— "The Curse of Kehama"— Scriptural character of "Thalaba"—Keble's "Christian Year"— Story of "Thalaba and Oneiza" — Southey's Odes — "The Retreat from Moscow" — "The Tale of Paraguay"—His playful poetry— Ode on the Portrait of Bishop Heber.

In the last lecture it was my intention to give a few words, at the close, to an author whom I wished to notice briefly; but I became entangled in the witchery of "Christabel," and the glittering eye of "the Ancient Mariner" held me too long to let me accomplish my purpose. It was a life-long friend of Coleridge's I was anxious to speak of; and I must find room for him now, before proceeding to the chief subject of the present lecture. Let me, therefore, present Charles Lamb between his two friends Coleridge and Southey. His intimacy with Coleridge began within the venerable precincts of Christ's Hospital, when they were blue-coat boys together in that time-honoured school. The friendship of boyhood, as is not usual, lasted into manhood and during life,—their minds, in many respects dissimilar, closely associated and identified. Coleridge died; and, in the brief interval of only a few months that Lamb survived, he was constantly reiterating, in a kind of soliloquy, and that confused state of feeling before we realize the absence in death of one whose presence has long been familiar,—he was reiterating, "Coleridge is dead! Coleridge is dead!" A poet who knew and loved them both has coupled their names in the same stanzas of his elegy on his brother-bards:—

> "Nor has the rolling year twice measured
> From sign to sign its steadfast course,
> Since every mortal power of Coleridge
> Was frozen at its marvellous source.
>
> "The rapt one of the godlike forehead,
> The heaven-eyed creature, sleeps in earth;
> And Lamb, the frolic and the gentle,
> Has vanished from his lonely hearth.
>
> "Like clouds that rake the mountain summit,
> Or waves that own no curbing hand,
> How fast has brother followed brother
> From sunshine to the sunless land!"

The early poetical pieces of Lamb were first published with Coleridge's; and it was Coleridge, he said, who first kindled in him, if not the power, yet the love, of poetry, and beauty, and kindliness. Poetry was gradually given up by them both. "You," said Lamb to his friend, now devoted to his philosophy, "now write no 'Christabels' nor 'Ancient Mariners,' and I have dwindled into prose and criticism." One of the most pleasing pieces in the small collection of Lamb's poems may illustrate both the depth and tenderness of his feelings and the peculiarity of his way of thought. The verses have the merit of giving currency to a very feeling phrase,—one of those happy combinations of words which poetry frequently incorporates into the language, serving to express some universal sentiment, and, therefore, soon acquiring the familiarity of a proverb. It cannot fail to be recognised, I think, as an expression of a feeling which has been experienced probably by every one who is now listening to me,—that painfully hollow sense of destitution when there comes across us the memory of faces familiar to some former period of life, —that desolate craving after the departed,—the missing of something which had been a portion of our very selves. Several of the stanzas go on to mention the memory of what has been and never more will be, and in language as simple as possible,—just such words as the feeling would express itself in, finding natural utterance in earnest conversation; but, as it is dwelt on, suddenly the imagination expands, and, as the shadowy recollections of childhood—memories of the old familiar faces—throng around him, the living man, moved by a stronger sympathy with the past than with the present,—nearer of kin, as it were, to the dead than to the living,—feels spectre-like visiting the scenes of his childhood, and, in the intensity of his loneliness, the earth becomes a very desert to him. The allusion in the latter part of the verses is to Coleridge:—

"I have had playmates, I have had companions,
In my days of childhood, in my joyful school-days:
All, all are gone, the old familiar faces!

"I have been laughing, I have been carousing,
Drinking late, sitting late, with my bosom cronies:
All, all are gone, the old familiar faces!

"I loved a love once, fairest among women;
Closed are her doors on me; I must not see her:
All, all are gone, the old familiar faces.

"I have a friend, a kinder friend has no man;
Like an ingrate I left my friend abruptly,—
Left him to muse on the old familiar faces!

"Ghost-like I paced round the haunts of my childhood;
Earth seemed a desert I was bound to traverse,
Seeking to find the old familiar faces.

"Friend of my bosom! thou more than a brother!
Why wert not thou born in my father's dwelling?
So might we talk of the old familiar faces!

"How some they have died, and how some they have left me,
And some are taken from me: all are departed:
All, all are gone, the old familiar faces!"

There is another set of verses of Lamb's, which very gracefully and feelingly, and with admirable truth and a certain indescribable sort of playful pathos, express the emotion, not amounting to strong grief, occasioned by the death of one who had been pleasantly known, and the perplexity of mind in associating the lately living with the grave:—

"When maidens such as Hester die,
Their place ye may not well supply
Though ye among a thousand try
With vain endeavour.

"A month or more hath she been dead;
Yet cannot I by force be led
To think upon the wormy bed
And her together.

"A springy motion in her gait,
A rising step, did indicate
Of pride and joy no common rate
That flushed her spirit.

"I know not by what name beside
I shall it call, if 'twas not pride;
It was a joy to that allied
She did inherit.

"Her parents held the Quaker rule,
Which doth the human feeling cool;
But she was trained in nature's school:
Nature had blest her.

"A waking eye, a prying mind,
A heart that stirs, is hard to bind:
A hawk's keen sight ye cannot blind;
Ye could not Hester.

"My sprightly neighbour, gone before
To that unknown and silent shore,
Shall we not meet, as heretofore,
Some summer morning?

"When from thy cheerful eyes a ray
Hath struck a bliss upon the day,—
A bliss that would not go away,—
A sweet forewarning."

The prose and criticism into which Lamb describes himself as having dwindled are those delightful essays which have given such a pleasant popularity to his assumed title of "Elia." I know of no essay-writing comparable to them, so full are they of an inimitable blending of thoughtfulness and playfulness,—that half-serious, half-sportive habit of mind, far more agreeable than wit, described by our word,—without, I believe, any equivalent in other languages,—our English word *humour*.

I pass now to a name of high worth in English literature,—the poet-laureate, Robert Southey. His life has been one of extraordinary literary industry,—a career of most honourable authorship, actuated by the most ardent impulses, and never lowered to the flattery of mean tastes or temporary fashions, but steadily devoted to the purpose of instructing, improving, and innocently pleasing his fellow-beings. I am not able to recall the name of any author who has accomplished so many, such varied, and such laborious literary plans. In prose he will be remembered as the historian of Brazil, of the Peninsular War, of the Church of England, as the biographer of Nelson, of Wesley, and of Cowper, and as the writer of various miscellaneous works and essays and translations. The excellence of his prose style is distinguished: such is its native purity and ease that you may read page after page with scarce a thought of the transparent veil of words interposed between your mind and his. But my present duty is with his poetry alone.

Three or four years ago Mr. Southey, at the age of sixty-three, undertook what he regarded as a kind of testamentary task,—the collecting, arranging, and editing his complete poetical works. The task has been well fulfilled, with becoming modesty and an equally-becoming manly spirit of self-assurance. More than forty years had passed over some of the early poems; and, with the memory of the distant days revived and the present thought of the approach of the evening of his life, truly does he exclaim, "What is this task but to bring in review before me the dreams and aspirations of my youth and the feelings whereto I had given that free utterance, which by the usages of the world is permitted to us in poetry, and in poetry alone? Well may it be called a serious task thus to resuscitate the past. But, serious though it may be, it is not painful to one who knows that the end of his journey cannot be far distant, and by the blessing of God looks on its termination with sure and certain hope." The honourable ambition of occupying a permanent place in the literature not only of his own country, but of all lands where the English language is spoken, could not fail to animate the breast of one whose gratitude was as deep as Southey's to the wise and good of other ages who had bequeathed their recorded thoughts and inspirations. The strong and placid feelings of the true-hearted man of letters were never better told than by him:—

"My days among the dead are past:
Around me I behold,
Where'er these casual eyes are cast,
The mighty minds of old:
My never-failing friends are they,
With whom I converse day by day.

"With them I take delight in weal
And seek relief in woe;

And, while I understand and feel
  How much to them I owe,
My cheeks have often been bedewed
With tears of thoughtful gratitude.

"My thoughts are with the dead; with them
  I live in long-past years;
Their virtues love, their faults condemn,
  Partake their hopes and fears,
And from their lessons seek and find
Instruction with an humble mind.

"My hopes are with the dead; anon
  My place with them will be;
And I with them shall travel on
  Through all futurity,
Yet leaving here a name, I trust,
That will not perish in the dust."

That trust will not be frustrated: the name of Southey will not perish in the dust, whatever clouds may have gathered round the evening of his days. If his strength has departed from him, it has not been wasted by slothful neglect or by unworthy uses. A life of unwearied and unintermitted industry and of pure and honourable aim has been his; he has done a giant's work in his generation; and it is a very sad thing to think that now, when he has not quite reached the limit of his threescore years and ten, powers so well cultivated and so well employed should, by an inscrutable visitation, be impaired. I do not know of any piece of literary intelligence that has grieved me more than that the faculties of Southey's fine mind have been shattered.

"What sight can sorrow find
Sad as the ruins of the human mind?'

The poetical fire inborn in Southey's heart began to make the motions of its first flames very early. Ardent in his feelings, and of a happy, buoyant temper, literary ambitions began very early to cross his mind. His passion for poetry happily took a fortunate and safe direction. At an age when it was thought the antiquated diction of the "Fairy Queen" must be unintelligible to him, he obtained a copy of that poem, on which his imagination at once fastened as most congenial; and from that early day Spenser was the acknowledged master of his poetic life. The taste thus acquired was confirmed by the reading of Chaucer and Shakspeare and the old ballads, and the study of Homer and the Bible. He is well justified in adding, significantly, "It was not likely to be corrupted afterwards."

Southey's poetic impulses were strong in childhood, and the quickness of his apprehensions raised high and flattering hopes of his success in life, as he tells us in the lines on his miniature-picture taken in very early life:—

> "They augured happily
> That thou didst love each wild and wondrous tale
> Of fairy fiction, and thine infant tongue
> Lisped with delight the godlike deeds of Greece
> And rising Rome; therefore they deemed, forsooth,
> That thou shouldst tread preferment's pleasant paths.
> Ill-judging ones! They let thy little feet
> Stray in the pleasant paths of poesy,
> And when thou shouldst have prest amid the crowd,
> There didst thou love to linger out the day,
> Loitering beneath the laurel's barren shade.
> Spirit of Spenser, was the wanderer wrong?"

There is scattered throughout Southey's poetry much of that personal interest which is communicated when the poet employs his imagination to express his own individual thoughts and feelings, speaking in his own person, and not with the more purely-imaginative voice of his creations. There is one of his smaller poems—a pleasing one, entitled the "Retrospect"—full of this kind of personal interest. It was suggested by a visit to the village of Corston, where he had spent some part of his boyhood, under the harsh tyranny of a boarding-school clouding the rightful gayety of those blithe early years. The stern look and voice of his old teacher rise up to his memory, and the recollections of the dismal feelings of his entrance into the school:—

> "Even now, through many a long, long year, I trace
> The hour when first with awe I viewed his face;
> Even now recall my entrance at the dome:
> 'Twas the first day I ever left my home!
> Years intervening have not worn away
> The deep remembrance of that wretched day."

But what I chiefly notice this poem for is an expression of the fine satirical power which is a trait of Southey's genius, well chastened, however, for it never tempted him into the indulgence of a vicious mockery. He is describing the interview between his parents and the proprietors of the school, and closes it with a significant allusion to the master's short-lived civility to his pupil:—

> "Methinks even now the interview I see,—
> The mistress's glad smile, the master's glee.
> Much of my future happiness they said,
> Much of the easy life the scholars led,
> Of spacious play-ground and of wholesome air,
> The best instruction and the tenderest care;
> And when I followed to the garden door
> My father, till through tears I saw no more,

How civilly they soothed my parting pain!
And never did they speak so civilly again."

Some sad feelings come over him, as after the lapse of some years he finds the spot the same, yet different, and the people estranged,—himself unknowing and unknown; but, after yielding to a momentary depression, he bids his spirit rise to worthier feelings, and closes the poem with a self-admonition, which, considering it was an effusion of his early manhood, is a fine indication of that upright manliness which has honourably characterized Southey's whole life:—

"Thy path is plain and straight; that light is given.
Onward in faith, and leave the rest to heaven."

This deep, confiding spirit seems never to have deserted him. Living in one unbroken mood of faith, he carried forward with him as he grew older not only the buoyancy of boyish years, but a steadier cheerfulness, forever brightening his own heart and his own home. In one of his early pieces, conceived quite in the spirit of old George Herbert's poetical moralizing, and with somewhat of its sound, he touches very pleasingly on the moral discipline of his temperament:—

"O reader! hast thou ever stood to see
The holly-tree?
The eye that contemplates it well perceives
Its glossy leaves,
Ordered by an intelligence so wise
As might confound the atheist's sophistries.

"Below, a circling fence, its leaves are seen,
Wrinkled and keen;

No grazing cattle through their prickly round
Can reach to wound;
But, as they grow where nothing is to fear,
Smooth and unarmed the pointless leaves appear.

"I love to view these things with curious eyes,
And moralize;
And in this wisdom of the holly-tree
Can emblems see
Wherewith perchance to make a pleasant rhyme,—
One which may profit in the after-time.

"Thus, though abroad perchance I might appear
Harsh and austere,—
To those who on my leisure would intrude,
Reserved and rude,—
Gentle at home amid my friends I'd be,
Like the high leaves upon the holly-tree.

"And should my youth (as youth is apt, I know)
Some harshness show,
All vain asperities I day by day
Would wear away,
Till the smooth temper of my age should be
Like the high leaves upon the holly-tree.

"And as, when all the summer trees are seen
So bright and green,
The holly-leaves a sober hue display
Less bright than they,—
But when the bare and wintry woods we see,
What then so cheerful as the holly-tree?—

"So serious should my youth appear among
The thoughtless throng,
So would I seem, among the young and gay,
More grave than they;
That in my age as cheerful I might be
As the green winter of the holly-tree."

It is a part of the history of Southey's mind, that, as he describes it, in his youth, when his stock of knowledge consisted of such an acquaintance with Greek and Roman history as is acquired in the course of a regular scholastic education, when his heart was full of poetry and romance, and Lucan and Akenside were at his tongue's end, he fell into the political opinions which the French Revolution was then scattering throughout Europe; at that time, and with those opinions—or rather feelings—he wrote the dramatic piece entitled "Wat Tyler," which was so often and so reproachfully coupled with his name. It was assailed on the floor of the House of Commons as seditious, and in various ways gained a notoriety remarkable in literary history for the crude production of a boy. Written hastily in three mornings, it was never given by the author himself to publication, till recently he has placed it in the collection of his works, just as it was first printed, when a stolen copy found its way to the press. It detracts nothing from the truth of Southey's pure and high-spirited review of his long literary career, when he records an author's best pride:—"In all that I have written, whether in prose or verse, there has never been a line, which, for any compunctious reason, living or dying, I could wish to blot." "Wat Tyler" had been written under the influences of an enthusiasm which hoped that the immutable division of society into rich and poor might be abolished. The author had taken up revolutionary notions in his youth; conscientiously he wrote what he sincerely thought and felt; and when he outgrew them they were left behind and frankly disavowed, in the same straightforward and manly spirit.

Southey's young ardent genius was busy with poetical

plans as well as with schemes of political and social regeneration. He was thus hurried into the execution of his early literary day-dreams when his powers should rather have been gradually maturing by such cautious development as the genius of his illustrious model, Spenser, had prescribed to itself. Southey first made himself known as a poet by a production in the fashion of an epic poem,—his "Joan of Arc," the bold enterprise of a youth of nineteen years of age, and composed in the short space of six weeks. This poem, as Southey himself has since very candidly described it, crudely conceived, rapidly executed, rashly prefaced, and prematurely hurried to publication, was nevertheless favourably received,—a success which, with equal candour and good sense, he attributes chiefly to adventitious circumstances. It was a work of greater pretensions than had appeared for some time, and, being composed in somewhat of a political spirit, at a period of political excitement, attracted more attention and favour than usually falls to the share of juvenile performances. Happily no one sooner discovered its deficiencies and faults than the young poet himself; and his vigorous good sense never suffered his early success to betray him into the fatal error of supposing that it gave him a dispensation from the careful cultivation of his natural endowment and the thoughtful study of the principles of his art. One single passage in the poem I wish briefly to notice, for the sake of a coincidence illustrative of the beauty-making power of imagination. The Maid of Orleans describes the death of a loved friend and playmate of her peasant-days, closing with these lines,—

> "I remember, as her bier
> Went to the grave, a lark sprung up aloft,

And soared amid the sunshine, carolling
So full of joy, that to the mourner's ear
More mournfully than dirge or passing bell
The joyous carol came, and made us feel
That, of the multitude of beings, none
But man was wretched."

At the opening of this course of lectures I had occasion to speak of what I have often since sought to illustrate,—imaginative truth,—such truth as poetry makes manifest,—better, brighter, and purer than what we commonly see around us, and therefore designed to elevate and refine our thoughts and feelings. That the product of imagination is still truth is sometimes forced upon our conviction when actual life presents that which equals the poet's inventions. I have just referred to an incident which existed only in Southey's imagination,—the caroling of the lark over the grave of one of the imaginary beings in his early poem. At the burial of Mrs. Lockhart, the favourite child of Sir Walter Scott, precisely the same incident actually occurred,—the notes of the jocund lark heard in the air above the mournful company, and mingling with the sounds of the solemn services for the dead. That which had been seen and heard by the imaginative sense of one poet was now witnessed by the bodily senses of another. One had recorded an imagination; the other has recorded a fact; but does not every one feel that each is a record of truth, and hold unimportant that one is imaginative and the other actual? The officiating clergyman over Mrs. Lockhart's grave was that chaste and excellent poet—deserving more than this casual allusion—Milman. He has told, in some stanzas as true in feeling as in poetry, of the incident, when the "Minstrel's darling child" was placed in earth:—

"O thou light-loving and melodious bird!
At every sad and solemn fall
Of mine own voice, each interval
In the soul-elevating prayer, I heard
Thy quivering descant full and clear,
Discord not inharmonious to the ear!
I watched thee lessening, lessening to the sight,
Still faint and fainter winnowing
The sunshine with thy dwindling wing,—
A speck, a movement in the ruffled light,—
Till thou wert melted in the sky,
An undistinguished part of the bright infinity.

"Meet emblem of that lightsome spirit thou!
That still, wherever it might come,
Shed sunshine o'er that happy home,
Her task of kindliness and gladness now,
Absolved with the element above,
Hath mingled, and become pure light, pure joy, pure love."

To resume the poetry of Southey: his works are remarkable for including a greater number of elaborate poems than I remember in the volumes of any other of the English poets. "Joan of Arc," "Madoc," "Thalaba," "The Curse of Kehama," and "Roderic the Goth," are the five extended poems which Southey completed amid all his multifarious literary work. His fame would perhaps have been greater had he written less; for the estimate of his poetical character is almost distracted by these numerous works of such variety and scope, and the occurrence of passages deficient in imaginative animation has depreciated the real value of other portions of his writings, distinguished for many of the highest qualities of poetry. The least interesting of his long poems seems to me to be the poem of "Madoc," founded on the tradition of the early voyages of the Welsh to America; and its failure to win the sympathies of the reader would be very apt to discourage further acquaintance with Southey's poetry. "Roderic" is a noble heroic narrative poem, founded on a grand historical period, the downfall of the Gothic monarchy in Spain, and filled with the lofty actors in that great national drama. It is a very spirited poem, the story conducted with all the interest of a romance, and not only abounding in passages both of beauty and sublimity, but finely sustained throughout. To resort to that very inadequate mode of illustrating the character of a poem, by giving isolated quotation, how true and how beautiful a description is in such a passage as this,—one of many like it:—

"The morn had risen o'ercast,
And, when the sun had reached the height of heaven,
Dimly his pale and beamless orb was seen
Moving through mist. A soft and gentle rain,
Scarce heavier than the summer's evening dew,
Descended,—through so still an atmosphere,
That every leaf upon the moveless trees
Was studded o'er with rain-drops, bright and full,
None falling, till, from its own weight o'erswoll'n,
The motion came."

One of the noblest passages (and it is one of true sublimity) is that in which Roderic, his royalty put off, disguised, and present in the priestly character, receives the vow pronounced by prince and people to the Lord of Hosts, upon the eve of war, and silently motions a blessing over the multitude:—

"Ne'er in his happiest hours had Roderic
With such commanding majesty dispensed
His princely gifts as dignified him now,
When with slow movement, solemnly upraised,

Towards the kneeling troop he spread his arms,
As if the expanded soul diffused itself,
And carried to all spirits, with the act,
Its effluent inspiration. Silently
The people knelt, and, when they rose, such awe
Held them in silence, that the eagle's cry,
Who far above them—at her highest flight,
A speck scarce visible—gyred round and round,
Was heard distinctly; and the mountain stream,
Which from the distant glen sent forth its sounds
Wafted upon the wind, grew audible
In that deep hush of feeling, like the voice
Of waters in the stillness of the night."

The most signal proof of the energy of Southey's imagination is the fact of his having, when a school-boy, conceived the design of exhibiting the most remarkable forms of mythology which have at any time obtained among mankind, by making each the groundwork of a narrative poem. The conception was a grand one, worthy of the strength and far-reaching vision of a mature imagination, and, if successfully executed, competent to enlarge the domains of poetry. It proved more than a dream of juvenile ambition; for he realized his plan in two important poems, founded on two of the mythologies,—that of the Arabs and of the Hindoos,—"Thalaba" and "The Curse of Kehama." The wildest of these poems is that which has for its framework the religion of Hindostan,—the most monstrous, perhaps, of all false systems in its fables and in its rites. The highest efforts of Southey's genius were called forth by this Indian poem, "The Curse of Kehama;" and, while the extravagant fictions of the superstition are not suffered to transcend his reach, and while the wonderful wildness and power of the work raise a mingled feeling of admiration and amazement, I find a perusal of the poem raises a sympathy with Charles Lamb's friendly criticism, when he said to Mr. Southey, "I confess the power of Kehama with trembling; but it puts me out of the pale of my old sympathies: my imagination goes sinking and floundering in the vast spaces of unopened-before systems and faiths."

The Arabian tale of "Thalaba" is, in this respect, different. It is not only an admirable poem, but one that lies within the range of our sympathies,—indeed a wild and wondrous song, but full of all emotions that have their home in every human heart. It is the finest achievement of what has been well styled Southey's judicious daring in the department of supernatural poetry. The one pervading moral of the poem is as pure and precious a one as the imagination of poet has ever glorified,—the war and victory of faith, the triumph over the world and evil powers. The imaginative lesson is conveyed through the types and forms of the Mahommedan religion purified and spiritualized; and it was on this point that an apprehension was entertained by the late Mr. Wilberforce that the poem conveyed a false impression of that religion, and that the moral sublimity which he admired in it was owing to that flattering misrepresentation. In this instance—as I am inclined to believe happens very often—that good man's imagination and feelings arrived at true conclusions; but, when he came to speculate and to criticize, his understanding misled him. With the moral sublimity of the poem he was impressed; nor is it possible that such impressions could have been attended for one instant with any misdirected feeling of admiration for a false religion. If the poem had the effect of misappropriating to a superstition that sentiment which is the rightful tribute to the faith of a true believer, an Israelite or a Christian, it would be as dangerous as delusive. But the truth takes no injury at the poet's hands. Indeed, "Thalaba" is one of the finest sacred poems in the language. It is not so much Mohammedism on which it is founded as something purified by the poet's imagination from the abominations of the false prophet,—a system such as we may conceive to have been developed under the covenant of Ishmael, a remnant of the patriarchal faith preserved by the pure and the faithful in Arabia. Instead, therefore, of discovering any reason for apprehension in the groundwork of "Thalaba," it is its glory that the poet has, by the might of imagination, spiritualized and Christianized Mohammedanism, much in the same way that Spenser hallowed the institution of chivalry, disfigured as it often was in actual life by martial and aristocratic atrocities. Southey's poem is a splendid exhibition of faith,—its spiritual birth, its might, its trials, and its victory:—a portraiture none but a Christian poet could have conceived. Let the poem be read with the belief that such is the principle of it; and, as you follow the hero along his wondrous career to its sublime and pathetic close, the only feeling your rapt imagination will return will be a deep sense of the majestic strength given to the soul of man when God breathes into it the spirit of faith. Indeed I do not doubt that the imaginative impression is better than if the narrative of the poem had been taken from Scripture history,—a consideration demanding, however, more of argument for its development than I can now attempt. Let me only say that there seems to me much force in a remark of Mr.

Southey's, in another connection, on the subject of poems, or fictions founded on themes drawn from Scripture:—that when what is true is sacred, whatever may be added to it is so surely known to be false that it appears profane. A poem conceived and executed with so spiritual a purpose and so fanciful a form is, in truth, an illustration how pure a thing is the fire of genuine poetic inspiration, no matter what it touches. True to its nature, it is beyond the reach of contamination, shining like the sunlight upon the cathedral-roof or the church-spire, and not less brightly on mosque or minaret. The poem of "Thalaba" accomplishes its lofty design of elevating and adorning the reader's idea of faith; and what matters it that it reaches his imagination through the innocent superstitions of mythology? What object is there so harmless to the sun, as it moves along his path in the skies, and indeed so gloriously attendant upon him, as a sunlit cloud? The Christian believer will find nothing in this Arabian tale that can wound his sense of truth, and much that can fortify the spirit of faith. Let him not regret—let him rather rejoice—that poetry, Christian poetry, has shed its light, its glory, upon the harmless superstitions of the once faithful Arabia. It beams upon them like the angel's face upon the fugitive bondwoman when he bade her turn her wandering footsteps home again, or when he spoke a blessing to her and the outcast Ishmael, opening a fountain to them in the desert. Admirable skill and taste are shown in the manner in which the poet causes a Bible strain to pass occasionally over the wild fancies of his Arabian story. This scriptural character is impressed upon the poem in the beautiful opening stanzas:—

"How beautiful is night!
A dewy freshness fills the silent air;
No mist obscures, nor cloud, nor speck, nor stain,
Breaks the serene of heaven.
In full-orbed glory, yonder moon divine
Rolls through the dark blue depths.
Beneath her steady ray
The desert circle spreads,
Like the round ocean, girdled with the sky.
How beautiful is night!

"Who, at this untimely hour,
Wanders o'er the desert sands?
No station is in view,
Nor palm-grove, islanded amid the waste.
The mother and her child,
The widowed mother and the fatherless boy,—
They, at this untimely hour,
Wander o'er the desert sands!

"Alas! the setting sun
Saw Zeinab in her bliss,—
Hodeirah's wife beloved.
Alas! the wife beloved,
The fruitful mother late,
Whom, when the daughters of Arabia named,
They wished their lots like hers,—
She wanders o'er the desert sands
A wretched widow now;
The fruitful mother of so fair a race
With only one preserved,—
She wanders o'er the wilderness!

"No tear relieved the burden of her heart;
Stunned with the heavy woe, she felt like one
Half-wakened from a midnight dream of blood.
But sometimes, when the boy
Would wet her hand with tears,
And, looking up to her fixed countenance,
Sob out the name of 'mother!' then she groaned.

At length, collecting, Zeinab turned her eyes
To heaven, and praised the Lord.
'He gave, he takes away!'
The pious sufferer cried:
'The Lord our God is good.'

"She cast her eyes around;
Alas! no tents were there
Beside the bending sands;
No palm-tree rose to spot the wilderness;
The dark blue sky closed round,
And rested like a dome
Upon the circling waste.
She cast her eyes around:
Famine and thirst were there.
And then the wretched mother bowed her head,
And wept upon her child!"

In vindicating the poem of "Thalaba" from a misapprehension respecting the impression caused by its Arabian framework, I have sought to show that poetry—Christian poetry—has the power of rescuing fictions and superstitions from the realms of error and bringing them into the alliance of truth. This leads to a further reflection, which I deem of sufficient importance to justify me in proceeding to it. It is that to Christianity belongs the privilege of appropriating to itself—of taking possession of—whatever is noble and grand and beautiful in the poetry of even paganism. This is the vantage-ground of our faith; and, standing there, the Christian imagination may look over all the earth,—over all time,—and, wherever it discovers a sublime aspiration rising from the human soul, even though that soul be not blessed with the light of revelation, it may make that aspiration its own. Broken tones of truth come to us from the odes of Pindar, and from the Greek tragedies, and from the dark allusions in Roman poems to the Sibylline prophecies; and when they strike upon the ear of Faith, they are tuned and harmonized to some celestial melody, and the discords of error mingled with them are lost in the air. It is thus the poetry of the heathen is given to us for an inheritance. All that is good and beautiful in it is part of the perfect truth of a true religion. This subject has been finely treated by the imagination of a living poet,—the Professor of Poetry in the University of Oxford. It is the theme of one of the poems in Keble's "Christian Year." Faith made the jewels of the Egyptians its own; it made the fertile land of the Canaanites its own; and it has the power to make its own the imaginative wealth of heathendom,—the rich domain of classic poetry:—

"See Lucifer like lightning fall,
Dashed from his throne of pride;
While, answering thy victorious call,
The saints his spoils divide,—
This world of thine, by him usurped too long,
Now opening all her stores to heal thy servants' wrong.

"So, when the first-born of thy foes
Dead in the darkness lay,—
When thy redeemed at midnight rose
And cast their bonds away,—
The orphaned realm threw wide her gates, and told
Into freed Israel's lap her jewels and her gold.

"And when their wondrous march was o'er,
And they had won their homes
Where Abraham fed his flock of yore,
Among their fathers' tombs,—

A land that drinks the rain of Heaven at will,
Whose waters kiss the feet of many a vine-clad hill;—

"Oft as they watched, at thoughtful eve,
A gale from bowers of balm
Sweep o'er the billowy corn, and heave
The tresses of the palm,
Just as the lingering Sun had touched with gold,
Far o'er the cedar shade, some tower of giants old;—

"It was a fearful joy, I ween,
To trace the Heathen's toil:—
The limpid wells, the orchards green
Left ready for the spoil,
The household stores untouched, the roses bright
Wreathed o'er the cottage walls in garlands of delight.

"And now another Canaan yields
To thine all-conquering ark;—
Fly from the 'old poetic' fields,
Ye Paynim shadows dark!
Immortal Greece, dear land of glorious lays,
Lo! here 'the unknown God' of thy unconscious praise!

"The olive wreath, the ivied wand,
'The sword in myrtles drest,'
Each legend of the shadowy strand
Now wakes a vision blest:
As little children lisp, and tell of Heaven,
So thoughts beyond their thought to those high bards were given.

"And these are ours; Thy partial grace
The tempting treasure lends:
These relics of a guilty race
Are forfeit to thy friends:
What seemed an idol-hymn now breathes of Thee,
Tuned by Faith's ear to some celestial melody.

"There's not a strain to Memory dear,
Nor flower in classic grove,
There's not a sweet note warbled here,
But minds us of thy Love.
O Lord, our Lord, and spoiler of our foes,
There is no light but thine: with Thee all beauty glows."

To return to "Thalaba:" it would be a delightful task to follow the course of this remarkable and beautiful poem; but, drawing now towards the close of these lectures, I have learned, by repeated experience, some little of the virtue of forbearance, and the necessity of passing over many more things than the large demands I have made on your patience would lead you to suppose. One or two passages I must allude to. No poem is adorned with a more beautiful love-story than that of Thalaba and Oneiza:—

"Oneiza called him brother, and the youth
More fondly than a brother loved the maid;
The loveliest of Arabian maidens she.
How happily the years
Of Thalaba went by!
. . . . . . In deep and breathless tenderness,
Oneiza's soul is centred on the youth,
So motionless, with such an ardent gaze,
Save when from her full eyes
She wipes away the swelling tears
That dim his image there.

"She called him brother: was it sister love
For which the silver rings
Round her smooth ankles and her tawny arms
Shone daily brightened? for a brother's eye
Were her long fingers tinged,
As when she trimmed the lamp

And through the veins and delicate skin
The light shone rosy? that the darkened lids
Gave yet a softer lustre to her eye?
  That with such pride she tricked
Her glossy tresses, and on holy-day
Wreathed the red flower-crown round
  Their waves of glossy jet?
  How happily the days
  Of Thalaba went by!
Years of his youth, how rapidly ye fled!"

A drear winter was to close over this happy spring,—a tragic ending to this bright promise. The trial of his faith which most heavily crushes the heart of Thalaba is when the angel of death invades the bridal chamber; and then follows that woeful description,—his ghastly wretchedness at Oneiza's grave:—

"By the tomb lay Thalaba,
  In the light of the setting eve.
  The sun, and the wind, and the rain,
  Had rusted his raven locks;
  His cheeks were fallen in,
  His face-bones prominent.
  Reclined against the tomb he lay,
  And his lean fingers played,
Unwitting, with the grass that grew beside."

When Thalaba's unwearied faith approaches its consummation,—the good fight nearly finished, the race nearly won,—the ministering spirits come closer to his path, and he hears a spiritual welcoming from the angel voice of his lost Oneiza:—

"Was there a spirit in the gale
  That fluttered o'er his cheek?

For it came on him like the new risen sun,
Which plays and dallies o'er the night-closed flower

"And woos it to unfold anew to joy;
For it came on him as the dews of eve
Descend with healing and with life
Upon the summer mead;
Or liker the first sound of seraph-song
And angel-greeting to the soul
Whose latest sense had shuddered at the groan
Of anguish, kneeling by a death-bed side."

It gives a vivid impression of the versatility of Southey's genius to turn from a spiritual and wildly-supernatural poem like "Thalaba" to his poetical odes. The finest of these were written during the long strife between his country and Napoleon. I cannot stop to characterize that contest, or to say how far I consider the poet's strain against the adversary to be justified. It is with the poetry, and not the politics, I have to deal. This only let me say: that the war with the French Empire is a grand chapter in British history, and that I know not where an American or a republican can find just ground for any sympathy with a military despotism. The trumpet-sounds of Southey's poetry came forth from his mountain dwelling to cheer and fortify the hearts of his countrymen. His heart never lost its faith that there is a moral strength mightier and more enduring than the perishable power of armies. He spake to the nation in the spirit of that noble line which he had spoken to himself in early manhood:—

"Onward in faith, and leave the rest to Heaven!"

And it is a grand thing to behold the poet, like his

own Thalaba, ever faithful, hopeful alike in seasons of victory and of doubt, and to hear him at last raising the exultant strain of triumph, as over the disastrous retreat from Moscow:—

> "Witness that dread retreat,
> When God and nature smote
> The tyrant in his pride!
> Victorious armies followed on his flight;
> On every side he met
> The Cossack's dreadful spear;
> On every side he saw
> The injured nation rise
> Invincible in arms.
> What myriads, victims of one wicked will,
> Spent their last breath in curses on his head!
> There where the soldiers' blood
> Froze in the festering wound,
> And nightly the cold moon
> Saw sinking thousands in the snow lie down
> Whom there the morning found
> Stiff as their icy bed!"

The highest and most impetuous of these strains is the ode written during the negotiations with Napoleon in 1814. Since Milton's tremendous imprecation against the Papal tyranny on occasion of the Piedmontese massacre, I know of no piece of political invective equal to it. It is hurled with the force and the fire of a thunderbolt, one burst of indignation following another, and closing with an accumulation of all the deeds of blood identified with the name of him who had been at once the terror and the wonder of Europe. Let me give the opening and ending stanzas of the ode:—

"Who counsels peace at this momentous hour,
When God hath given deliverance to the oppressed,
And to the injured power?
Who counsels peace when vengeance, like a flood,
Rolls on, no longer now to be repressed;
When innocent blood,
From the four quarters of the world, cries out
For justice upon one accursed head;
When Freedom hath her holy banners spread
Over all nations, now in one just cause
United;—when, with one sublime accord,
Europe throws off the yoke abhorred,
And loyalty and faith and ancient laws
Follow the avenging sword?

"Woe, woe to England! woe and endless shame,
If this heroic land,
False to her feelings and unspotted fame,
Hold out the olive to the tyrant's hand!
Woe to the world if Buonaparte's throne
Be suffered still to stand!

"France! if thou lovest thine ancient fame,
Revenge thy sufferings and thy shame.
By the bones which bleach on Jaffa's beach;
By the blood which on Domingo's shore
Hath clogged the carrion-birds with gore;
By the flesh which gorged the wolves of Spain,
Or stiffened on the snowy plain
Of frozen Moscovy;
By the bodies which lie all open to the sky,
Tracking from Elbe to Rhine the tyrant's flight;
By the widows' and the orphans' cry;
By the childless parents' misery;
By the lives which he hath shed;
By the ruin he hath spread;
By the prayers which rise for curses on his head,—
Redeem, O France! thine ancient fame!
Revenge thy sufferings and thy shame!

"Open thine eyes! Too long hast thou been blind!
Take vengeance for thyself and for mankind!
By those horrors which the night
Witnessed when the torch's light
To the assembled murderers showed
Where the blood of Condé flowed;
By thy murdered Pichegru's fame;
By murdered Wright,—an English name;
By murdered Palm's atrocious doom;
By murdered Hofer's martyrdom;
Oh! by the virtuous blood thus vilely spilt,
The Villain's own peculiar, private guilt,—
Open thine eyes! Too long hast thou been blind!
Take vengeance for thyself and for mankind."

From these notes, tuned in tumultuous times, and fit to cope with the tempest's swell, let me further illustrate the varied power of Southey's genius by turning to a passage in his pleasing poem, "The Tale of Paraguay." It is an exquisite specimen of purely pathetic poetry,—full of the truth of feeling and of fancy,—the description of the death-bed of a young and innocent female. What can be more beautiful or more touching than the line which actually pictures to your imagination the sweet smile of the dying one?—

"Who could dwell
Unmoved upon the fate of one so young,—
So blithesome late? What marvel if tears fell
From that good man, as over her he hung,
And that the prayers he said came faltering from his tongue?

"She saw him weep, and she could understand
The cause thus tremulously that made him speak.
By his emotion moved, she took his hand;
A gleam of pleasure o'er her pallid cheek

Past, while she looked at him with meaning meek,
And for a little while, as loth to part,
Detaining him, her fingers lank and weak
Played with their hold; then, letting him depart,
She gave him a slow smile, that touched him to the heart.

"Mourn not for her; for what hath life to give
That should detain her ready spirit here?
Thinkest thou that it were worth a wish to live,
Could wishes hold her from her proper sphere
That simple heart, that innocence sincere
The world would stain. Fitter she ne'er could be
For the great change; and, now that change is near,
Oh, who would keep her soul from being free?
Maiden beloved of Heaven, to die is best for thee!

"She hath passed away, and on her lips a smile
Hath settled, fixed in death. Judged they aright,
Or suffered they their fancy to beguile
The reason, who believed that she had sight
Of heaven before her spirit took its flight?—
That angels waited round her lowly bed,
And that, in that last effort of delight,
When, lifting up her dying arms, she said,
'I come,' a ray from heaven upon her face was shed?"

I might exhibit yet another phase of Southey's poetry in his humorous pieces. No man has better shown that one trait of genius,—the carrying forward the feelings of childhood into the powers of manhood:—

"My days have been the days of joy,
And all my paths are paths of pleasantness;
And still my heart, as when I was a boy,
Doth never know an ebb of cheerfulness.
Time, which matures the intellectual part,
Hath tinged my hairs with grey, but left untouched my heart."

This natural and cultivated cheerfulness has vented itself in his playful poetry, to relieve his own exuberant feelings, and to gladden his happy household group. There is something exceedingly fine in hearing him at one time uttering strains that sound from Arabia, or Gothic Spain, or the wilds of America, or from the magic supernatural caverns under the night of the ocean, —at another time sounding one of those tremendous imprecations on the head of Bonaparte,—and then to find him writing, from the fulness of a father's heart, poetic stories for his children. This he deemed part of his vocation; for, as he sings in one of his sportive lyrics:—

"I am laureate
To them and the king."

No man ever clung with deeper or manlier devotion to his household gods. For his children's sake, and for the sake of his own moral nature, he ever kept the young heart alive within him. There was wisdom in this, as he has shown in the plea that he has appended to one of his wild ballads:—

"I told my tale of the Holy Thumb,
That split the dragon asunder;
And my daughters made great eyes as they heard,
Which were full of delight and wonder.

"With listening lips and looks intent,
There sate an eager boy,
Who shouted sometimes and clapt his hands,
And could not sit still for joy.

"But when I looked at my mistress' face,
It was all too grave the while,
And when I ceased, methought there was more
Of reproof than of praise in her smile.
That smile I read aright, for thus,
Reprovingly, said she :—
'Such tales are meet for youthful ears,
But give little content to me.
From thee far rather would I hear
Some sober, sadder lay,—
Such as I oft have heard, well pleased,
Before those locks were grey.'

"'Nay, mistress mine,' I made reply;
'The autumn hath its flowers,
Nor ever is the sky more gay
Than in its evening hours.
That sense which held me back in youth
From all intemperate gladness,
That same good instinct bids me shun
Unprofitable sadness.
Nor marvel you if I prefer
Of playful themes to sing:
The October grove hath brighter tints
Than summer or than spring;
For o'er the leaves, before they fall,
Such hues hath nature thrown,
That the woods wear in sunless days
A sunshine of their own.
Why should I seek to call forth tears?
The source from whence we weep
Too near the surface lies in youth;
In age it lies too deep.

"'Enough of foresight sad, too much
Of retrospect, have I;
And well for me that I sometimes
Can put those feelings by.

"'From public ills and thoughts that else
Might weigh me down to earth;
That I can gain some intervals
For healthful, hopeful mirth.'"

It only remains for me to show that that spirit of mirth was healthful,—a help to his moral strength, and consistent with a profound spirit of meditation. Let us turn, therefore, to the sublime closing strains of the most spiritual of his lyrical poems,—the noble ode on the portrait of Bishop Heber. They had been friends; and, when India's saintly bishop was no longer upon the earth, Southey's heart was strongly stirred as he gazed upon his portrait:—

"O Reginald! one course
Our studies and our thoughts,
Our aspirations, held.

* * * *

We had a bond of union, closely knit
In spirit, though in this world's wilderness
Apart our lots were cast.

* * * *

"Hadst thou revisited thy native land,
Mortality, and Time,
And Change, must needs have made
Our meeting mournful. Happy he
Who to his rest is borne,
In sure and certain hope,
Before the hand of age
Hath chilled his faculties
Or sorrow reached him in his heart of hearts!
Most happy if he leave in his good name
A light for those who follow him,
And in his works a living seed
Of good, prolific still!

"Yes, to the Christian, to the heathen world,
Heber, thou art not dead,—thou canst not die
Nor can I think of thee as lost.
A little portion of this little isle
At first divided us; then half the globe:
The same earth held us still; but when,
O Reginald! wert thou so near as now?
'Tis but the falling of a withered leaf,
The breaking of a shell,
The rending of a veil!
Oh, when that leaf shall fall,
That shell be burst, that veil be rent, may then
My spirit be with thine!"

LECTURE XIV.

Byron.

A catholic taste in literature—Difficulties of a course of critical lectures—Southey and Byron—The spirit of criticism, the spirit of charity—Roger's plea for Byron's memory—Popularity of his poetry—"English Bards and Scotch Reviewers"—"Childe Harold"—His love of external nature—Formation of his literary character—Admiration for Pope—Success of "Childe Harold"—His Oriental tales—Literature of the last century—Story of Byron's marriage—Noctes Ambrosianæ—Contrast between the "Corsair" and the "Prisoner of Chillon"—"The Dream"—Materialism in his poetry—Manfred—Venice—The Dying Gladiator—Strains for liberty—Beauty of womanly humanity—"Sardanapalus"—Byron's selfishness—His Infidelity.

In one of the introductory lectures of this course I took occasion to advert to the importance of cultivating a *catholic* taste in literature, and, in so doing, gave at least an implied pledge that it should be one of my chief efforts to carry the same spirit into what I might wish to say to you on the many and multiform productions of English poetry. A rash or a mock originality lies not within my ambition; and I have striven so to govern my voice that it should not convey to your ears old errors or old truisms disguised as startling paradoxes, that you should not turn from my opinions as prejudices or feel a wound given to your own prepossessions. Indeed, I have desired to introduce into these lectures no more of my own opinions than the very nature of my position made necessary, and, avoiding the spirit of the judge or the advocate, simply to set before your minds the poets as they have risen in succession on the glorious registry we have been examining, to open and illustrate the hidden nature of their genius, and then to leave you to know and to feel the character and spirit of their poetry. Believing that every profession has its peculiar temptation and peril, and that the professional teacher has most need to be on his guard against the insidious habit of dogmatizing, I have arrogated no authority for my opinions. But when I have felt assured that they had a root of truth, and branching aspirations after truth, I have given them utterance, trusting that the sounds awakened by the breath of poetic inspiration would prove sounds of truth.

I have refrained from adverting at any time to the difficulties which may attend the prosecution of a course of lectures such as we have been engaged in, for the simple reason that it belongs to the lecturer alone to measure and meet them, and it is a matter of small moment whether they are appreciated or not by his hearers. One difficulty may be made in some measure an exception to the rule of silence, for partially it is shared by both parties. I mean the difficulty, consequent on a rapid succession of criticisms, of making the requisite transfer of the mind from one subject to another. No one, whether for the purpose of forming a critical opinion or of reading without any thought of criticism, can gain a real knowledge of an author, and, most of all authors, of a poet, without entering into the spirit of his writings, be that spirit a right spirit or a wrong spirit. It is almost essential to stand upon his place of vision, and then, when it becomes necessary, to change that for the position of another poet,—to pass quickly from sympathy with one to sympathy with another, the elements of sympathy being often in all respects different. Let me say, without, I hope, subjecting myself to the imputation of seeking indirectly to magnify the labours of my course, the task is no easy one. It brings perplexity of mind with it. The transitions must often be sudden and violent: one set of feelings must be laid down and another taken up with a promptness and dexterity which, to employ a familiar illustration, may be likened to the attempt to accommodate our raiment to the changes of a fickle climate with its hasty revolutions of heat and cold. Each poet of original genius dwells in an atmosphere of his own, and he who seeks to know him must learn to breathe it, whether it be pure or noxious: he must needs live in it for a brief space.

But I can fancy that some of you are beginning to ask, Why this unwonted preface? Unwonted, because, whatever sins of tediousness may rest upon me, there has been no introductory loitering; for the first sentence of my lecture has, I believe, for the most part, taken you straightway into the very subject of it. If a different style of introduction is given to the present lecture, it is because in no instance has the transition been so toilsome to my mind. Between the requisite sympathy with the genius of the poet I last parted with, and that with him I am approaching, lies a wide and dreary gulf What is it that I am passing from? and what is it I am coming to? It was but a few days ago that I was dealing with the faithful, pure, single-hearted, cheerful Southey, whose imagination seemed to have been strengthened and steadied by the resolution in that admirable line, which has been sounding to my heart since I first found it :—

"Onward in faith, and leave the rest to Heaven!"—

so that, as I followed his footsteps and his flights, I felt that there was a path in which as firm a pace might be taken. From this I have to turn away and enter on the faithless, hopeless, wayward, and wondrous career of the darkened and distempered genius of Byron. I have been guided in the study of the various powers of the poets who have gone before, by principles of the nature of poetry, its constituent properties, and its purposes, in which I have yet found no reason to believe my confidence misplaced. Should they bring me to conclusions, respecting the true measure of Byron's endowments, different from the general estimate that has been formed of them, I cannot believe that his genius transcends the reach of principles that serve for the measurement of the poetry of Shakspeare and Spenser and Milton. The aberrations of Byron's talents may perplex and baffle the application of those principles; but surely it is better to hold fast to them than, casting them aside, to indulge in indiscriminate panegyrics or indiscriminate censure. If, therefore, the tone of criticism in this lecture should sound differently from what has preceded it, the source of that change may be sought in the nature of the subject.

There may be among those who are listening to me not a few ardent admirers of Lord Byron's poetry; there may be some—a far smaller number—who find in it ground only for reprobation. To both these this lecture can scarce fail to prove unsatisfactory, but not more than to a third party,—the lecturer himself. If I brought to the task powers of criticism greater than any I can lay claim to, still, the discussion must be singularly imperfect, because there are qualities in Byron's poetical character—essential characteristics in the very heart of it—which I have not the audacity, even if I had the inclination, to speak of. If, casting off all the restraints instinctively recognised by every—I will not say only gentleman, but every decent man,—I were to take the full scope of his powers and attempt a complete discussion of the subject, men would cry out "Shame!" and the cheek of every woman would burn with crimson blushes; and yet the offensive topics would be unexceptionably appropriate to them. I have encountered no such difficulty as this before, from the age of old Chaucer down; for while, indeed, the pages of the elder poets were sometimes defaced by impurities, the grossness of a gross age, they were extrinsic, and, as it were, accidental, and, therefore, might properly and justly be cast aside as unimportant in the estimate of those poets. In the present case, however, you cannot escape from the impurities; for I put it to the candour of those who are most thoroughly acquainted with Lord Byron's writings, whether there is one volume of them in which you will not encounter either infidelity, or profanity, or obscenity, or vulgarity, and not unfrequently all of them? I make this remark, not because I am going on thus to characterize Byron's character, but merely to suggest how much the interest is impaired in the discussion of an author's character when there is imperative necessity of passing in silence over some of its prominent features. I have no desire to say harsh things of the poet and to repeat the often-repeated charges against his works. Far more pleasing would be the task of vindicating their errors, and of showing that, like the frailties of Burns, they might be detached so as to leave unimpaired and uncontaminated the other and better aspirations connected with them. I would gladly seek to save the glory of a true poet; for each one added to the list, already so rich in names, is so much added to the glory and the value of the literature of our language. I know, too, that the true spirit of criticism is the spirit of charity and of candour; and, where there are faults which do not enter into the very constitution of an author's mind, it is far better to throw over them the veil of silence and forgetfulness. I am not conscious that the evil spirit of censoriousness has insinuated itself into my course, and trust I shall not be regarded as suffering it now to get the advantage of me. In entering upon some revision of Byron's poems for the preparation of this lecture, I chanced to encounter the touching plea for his memory from the pen of a brother-poet who knew and loved him, that kind-hearted veteran, the poet Rogers:—

"He is now at rest;
And praise and blame fall on his ear alike,
Now dull in death. Yes, Byron, thou art gone,—
Gone like a star that through the firmament
Shot, and was lost in its eccentric course,
Dazzling, perplexing.

* * * * * *

"If in thy life
Not happy, in thy death thou surely wert,—
Thy wish accomplished: dying in the land
Where thy young mind had caught ethereal fire,—
Dying in Greece, and in a cause so glorious.

"Thou art gone:
And he who would assail thee in thy grave,—
Oh, let him pause! For who among us all,
Tried as thou wert even from thy earliest years,
When wandering yet, unspoilt, a Highland boy,—
Tried as thou wert, and with thy soul of flame,—
Pleasure, while yet the down was on thy cheek,
Uplifting, pressing, and to lips like thine,
Her charmèd cup,—ah! who among us all
Could say he had not erred as much and more?"*

The feeling which prompted this appeal, and its source, entitle it to a respectful consideration. It would indeed be unmanly and irrational to assail the poet in his grave, especially when we remember his life full of wretchedness and his death-bed clouded with spiritual darkness. But his poems are living things: the sanctity of the grave does not belong to them. They will live, though not in the full vitality of their first fame. And equally unmanly and equally irrational appears to me the habit of silencing the voice of even-tempered opinion by the sickly, sentimental commiseration for poor Byron.

I shall make no attempt, in illustration of my subject, to follow, regularly, the irregular course of the poet's life. It is a well-known story, from his boyish rambles in the Scottish Highlands, his London life, with all its metropolitan pleasures, his adventurous wanderings on the Continent, his years of Italian profligacy, down to

* "Italy."

the dismal expiring amid the marshes of Missolonghi. The annals of English poetry present nothing equal to the popularity which was gained by Lord Byron's poetry. It was speedy, it was strong, it was wide-spread, and during his life did not, perhaps, suffer a very serious decline. The literary student well knows that mere popularity does not surely betoken an abiding fame. In the extraordinary reception of Byron's poetry, I am disposed to think that there is proof of both the poetic virtues and vices which characterize it. How could he have found entrance into so many hearts if he possessed not some of those powers of imagination which sooner or later find their path? How, on the other hand, is it possible that he could have found that entrance so speedily, if the strains he was uttering were strains of the loftiest and best poetry? The world never yet, in any of its ages, has been ready for the prompt and intelligent reception of a great poet of original powers. It is not incredible that the fourteen thousand copies of a poem like "The Corsair" might be sold in one day, soon finding more, probably, than that number of readers; but, when poetry speaks in its mightiest tones,—those which have an echo of eternity in them,—the one living generation of mankind to whom they are addressed does not, the first moment, the first month, or the first year, open its heart to the sounds. Poetry which is addressed to the feelings, the fancy, and the imagination, in some of its lighter moods, is listened to and admired in its earliest hour; but that poetry for which fame, as distinguished from mere popularity, is in store, as surely as it comes from the depths of the poet's soul, so surely it travels slowly, often toilsomely, sinking into the deep places of the souls of men,—its resting-place for ages. A brilliant and rapid popularity dazzles and misleads the judgment: a rocket-fire will leap up into the heavens, outshining and outstripping the stars, while the steady orb of a planet—its golden urn filled at the fountain of the sun—is climbing, imperceptibly and noiselessly, up the eastern region of the firmament. The memory of an author's popularity—the recollection of the feelings with which he was once read—will continue to mislead. If, for instance, any one desire to form a safe and permanent opinion of Byron's poetry, let me warn him not to trust to the impressions remaining from former intercourse with it; but, examining it anew, more calmly, more cautiously, and, if possible, with a judgment fortified by the study of those masters of English song whose fame is undisputed, and then, but not till then, whatever conclusion he may arrive at, will it be his right to speak with confidence.

The juvenile poems which introduced Lord Byron into literary life gave little promise of his future career, and have their chief interest in indirectly leading to his next publication,—one of a widely-different character,—the "English Bards and Scotch Reviewers." The contemptuous treatment of his youthful verses by the "Edinburgh Review" wounded him deeply, and helped to injure a mind easily swayed by any untoward influence. He felt a consciousness of more poetic power than he had been able to express, which made him more sensitive to the wrong and more ready to seek his revenge. The satirical poem he was thus prompted to write served to fix on his character that splenetic and malevolent habit which it became more and more his delight to indulge in; and, in this instance, the shaft which had pierced him seems so to have poisoned his heart, that he rushed forth to scatter his darts in an indiscriminate warfare alike upon reviewers and his brother-poets. It was the beginning of a system of hostilities such as no poet ever waged before. Dryden and Pope had each of them laid a heavy hand upon the poetasters and scribblers of their times; but never before Byron was a poet found who could seek to soil with bitter and contemptuous insults the fair fame of his contemporaries, whose merits he was constrained, in some chance moods of better feelings, to recognise. His youthful satire was a bold assault upon the citadel of criticism, and served, no doubt, to prompt a very ready attention to his next work, his first important poem, and the one on which his general reputation chiefly rests,—"The Pilgrimage of Childe Harold."

The first and second cantos of "Childe Harold" appeared, it will be remembered, some years earlier than the third and fourth; and, as they gave him rank as a poet, let us briefly notice their relation to his personal life. When Byron reached the limit of manhood, he had already run no short distance in his unbridled race of self-indulgence. He revelled in the voluptuousness of the looser portion of the British aristocracy; and no wonder, therefore, that, to apply to him the words of one of his own dramas, he was full of pride,—

> "And the deep passions fiercely fostered by
> The uses of patricians."

He was not in habits of healthy intercourse with his

fellow-beings. The love of external nature, which became a passion with him, and which he himself regarded, probably, as the predominant trait of his genius, does not seem to have been developed by the familiar prospect of his own country. It was rather awakened by the more active stimulant of the strange scenery presented by foreign travel. Previously his communion with nature—that precious discipline for the poet's mind—was little more than in the way of some of the strenuous bodily exercises, the favourite and most innocent modes of excitement in which he luxuriated,—the delight, for instance, of wrestling with the billows of the sea, "borne, like its bubbles, onward,"—or, as he has somewhere said in a figure which seems an image of his life, with no mastery over his passions, but hurried, a helpless thing, wherever their tides might drift him,—

> "Swept like a weed upon the ocean waves!"

The passionate pleasure of a lusty swimmer was a real emotion with him,—an active emotion too, and not, like many of his feelings, unreal and ending in empty and morbid affectations. The thought of it coming over his mind had the power—for this was a thing of truth—to kindle his imagination into the finest description poetry has perhaps ever given of a swimmer's intense and earnest delight. It occurs in one of his tragedies, and will be found a passage of more genuine poetry than the more celebrated apostrophe to the ocean at the close of "Childe Harold." It is superior both in imagination and expression :—

"How many a time have I
Cloven, with arm still lustier, breast more daring,
The wave all roughened with a swimmer's stroke;
Flinging the billows back from my drenched hair,
And laughing from my lip the audacious brine
Which kissed it like a wine-cup, rising o'er
The waves as they arose, and prouder still
The loftier they uplifted me; and oft,
In wantonness of spirit, plunging down
Into their green and glassy gulfs, and making
My way to shells and seaweeds, all unseen
By those above, till they waxed fearful; then,
Returning with my grasp full of such tokens
As showed that I had searched the deep, exulting
With a far-dashing stroke, and drawing deep
The long-suspended breath, again I spurned
The foam that broke around me, and pursued
My track like a sea-bird. I was a boy then."

This is a description full of imagination and truth, and well describing the poet's own active communion with nature and the elements.

It is a consideration, in examining a poet's character, not to be overlooked, how far his natural endowments have been cultivated by study of the principles of his art as exemplified in the approved productions of his predecessors. This cultivation no one, no matter what may be his native gifts, can venture to despise; indeed, the greater his powers the more valuable is such discipline, for it seems to chasten and to strengthen, without the peril of servility of imitation. Every one of the greatest poets in our language, holding an independent and majestic attitude of originality, yet deemed it a worthy thing to study with a docile spirit the inspirations of the mighty bards who had gone before. In the formation of Byron's literary character this cultivation was grievously wanting. His knowledge derived from books was no more than the casual results of the light and purposeless reading of a gentleman of the ordinary degree of accomplishment. Neither his habits of study, nor his attainments, were calculated to invigorate his intellectual or imaginative faculties. His acquaintance with English poetry was by no means extensive, and his tastes singularly contracted. Of Chaucer his only mention is in terms of strong and supercilious—and, let me add, ignorant—contempt. There is no evidence of familiarity with either Spenser, or Shakspeare, or Milton, and, indeed, proof that his sympathy with their immortal works was small and sluggish. They had no place in his affections. Now, some may be inclined to discover in this signs of Byron's power and his originality; but the history of the minds of his most illustrious predecessors is an insuperable obstacle to all this sophistry. Besides, this imperfect and careless cultivation led to no such independence. It did lead to literary bigotry and intolerance, narrow tastes, and acrimonious opposition to whatever thwarted them. His critical opinions were often so perversely peculiar, that we might rather attribute them to his habitual recklessness of truth, were there not sufficient reason to believe him sincere in them. What but the dogmatism of a half-educated and ill-disciplined mind could speak in such words as these, to be found in one of Byron's prose pieces?—"I would no more say that Pope is as high a poet as Shakspeare and Milton, than I would, in the mosque, (once St. Sophia's,) that Socrates was a greater man than Mohammed. But, if any great natural or national convulsion could or would sweep Great Britain from the kingdoms of the earth, and leave only that after all the most living of human things, a dead language, to be studied and read and imitated by the wise of future and far generations, upon foreign shores,—if English literature should become the learning of mankind, divested of party cabals, temporary fashions, and national pride and prejudices,—an Englishman, anxious that the posterity of strangers should know that there had been such a thing as a British Epic and Tragedy, might wish for the preservation of Shakspeare and Milton; but the surviving world would snatch Pope from the wreck and let the rest sink with the people. He is the moral poet of all civilization; and, as such, let us hope that he will one day be the national poet of mankind." Was there ever such extravagance? Shakspeare and Milton sinking with the people, and Pope, snatched by the surviving world from the abyss of perishing England, be the national poet of the whole human race! But, so far was Byron's want of cultivation from increasing his originality by separating him from other influences, that it was the very cause which impaired it; for, unarmed with settled principles of his art, no one more frequently lapsed into unconscious imitations of his contemporaries,—the very poets whom he reviled, but from whose influences he could not wholly isolate himself. It was this, too, which may explain the changeable character of his poetry. One while you meet with what may be pronounced uncontrolled poetic inspiration; another while it becomes with him a thing of mere art. His mind seems to have reeled from one system to another, and never caught a steady view of the principle that poetry is both an inspiration and an art, demanding, therefore, natural endowment and studious cultivation. No art could ever give the poet's creative, shaping faculty of imagination; but equally true is it that no great poet has ever safely ventured to approach the principles of his art lightly and carelessly. Strange indeed would it be if that, the most precious talent intrusted to man, should multiply without the laborious cultivation which is a law to fallen humanity. The primal curse is upon the poet not less than on other men. He must *labour* in his vocation for the last sounds of spontaneous poetry,—the instinctive imaginations, the natural melodies which made happy the heart of the new-created man,—past away with the last gales that blew over Eden.

The merit of "Childe Harold" lies in the latter cantos; and, on turning at the present day to those which formed the first publication of the poem, the reader cannot there find the brilliant success, which instantly welcomed it, justified. "I woke," said Byron, "one morning and found myself famous." He had made his name known by his earlier poems; he now had newly returned from his foreign travels in Spain and Greece. Just entered into manhood,—a peer,—distinguished, too, for his personal beauty,—he had succeeded in throwing an air of romance around himself which was greatly increased by a mystical correspondence with the fictitious personage of the poem. There were flashes of skepticism and misanthropy which heightened the fascination; for they seemed strangely to accord with the feelings of a young nobleman, surrounded by wealth and fashion, returning from travels full of enterprise and an activity undiminished by luxurious habits of sensuality,—returning to take his seat in the House of Lords and to publish a poem which had been conceived and executed in distant lands. There were all the elements of a speedy and unbounded popularity. The form of the poem—travels in poetry—was attractive; and, making no demand upon the reader for any great sympathetic effort of imagination or reflection, it is not surprising that it was at once read and admired by thousands. The finest passages in the early cantos are those which were inspired upon the soil of Greece. The young poet's emotions awakened there were strong, and they were real; and with such impulse his imagination rises to a vivid vision of the ancient battle-field :—

"First bowed beneath the brunt of Hellas' sword,
As on the morn, to distant glory dear,
When Marathon became a magic word,
Which uttered, to the hearer's eye appear
The camp, the host, the flight, the conqueror's career!

"The flying Mede, his shaftless, broken bow;
The fiery Greek, his red pursuing spear;
Mountains above, earth's ocean's plains below,
Death in the front, destruction in the rear!—
Such was the scene. What now remaineth here?
What sacred trophy marks the hallowed ground,
Recording Freedom's smile and Asia's tear?—
The rifled urn, the violated mound,
The dust thy courser's hoof, rude stranger, spurns around."

In quick succession followed the Oriental Tales, everyway fitted to sustain and increase the poet's popularity, not less by passages of brilliant poetry than by the dazzling melodramatic effect resulting from the frameworks of the poems, the pomp and circumstance of Eastern life, with names and words known only in fanciful associations,—these, the accidents, as I may call them, the costume and scenery, greatly enhances the interest of these productions. They fostered Byron's propensity to deal with exaggerations of depravity,—the moral monsters, like his Corsair, "linked with one virtue and a thousand crimes." Surely it was a small game for one gifted like Byron to be playing over again the exploded extravagancies of the sickly romantic novel, by once more bringing forward that unnatural, unmeaning race of imaginary beings,—the sentimental villains. It had grown to be ridiculous in those prose fictions which, imitating humanity so abominably, had given way before the true and manlier novel of the Waverley school; but literary heresies, like worn-out heresies in the church, often revive in a new disguise, to be again welcomed by a morbid and unchastened taste, the appetite that feeds on criminal records and the dying confessions of murderers, and stories of inhuman and superhuman atrocity. The stock-players in the worthless novels and romances which filled the circulating libraries of the last century were bravos and bandits and assassins; and Lord Byron should have known that fictions, whether in prose or verse, with such heroes, were the meanest efforts of imagination, and addressed to a vulgar as well as an undisciplined spirit. It was a pitiful thing for a man to pander to and stimulate such tastes.

It has been my determination to have in this lecture as little to do as possible with Lord Byron's personal character, and to advert to it only when absolutely necessary, and where it is illustrative of the spirit of his writings. He has mingled the story of his marriage with his poetry. It was no strange thing that that marriage was an unhappy one. There was little, if any, love in it. It was one of those cool connections more common in a highly-artificial state of society than, happily, they are among us. I do not mean to say much about it; not that there can be doubt to whom the rupture and final separation were owing. The specific causes of it have not been revealed; but I want nothing more to satisfy me where the guilt lay, than a few incidents that are known. The story of Byron's life, as told by his friend and apologist, convicts him of that which is a man's most unmanly and pitiful habit,—*quarrelling with the women.* If any blind idolater of the poet can find in his heart to palliate this dark spot, let him only contrast the conduct of the parties. Lady Byron, with a womanly fortitude, preserving on the causes of their separation an indomitable silence, which cannot be too highly respected: he—the man with less than a man's sense of honour—assailing the mother of his child with published verses, an unnatural compound of sentiment and satire, proclaiming his boastful resolution never to touch a shilling of his wife's fortune, and then breaking through his vain determination by grasping all that he could reach of it,—sentimentalizing about his daughter, and then plunging into a career of debauchery which left to that daughter the blackest of all legacies,—the memory of a parent's worst guilt.

This epoch of Byron's life I touch upon chiefly for the sake of noticing some of the matchless sophistry which has been employed in his apology. The biography of the poet was intrusted to an amiable and accomplished brother-poet, a writer overflowing with that fanciful style of feeling, styled "*sentimentality*." According to Moore's theory, what was the cause of Byron's matrimonial infelicity? His genius. For the sake of veiling the moral deformities of the noble poet, the biographer has raised a cloud of gaudy sophistry which casts a shade upon the grandest endowments of the human intellect. He would teach the dangerous fallacy that there is a dreary gulf between poetic power and domestic virtue and happiness; that genius of the higher order is a wild thing, "not to be tamed and domesticated in society;" that it must dwell in what he calls "the lonely laboratory of self:" to take up his words, that "genius ranks but low among the elements of social happiness; that, in general, the brighter the gift the more disturbing its influence, and that in married life particularly its effects have been too often like that of the 'wormwood star,' whose light filled the waters on which it fell with bitterness." "It is," he adds, "a coincidence no less striking than saddening, that on the list of married poets who have been unhappy in their homes there should already be found four such illustrious names as Dante, Milton, Shakspeare, and Dryden, and that we should now have to add as a partner in their destiny a name worthy of being placed beside the greatest of them,—Lord Byron."

A passage like this calls for remark, not only for its own sake, but because it is a specimen of the systematic sentimental sophistry that has been woven around Lord Byron's memory. There is an evil spirit at work in it, confounding the sense of right and wrong, defacing and mutilating the landmarks of virtue and vice :—"fair is foul and foul is fair." The doctrine is deliberately taught that the higher a man's intellectual powers the further they are removed from the best elements of his moral being; that the qualities of the head and the heart travel in different and opposite roads. It is the old and shallow but not obsolete fallacy that genius is privileged to claim exemption from moral obligation; as if a human being were any the less a man because he is a poet!—a lawlessness which no truly great poet ever dreamed of arrogating. It is the fatal sophistry which would divorce genius from its natural alliance with all that is good and noble and spiritual, and drive it to batten with the base, the selfish, and sensual. Moore brought to his argument all the force of his brilliant fancy; but it has been swept away by an answer, full not only of fancy but of truth, which was called forth in one of that remarkable series of papers, the "*Noctes Ambrosianæ*,"* — witty, imaginative, and thoughtful. The vindication of genius and its capacity for domestic happiness is put in the mouth of the Ettrick Shepherd; and, after a careful refutation, it closes with this glowing prose rhapsody :—

"I have read Shakspeare and Milton many thousand times; and, Master Moore, you had no right, sir, by your *ipse dixit*, to place Byron by the side of them two,—the greatest of all the children of men : he must sit, in all his glory, far down beneath their feet." And then, as to the domestic virtues :—"Why, it is in the power of any one man of the higher order of genius — say poetical

* Blackwood's Magazine.

genius — to lavish, in the prodigality of his soul, more love on his wife during any one day—ay, any one hour—than it is in the capacity of a blockhead to bestow on his during fifty years, beginning with the first blink of the honeymoon and ending with the last hour that falls upon her coffin. Oh, what a fearful heap of passion can the poet cram into one embrace—one kiss—one smile—one look—one whisper—one word—towards the partner of his life, the mother of his weans! What though the poet's marriage-life be sometimes stormy?—what though sometimes

> 'Blackness comes across it like a squall,
> Darkening the sea'?

Yet who can paint the glory and the brightness of the celestial calm, when the world of them two—of him and his wife—may be likened to the ocean and all her isles in the breezy sunshine, and them two, themselves to consort-ships steering along with all their sails and all their streamers—no fear of shoals or lee-shore rocks—on, on, on, together, towards the haven of everlasting rest among the regions of the setting sun! Or when it may be likened—that is, the world of them two, of him and his wife—to the blue lift all a-lilt with laverocks, and themselves, too, like consort-clouds, now a wee way apart, and now melting into one another, pursued by eyes looking up from below along their sky-course, of which the goal is set, by God's own hand, far away among the stars of heaven!"

Byron, his home desolate and his popularity followed by public odium, left his native land, never to revisit it. He found a dwelling for a time in the region of the

Alps, and then passed into Italy; and this was the period of his best poetry. The tumultuous passions which had agitated him not long before subsided into a gentler feeling than marked any other portion of his life. The tempest which had driven him from his domestic mooring was followed by a fitful calm. It is worthy of reflection that, in this mood of mind, his imagination displayed more true power than in the seasons of its false and morbid energy. The one was the vigour of health, the other, the force of fever. The mock and exaggerated sentiment which he dallied with in so many of his poems made room for that which was genuine pathos. This will be understood by all who are familiar with Byron's poetry,—and I am this evening calculating peculiarly on a general familiarity with the subject of the lecture,—it will be understood by suggesting to your recollections the contrast between "The Corsair" and that beautiful poem, "The Prisoner of Chillon." To this period also belongs one of his pieces which seems to me to display more of genuine imagination, more chaste and better sustained, than any poem he has left. I refer to that entitled "The Dream." The marked years of his life are brought together by a fine imaginative effort, which blends also, with admirable effect, the actual and the spiritual. There is nothing counterfeit in it. The lights and shadows, glimmer and gloom, pass over the spirit of this dream, with all the reality of truth and imagination. The descriptions are worthy of all praise. How perfectly picturesque is the Eastern scene!—

"A change came o'er the spirit of my dream.
The boy was sprung to manhood: in the wilds

Of fiery climes he made himself a home,
And his soul drank their sunbeams: he was girt
With strange and dusky aspects; he was not
Himself like what he had been; on the sea
And on the shore he was a wanderer;
There was a mass of many images
Crowded like waves upon me; but he was
A part of all; and in the last he lay
Reposing from the noontide sultriness,
Couched among fallen columns, in the shade
Of ruined walls that had survived the names
Of those who reared them; by his sleeping side
Stood camels grazing, and some goodly steeds
Were fastened near a fountain; and a man
Clad in a flowing garb did watch the while,
While many of his tribe slumbered around;
And they were canopied by the blue sky,
So cloudless, clear, and purely beautiful,
That God alone was to be seen in heaven!"

It was now, too, that the poet's love of external nature expanded more. No poet ever enjoyed finer or more various opportunities of communion with the earth and the elements. He was a denizen of ocean and of lake, of Alpine regions and of Greek and Italian plains. He had a poet's quick susceptibility to the tumultuous sublimity and the placid beauty of the world of sense that surrounded him. There were times when his heart was open to these natural influences, so that there arose the true poetic sympathy between the inner world of spirit and the outer world of sense. The finest passages of the "Childe Harold" are those in which nature had her will with this wayward child:—

"Clear, placid Leman! thy contrasted lake,
With the wild world I dwelt in, is a thing

Which warns me, with its stillness, to forsake
Earth's troubled waters for a purer spring.
This quiet sail is as a noiseless wing
To waft me from distraction. Once I loved
Torn Ocean's roar; but thy soft murmuring
Sounds sweet as if a sister's voice reproved
That I with stern delights should e'er have been so moved.

"It is the hush of night, and all between
The margin and the mountains, dusk, yet clear,
Mellowed and mingling, yet distinctly seen,
Save darkened Jura, whose capt heights appear
Precipitously steep; and, drawing near,
There breathes a living fragrance from the shore,
Of flowers yet fresh with childhood; on the ear
Drops the light drip of the suspended oar,
Or chirps the grasshopper one good-night carol more.

* * * * *

"The sky is changed!—and such a change! O night,
And storm, and darkness, ye are wondrous strong,
Yet lovely in your strength, as is the light
Of a dark eye in woman! Far along,
From peak to peak the rattling crags among,
Leaps the live thunder! Not from one lone cloud,
But every mountain now hath found a tongue,
And Jura answers, through her misty shroud,
Back to the joyous Alps, who call to her aloud!

"And this is in the night. Most glorious night!
Thou wert not sent for slumber! Let me be
A sharer in thy fierce and free delight,—
A portion of the tempest and of thee!
How the lit lake shines,—a phosphoric sea,—
And the big rain comes dancing to the earth!
And now again 'tis black."

I would gladly break the quotation here, in the middle of the stanza, in order not to break the impression of a passage of such true poetry, which I would always wish to leave unimpaired; but (it vexes me to be obliged to use this qualifying particle but) there follows a striking exemplification of those tumid exaggerations which are the weakness mingled with the poet's power :—

> "And now the glee
> Of the loud hills shakes with its mountain-mirth,
> *As if they did rejoice o'er a young earthquake's birth."*

The love of nature with Byron was passionate rather than either thoughtful or imaginative :—

> "A feeling, and a love,
> That had no need of a remoter charm
> By thought supplied, nor any interest
> Unborrowed from the eye."

He knew, however, that it was necessary to make it something more,—that a great descriptive poet cannot rest contented with what is an appetite and a rapture. One of poetry's grandest purposes—the showing how the external world and the mind of man fitted to each other —was before him. His strong poetic instincts struggled towards it, but the moral weakness of his genius perverted and lowered his aspirations. The blindness of idolatry came over him; the world of sight and sound became a divinity to him. That which was intended for only the means for higher ends became all in all to him. The material world, which its Creator formed to minister food not only to our bodily wants but to the imaginative appetites, which feed on the grand and beautiful that meet the senses, hemmed his faithless spirit in, not because of its strength, which many have mistaken its turbulence for, but because of its weakness. In this I do not fear to say the imagination of Byron failed: it had not strength to extricate itself from the sophistries of materialism. The strong passion for nature with which he was doubtless gifted, the moment he strove to make it any thing more than a passion, spent itself in misty, cloudy rhapsodies, meaningless of every thing but the old errors of a sensual philosophy. The days of fascination gone by, it is time to understand that when Byron's poetry begins to utter materialism it begins to utter folly, and then it ceases to be poetry, for poetry is allied to wisdom and madness. The poet had set up for his worship an idol as helpless as the headless trunk of Dagon. Quenching the true and spiritual love of nature, he talked of making the mountains his friends, and boasted that it was man's noblest companionship; but his heart told him, "Miserable friends are ye." It was his pride to love earth only for its "earthly sake," and to talk unmeaningly of becoming "*a portion of that around him,*" of "*high mountains being a feeling to him,*" and that he could see

"Nothing to loathe in nature, save to be
A link reluctant in that fleshly chain,
Classed among creatures, when the soul can flee,
And with the sky, the peak, the heaving plain
Of ocean, and the stars, mingle, and not in vain.

"And when at length the mind shall be all free
From what it hates in this degraded form,
Reft of its carnal life, save what shall be
Existent happier in the fly and worm,—
Where elements to elements conform
And dust is as it should be,—shall I not
Feel all I see, less dazzling but more warm?
The bodiless thought,—the spirit of each spot,—
Of which even now I share at times the immortal lot?"

Now, strip this, and the multitude of passages like it in Byron's poems, of all that is fantastic; measure it, as you please, either by the practical rules of common sense, or by the ethereal standard of the imagination, and what is it but the perplexity and the folly of materialism? What natural instinct is there, let me ask, so strong in the human heart as that which recoils from the dread anticipation that this living flesh of ours, or the cherished features of those that are dear to us, will be fed upon by worms in the grave?—a thought that would crush us down in helpless abasement but for the one bright hope beyond. And then to think of a poet exulting in the prospect of that remnant of his carnal life *"existent happier in the worm"!* When Byron is honoured as the great poet of nature, I wish you to understand where he will lead his disciple and where he will desert him. The material world has high and appropriate uses in the building up of a moral being: the study of it in the right spirit is full of instruction, but worthless and perilous if we lose sight of the great truth of the soul's spiritual supremacy over it,—that there is implanted in each human being an undying particle, destined to outlive not this earth alone, but the universe. The poet sent his materialized imagination to roam over the world of sense, ocean and mountain, seeking what the world could not give. *"Where shall wisdom be found, and where is the place of understanding? The depth saith, It is not in me; and the sea saith, It is not with me."**

The frailty of Byron's imagination is betrayed not only in his abandonment of the spiritual principle within

* Job, chap. xxvi. 2.

him instead of subordinating the world of sense to it, but also in the inability to accomplish what he undertook, of imaginatively identifying himself with the material objects around him. This is a prime function of the faculty of imagination:—to fuse together things in their nature different, giving them a harmonious existence and making them as one. Remember how the passion with which Shakspeare invests any of his creations shapes and colours all it touches. When Byron labours to combine his own personal feelings with the influences of nature, he throws the elements together, but for the most part leaves them unmingled and in confusion. You find unconnected and incongruous sentiments,—the admiration of earth's loftiest scenes, with morbid and restless social passions: indeed, so incoherent does his imagination become, that the chief element in his love of nature is hatred of mankind. The most strenuous effort of his imagination was the dramatic poem "Manfred," where he shapes into a visible form the beauty of inanimate foam,—the apparition of the beautiful witch of the Alps rising from the sunlit spray of the cataract. There is a passage in one of Byron's poems forming a splendid exception to the absence of the perfect combining power of imagination in so much of his descriptive poetry. It has the unaffected reality of true poetic sublimity in all the simplicity of imaginative truth. The lofty range of mountains, the history-hallowed battle-ground, the vast space of the ocean, are all vivified with the deep emotion of the one human being standing in the midst of them. The associating harmonizing energy of the poetic faculty blends all the elements in perfect union:—

"*The mountains look on Marathon,*
And Marathon looks on the sea;
And, musing there an hour alone,
I dreamed that Greece might still be free;
For, standing on the Persian's grave,
I could not deem myself a slave.

"A king sat on the rocky brow,
Which looks o'er sea-born Salamis;
And ships by thousands lay below,
And men in nations: all were his!
He counted them at break of day;
And, when the sun set, where were they?"

Italy opened to the poet her ancient cities and her glorious works of sculpture, painting, and architecture; and, in this world of art, his imagination expatiated with more power and thought than in the world of nature. He stood in the Adriatic City, and its ancient splendour rose to his vision:—

"A thousand years their cloudy wings expand
Around me, and a dying glory smiles
O'er the far times, when many a subject land
Looked to the wingéd lion's marble piles,
Where Venice sat in state, throned on her hundred isles!"

He beheld *the Eternal City*, the

"Childless and crownless, in her voiceless woe,
An empty urn within her withered hands,
Whose holy dust was scattered long ago."

He gazed upon the marble of the world-renowned Apollo:—

"The lord of the unerring bow,
The god of life and poesy and light,—
The sun in human limbs arrayed, and brow
All radiant from his triumph in the fight:

The shaft hath just been shot,—*the arrow bright*
With an immortal vengeance; in his eye
And nostril beautiful disdain, and might,
And majesty, flash their full lightnings by,
Developing in that one glance the deity."

He mused within the Coliseum; and, though mingling with his musings the spite of his petty quarrels, his weak hatred of man, and the worse and weaker hatred of woman,—the swelling subterfuge of moral littleness,—yet rising to the rapt vision of the dying athlete:—

"I see before me the gladiator lie:
He leans upon his hand; his manly brow
Consents to death, but conquers agony;
And his drooped head sinks gradually low,
And through his side the last drops, ebbing slow,
From the red gash fall heavy, one by one,
Like the first of a thunder-shower: and now
The arena swims around him: he is gone
Ere ceased the inhuman shout that hailed the wretch who won.

"He heard it, but he heeded not: his eyes
Were with his heart, and that was far away;
He recked not of the life he lost, nor prize,
But where his rude hut by the Danube lay:
There were his young barbarians, all at play;
There was their Dacian mother, he, their sire,
Butchered to make a Roman holiday:
All this rushed with his blood. Shall he expire,
And unavenged? Arise, ye Goths, and glut your ire!"

In this instance, the poet's morbid feelings passed into a pure channel,—the thought of his own separation from his child awakening, no doubt, a fine sympathy with the gladiator's dismal dying emotions for his young barbarians on the distant Danube.

Passing from Byron's claims as the poet of nature, he has been styled the poet of freedom. Spirited lines have burst from him on this theme:—

"Yet, Freedom! yet thy banner, torn but flying,
Streams like the thunder-storm against the wind;
Thy trumpet-voice, though broken now and dying,
The loudest still, the tempest leaves behind."

He harped upon the lost liberties of Italy and Greece, and the living liberties of America. Let us look, before rashly welcoming the alliance. The love of freedom with Byron was a sentiment, but it had no depth beyond that; and, when you come to analyze it carefully, its elements are misanthropy and *lawlessness.* I never hear his tributes to our institutions quoted, without an instinctive regret that any countryman of mine should, in his avidity for foreign flattery, be thus deluded. The name of Washington is met with more than once in Byron's poems in terms of praise: that name is beyond the reach of contamination; but still I recoil, as if it were profaned, when I contrast the manly, dutiful, genuine spirit of freedom in which he was nursed, with the spurious, fitful, sentimental licentiousness of the poet. When the tribute of a foreigner is rendered to our country or its men, I wish first to know whether that foreigner's heart is true to his own country, and not poisoned with a counterfeit liberality and a morbid hostility to that which nature and wisdom and truth all bid him hold dear. When a man like Southey points to this country as the land

"Where Washington hath left
His awful memory
A light to after-times!"

the tribute is worth something. But the spirit of freedom which gave that light could not be truly reverenced by one whose heart had grown hard in aristocratic licentiousness; who, running the wild career of profligacy, sought the last stimulant of his morbid tastes in the sentimental luxury of a romantic crusade.

"*The sensual and the dark rebel in vain;*"

and I deny the sincerity of Byron's professions and his power of knowing a genuine freedom, from the whole story of his life and mind. The true and the manly part was not a share in petty Italian tumults or in Greek revolutions, but to hold the responsible post at which his birth had placed him; for if, as he proclaimed, the liberties of England were in danger, the plainer and the stronger was it the duty of one gifted like him to battle for them to the last. That would have been indeed true energy, instead of its gaudy counterfeit in his sentimental recreancy.

If Lord Byron's descriptions of nature and his sense of freedom were imperfect and unequal, his portraiture of human characters is marked with the same imperfections. His imagination could not rise above the range of his own individual and morbid impulses. All his creations were of the same family, and all imaginatively kindred to himself,—impersonations of the same moral disease in some or other of its forms, and all betraying a woful, wilful ignorance of the better elements of human nature. Coloured by the poet's vivid fancy, they passed for heroes; but strip them of their disguise,—their playhouse finery,—and there is not one among them who rises—I will not say to the heroic standard, but—even to the level of real manliness. How opposite, it has been well said,* was Shakspeare's conception of a hero!—

"Give me that man
That is not passion's slave, and I will wear him
In my heart's core,—ay, in my heart of hearts."

I need scarcely remark that a true idea of the strength and beauty of *womanly* humanity had no place in Byron's mind. It was almost an unknown world to him, abounding, at the same time, as his poems do, with bright romantic creations of fancy and sentiment. Of these, when placed in situations calling for masculine energy, he gives some striking images, as the description in "Sardanapalus:"—

"She urged on with her voice and gesture, and
Her floating hair and flashing eyes, the soldiers
In the pursuit. * * * * I paused
To look upon her, and her kindled cheek;
Her large black eyes, that flashed through her long hair
As it streamed o'er her; her blue veins that rose
Along her most transparent brow; her nostril
Dilated from its symmetry; her lips
Apart; her voice that clove through all the din
As a lute's pierceth through the cymbal's clash,
Jarred, but not drowned, by the loud brattling; her
Waved arms, more dazzling with their own born whiteness
Than the steel her hand held, which she caught up
From a dead soldier's grasp;—all these things made
Her seem unto the troops a prophetess
Of Victory, or Victory herself
Come down to hail us hers."

* See preface to Henry Taylor's "Philip Van Artaveldte."

What was the meaning of the fitful irregularity of Byron's poetry, which we have been passing over with praise and blame mingled, and, perhaps, perplexed? Why is it that, with passages of true poetry scattered through all his volumes, he produced no important poem for which his most impassioned admirer can claim the fame of sustained imagination? And why, at last, unable either to quench or to feed the flame of poetry, did he ignominiously retreat into that base production in which, the very instant his better powers failed him he could exchange them for a vulgar ribaldry and all the vile elements of his nature,—the leprosy rising up in his forehead while standing beside the incense-altar? Was there any mystery in his inequalities? We are told that it was owing to his *genius*. Let me say that weakness is no attribute of genius. Here lies the grand fallacy respecting Byron's mind,—that which was its weakness mistaken for its strength, confounding the violence of his passions with power. Strength is shown by the victory over them, and not by the defeat. Byron deluded himself in these respects, when he should have known that really it is moral and intellectual weakness to be a misanthrope and a skeptic. It is an easy thing to fall into the way of hating the world, and into that confused, blind, stupid state of mind which is called unbelief. The greatest of all weaknesses—the cancer which eat into the very heart of Byron's genius—was his unmitigated *selfishness*. It weakened and wasted him, and perverted and defiled his great endowments, and brought him down to the grave, superannuated, at the age of thirty-six. It was the foul fiend which haunted his existence, tearing him like the wretched demoniacs who dwelt among the tombs and cried out words of blasphemy and defiance.

I am not going now to qualify my language with exceptions and reservations. That has been done, to the best of my ability, scrupulously throughout the lecture; and I am therefore justified in now saying that, taking the whole spirit of Byron's poetry,—its skepticism, its profanity, its blasphemy, its lewdness, its warfare upon religion and social and domestic morals,—it stands the blackest monument of intellectual depravity in the annals of our language. Never had our poetry been so profaned. The same corrupt spirit had been known before; it had disguised itself in one generation in the stately robe of philosophy,—in another it had snatched the myrtle-wreath of political freedom; but never before had it worn the garland of poetic inspiration. There had been one phase of infidelity with Bolingbroke and his disciples, and another with Paine and his crew; but the most insidious was that which came from the bright, dark fancy of Byron.

With all the wrong he did, there was mingled, too, a bitter contempt for poor, suffering humanity. Yes; it is true, as he reproached his fellow-mortals, that mankind is prostrate in his fallen nature. Look forth upon the human race, and, behold! they are lying—the wounded, the dying, and the dead—on the vast battle-plain, stricken by their spiritual enemies. But it ill became a poet to steal forth in the night, like one of those wretches that dog the footsteps of an army and prowl over the field fresh with the fight, plundering the expiring soldier, and stripping the bloody raiment from the dead and the dying.

Above all, let me entreat that no one will yield to that poor fallacy which teaches that Byron's infirmities and vice were attributes of genius :—

"If thou be one whose heart the holy forms
Of young imagination have kept pure,
Henceforth be warned, and know that pride,
Howe'er disguised in its own majesty,
Is littleness; that he who feels contempt
For any living thing hath faculties
Which he has never used; that thought, with him,
Is in its infancy. The man whose eye
Is ever on himself doth look on one
The least of Nature's works,—one who might move
The wise man to that scorn which wisdom holds
Unlawful ever. Oh, be wiser, thou!
Instructed that true knowledge leads to love;
True dignity abides with him alone
Who, in the silent hour of inward thought,
Can still suspect and still revere himself
In lowliness of heart."*

* Wordsworth.

LECTURE XV.

Wordsworth.

Difficulties in the way of a proper appreciation of contemporary genius — Candour rare in criticism — Controversy in regard to Wordsworth's school of poetry—Comparative criticism between the poetry of Wordsworth and Byron — Correspondence of Wordsworth's life with the spirit of true poetry—Continuity of his moral life — Recollections of his childhood — His love of nature and of man—His sympathy with the French Revolution—His seclusion—Communion with his brother-poets—Aim of his career of authorship—Lines composed in the neighbourhood of Tintern Abbey—"The Excursion"—"Sonnet on Westminster Bridge"—"Lines on the Death of Mr. Fox"—"Tribute to a favourite Dog"—"Simon Lee" — "Story of the Deserted Cottage"—His political poems—Conclusion.

We are now nearing the close of that glorious registry we have been engaged in examining. When I placed my mind, upon the imaginative point of vision, by the side of Chaucer, the father of English poetry, and looked forward, over the tract of nearly five hundred years, to the noble company of his successors, it was a joy to know that modern times would not be found to bring with them modern degeneracy.

There was encouragement in the assurance that, in quitting the companionship of the mighty men of old we should not pass into the society of a dwarfish and dwindling race. It is a proud feeling, too, that there is shining upon us not only those rays which travel down from former generations, but the light of the living genius of our own. I have been zealous to display the vast spaces of our English poetry; and especially to show how that domain has been, in successive eras, acquired, whenever a poet of original powers has arisen to discover and reclaim the unknown and neglected region. Remember how we have seen one territory after another thus appropriated and added to our imaginative literature. There was a time when the language was almost without form and void, and darkness was upon the face of its literature. The rude inventions of a barbarian minstrelsy appeared; but soon came Chaucer, the great poet of the fourteenth century. Like the Ancient Mariner, "he was the first that ever burst into that silent sea." It is only necessary to recur to the progress of the English Muse to learn how wrong is the notion which leads to the belief that the dominion of poetry has reached its utmost confines. The poorest pedantry is that which, not unfrequently, has taught implicit, passive obedience to the authority of a few models, and bound down genius to the servile toil of reiterated imitation. This cannot be: the universe is infinitely wide; and the highest proof is when it holds on high a light which reveals to the world realms which had been unknown as belonging to the sovereignty of imagination. It is the highest attribute of original powers to enlarge the sphere of human sensibility. Think, for instance, how the light of Spenser's imagination at once disclosed to view the untravelled latitudes of his marvellous allegory,—how there soon came the discovery of what may be called the world of Shakspeare,—and how all to whom the spirit and the sounds of our sublimest poetry are dear have been borne, by the imagination of Milton, through regions radiant with angelic light, through the happy home on the infant and sinless earth, and through the dark and dismal dwellings of the lost spirits. It is grand to find our language made subservient to such uses, and ennobling to contemplate the powers with which the most gifted of our race are endowed, employed to enlarge the compass of human thought. In the history of any department of knowledge, it is easier to recognise how this has been accomplished by those whose approved fame time has sanctioned, than to understand and appreciate similar services rendered by contemporary genius. Nor is this strange. Fame is a slow, and often a reluctant, gift. There is a constitutional frailty in us which explains why it is so. The actual presence is an obstacle to that honour which should be rendered to prophet and poet in his own country or his own generation. This must needs be so in poetry above all. When a poet of truly original powers arises, his very originality can be shown only by extending the light of his genius to regions of thought and feeling unillumined before. Now, too often this is regarded not so much as an enlargement of our ancient and best possession, but an encroachment upon them, and therefore to be resisted. Old landmarks are changed, and time is not taken to inquire whether the change has increased or contracted the territory. Settled literary opinions and tastes, carelessly acquired at first, are disturbed; and this, it seems to me, is one solution of the antagonist reception which every original poet of the higher order of genius is doomed to encounter from the world. It is a warfare that he must wage,—a conquest to be effected,—happily if controlled by the meek spirit of magnanimity. In criticism, candour, with its comprehensive sympathies, is as rare as bigotry is frequent; and therefore the world has never yet been quick to welcome the greatest poets that have blessed it. The seclusion of Stratford, and the deeper seclusion of the grave, had long closed over Shakspeare before a thousandth part of his genius was known. The pure and gentle heart of Edmund Spenser wasted beneath neglect and the frustrated hope of his unfinished poem. The indomitable spirit of Milton calmly knew how little he had to expect from his contemporaries. So it has ever been. What else is the reason of that tradition which, when all else that is personal respecting the father of poetry has perished, has come down to us upon the cloudy wings of three thousand years,—the tradition that Homer was a beggar? It has been finely said, "What a glorious gift God bestows upon a nation when he gives them a poet!" It might be added, with a sadder truth, that, when the poet enters upon his mission of gladdening and purifying and spiritualizing the hearts of men, the world is ready with the insult, the scoff, the ridicule, and all the weapons of a stupid and ignorant enmity. There is a blindness blinder than the mole's; there is a deafness deafer than the adder's: it is the blindness, the deafness of literary bigotry!

The character of the poetry which forms the subject of the present lecture has been peculiarly the subject of controversy,—advocated by an earnest, affectionate, and grateful sense of admiration, and assailed by misapprehension, contempt, and a rancorous and reckless hatred. It is not my intention to deal with my subject in a spirit of controversy, for two reasons. I have not done so in any part of the course. I have neither attacked nor defended any one of the poets in a controversial spirit; and surely it could not be worth while to assume the tone of polemics now, when just about to part with you. In the second place, it would be a form of discussion wholly unworthy the poet. The time has gone by for it. The poetry has wrought out its own vindication,—one of the noblest victories, in the annals of literature, of truth and the magnanimous self-possession which is its best attendant, over error, with all its alliance of vulgarity and violence and bitterness. Criticism did its worst; but the citadel on which it beat had its foundation deep set in the rock of nature; and we have lived, and—what is more precious to think of—the poet himself has lived, to see the waters of that insolent tide gradually trickling down; and now all that is left—the froth, the foam, the dirt, heaved up from the bottom, and the drift-wood on the surface—are fast floating out of sight.

There has been expended a great deal of comparative criticism between the poetry of Wordsworth and Byron. During this whole course I have refrained from entering upon comparisons between the poets, because it is a mode of criticism as unsatisfactory as it is easy. There would not be the least difficulty in placing them in comparison and in contrast, and in describing the true relation between the minds and the aspirations of these two poets; but it would be an uncalled-for deviation from the habit of my lectures. To any who are disposed to measure their worth by comparisons rather than independently, let me only suggest for reflection one significant forewarning of the abiding judgment of posterity,—the final award of fame:—the fact, indisputable by any one, that every succeeding year has worn away some crumbling portion of Lord Byron's splendid popularity, while the majestic splendour of Wordsworth's poetry has steadily been rising to a loftier stature amid the permanent edifices of the great poets of the English language.

It is with some reserve that I allude to the personal history of a living poet; but so truly has the course of Wordsworth's life corresponded with the spirit of his poetry,—so intimate the communion,—that I may avail myself of the autobiographical allusions in his works, and some other authentic materials. The earliest date attached to any of his pieces is the year 1786,—more than half a century ago; and now, when he has passed the solemn limit of seventy years, his imagination—that faculty which age so often quenches—is held in undiminished vigour. It has been a life devoted to the cultivation of the art for its best and most lasting uses,—a self-dedication as complete as any the world has ever witnessed. Among the great English poets, Edmund Spenser perhaps alone presented a career of as sedulous cultivation, equally the existence of one as entirely a poet. It is one of the causes which have given such perfect symmetry to the various periods of Wordsworth's existence,—a realization of one of his imaginative wishes,—that fine aspiration in the first words with which he meets the reader. It is the hope of a fulfilment of that grand law of our moral being which seeks to preserve the sympathy between the successive eras of life,—a law worthy of reflection; for it is a happiness to look back into past and distant years without the desolating sense of thoughts and feelings swept away by time. It is a happy thing for meditation, standing on the promontory of the present, to feel the air rising from the shadowy waters of the past and sweeping on to sink to rest upon the dim waves of the future. Injury is done to the health of our moral being when the principle of its continuity is broken. Feelings that were meant to be cherished are suffered to perish. This is worse than the work of time; for that which time should only ripen withers and runs to waste. It is the mischief of custom, and not of time; and thus one period of our life is alienated from another. The connection between them is broken, and former days are forgotten or despised. Childish things must, indeed, be put away with childhood; but too often worse than childish things are put in their stead. The uncalculating, unsuspicious fervour of youth, instead of being chastened into a manly fashion of the same feeling, is transformed into selfishness and distrust. Young enthusiasm does not grow into a mature and steadier spirit, but is changed into apathy, or the worse condition,—the habit of weak and morbid ridicule of all that is elevated and impassioned. To take an instance of two periods of life, standing in close connection, and yet often lamentably destitute of that natural piety which should bind them together for happy and salutary meditation and memory:—the ardent devotion of the lover evaporating in matrimony, when he settles down, as the phrase is, into the married man. From the cool region into which he has passed, he looks back upon his former self with something of contemptuous commiseration, disowning the chivalry, the deference, the adoration, as so much obsolete delusion. In Byron's fine poetic phrase, "a change comes o'er the spirit of his dream." He is a different being: his friends scarcely recognise him, and his wife hardly knows the man. I speak of this only as an example of this unnatural decomposition of the feelings of different periods of life, as one of the most striking and most dangerous. It was the poet's purpose to proclaim a law of our moral nature which gives harmony and consistency to life amid all its inevitable vicissitudes. But the lessons poetry teaches must be simple, strong, and touching: they must be imaginative. It was important, too, that the moral should be illustrated by some feeling at once pure and universal,—something all might sympathize with; and, accordingly, he has selected that phenomenon in the heavens which even the feeblest sense of the beauty of nature is touched with:—

"My heart leaps up when I behold
    A rainbow in the sky!
So was it when my life began;
So is it now I am a man;
So be it when I shall grow old,
    Or let me die!
The child is father of the man;
And I could wish my days to be
Bound each to each by natural piety."

The days of Wordsworth's life have been thus bound together by a natural piety; and hence the matchless symmetry of his career,—at once a cause and an effect of his well-disciplined genius. His childhood was spent on the borders of that romantic region in the North of

England where he was to find the happy home of his manhood and old age,—the blue outline of the Cumberland Mountains present to his sight,—a lofty and shadowy region for his young imagination to travel to.

The emotions of the early years of his life have been rescued from oblivion with a power which manifests both the depth of his childhood's impressions and the strength of his imagination in reviving them. I think that every one who has ever reflected on the movements of his own mind must have realized the difficulty of marking the boundary of his memory when it journeys back into past and early years, and at the same time be conscious of the flitting of dim recollections of childhood, —perhaps, after all, the most thoughtful period of our whole life. Feelings will often pass across the mind, coming you cannot tell whence, but only that they come from far away, from the dim distance of childhood. Which of its visionary realms could poetry more happily expatiate in? When the effort is made by a juvenile writer of verses to clothe his impulses in language, it is a weak expression of feeling which yet may be in all respects fit for poetry. But that fitness becomes beautifully apparent when a mature imagination is able to redeem feelings which, in almost all cases, perish entirely, or vanish into the most mysterious chambers of the memory,—such shadowy things that you can scarce tell whether they are recollections, or fancies, or dreams. The more you reflect on these things, the more you will appreciate the imaginative energy necessary to reanimate the impressions received in early life and give them a poetic shape. There is one of Wordsworth's small pieces which exemplifies this power of recalling some of the most evanescent feelings which could have flitted across a boy's mind. He remembers a distant day, bright both with its blue sky and with boyhood's buoyant happiness,—

> "One of those heavenly days that cannot die,"—

on which he sallied forth upon a boyish enterprise of foraging upon the hazel-trees. The eagerness of his hope, the luxury of animal delight, are vividly remembered, but not more so than the rapid transition of feeling,—one of those sudden reactions common to the quick heart of childhood, which rises from its unexpected sense of pain to an exquisite sympathy, by which imagination spiritualizes the insensate world of nature —

> "O'er the pathless rocks, I forced my way
> Until, at length, I came to one dear nook
> Unvisited, where not a broken bough
> Drooped with its withered leaves, ungracious sign
> Of devastation, but the hazels rose,
> Tall and erect, with milk-white clusters hung,—
> A virgin scene! A little while I stood,
> Breathing with such suppression of the heart
> As joy delights in, and, with wise restraint
> Voluptuous, fearless of a rival, eyed
> The banquet; or beneath the trees I sat
> Among the flowers, and with the flowers I played:—
> A temper known to those, who, after long
> And weary expectation, have been blest
> With sudden happiness beyond all hope.
> Perhaps it was a bower beneath whose leaves
> The violets of five seasons reappear
> And fade unseen by any human eye:

Where fairy water breaks do murmur on
Forever; and I saw the sparkling foam,
And with my cheek on one of those green stones
That, fleeced with moss, beneath the shady trees,
Lay round me, scattered like a flock of sheep,
I heard the murmur and the murmuring sound,
In that sweet mood when pleasure loves to pay
Tribute to ease, and, of its joy secure,
The heart luxuriates with indifferent things,
Wasting its kindliness on stocks and stones
And on the vacant air. Then up I rose,
And dragged to earth both branch and bough with crash
And merciless ravage, and the shady nook
Of hazels, and the green and mossy bower,
Deformed and sullied, patiently gave up
Their quiet being: and, unless I now
Confound my present feelings with the past,
Even then, when from the bower I turned away
Exulting, rich beyond the wealth of kings,
I felt a sense of pain when I beheld
The silent trees and the intruding sky.
Then, dearest Maiden! move along these shades
In gentleness of heart; with gentle hand
Touch; for there is a spirit in the woods."

The foundations of Wordsworth's mind were thus laid in communion with the grand and beautiful scenery of his native region:—

"He had felt the power
Of nature, and already was prepared
By his intense conceptions, to receive
Deeply the lesson deep of love which he
Whom Nature, by whatever means, has taught
To feel intensely, cannot but receive."

Conjoined with this,—the first virgin passion of a soul

"Communing with the glorious universe,"—

was his studious, reverential communion with the pages of his great predecessors,—the masters of English poetry, —and chiefly of Milton. Another element of his genius began very early to display itself,—his ever-active sympathy with his fellow men. Deep as his passion for nature has always been, the living nature of mankind has been dearer to him; and it is part of the history of his mind that he hoped greatly and enthusiastically for the cause of social and political regeneration, when for a short season, at the close of the last century, the whole earth

> "The beauty wore of promise,—that which sets
> The budding rose above the rose full blown."

His young spirit, which had fed upon its lonely musings in the mountains and its poetic sympathies with the souls of the dead poets, was prompt to change them for the more active fellow-feeling with mankind struggling for freedom:—

> "Farewell, farewell! the heart that lives alone,
> Housed in a dream, at distance from the kind!
> Such happiness, wherever it is known,
> Is to be pitied, for 'tis surely blind."

Full of hope, Wordsworth passed over into France in the early part of the French Revolution, and was an eye-witness of some of its terrific commotions. His heart was with the down-trodden people, and he was elated with the pure enthusiasm which trusted in the virtues of what proved a worthless cause. He witnessed the wretchedness that had been wrought by tyranny; and, young and ardent, he over-estimated the restraining influences on the people's vengeance. One of the darkest reproaches which rests on the Revolution of France is the wrong done to the eternal cause of freedom; for, when at the present day we seek to appreciate the sufferings which first heaved that vast commotion, there rise up, intercepting the view, the blood-boltered spectres of the hideous agencies in that drama. The sympathies of Wordsworth were with only the pure elements of the cause, especially because of what he witnessed in the miseries of the peasantry. The incident is told, that, walking one day, in the neighbourhood of Orleans, in company with a citizen of France, fervid with republicanism, they came suddenly on the spectacle of a girl of seventeen or eighteen years old, hunger-bitten and wasted to a meagre shadow, knitting in a dejected, drooping way, whilst to her arm was attached by a rope the horse, equally famished, that earned the miserable support of her family. The spectacle told, in one instant, the whole story of wretchedness; and, seizing Wordsworth by the arm, his companion exclaimed, "Dear English friend, brother, from a nation of freemen! *That* it is that is the curse of our people, in their widest division; and to cure this it is, as well as to maintain our work against the kings of the earth, that blood must be shed, and tears must flow, for many years to come."

The atmosphere of the Revolution grew more and more murky. France was stricken with the worst of Egypt's plagues: benighted in moral darkness, it was visited with the pestilence of blood throughout the land. Wordsworth sought the homeward road to England,—the innocent delusion of his enthusiasm scattered, but his heart unembittered by disappointment, and its pulse of genuine freedom beating as strongly as ever. Whilst travelling back to his native region, in crossing the sands of one of the great estuaries, he chanced to inquire of a horseman who overtook him, "Is there any news?" and to hear the tidings, "Yes: Robespierre has perished." Forgetful of the returning tide coming in over the waste of sands, he stopped to utter a heartfelt thanksgiving for that vindication of justice and outraged liberty.

When Wordsworth retired to dwell in the mountain-district of the North of England, there was in the spirit of his seclusion nothing of a morbid solitariness. It was a retirement sought as favourable not only to the genial and studious culture of his endowments, but also to the most propitious intercourse with his fellow-men. There was nothing of that faint and false-hearted flight from society of which genius has sometimes been guilty; but retirement was chosen as the vantage-ground of imagination and meditative truth, and in his solitude he has nursed his heart in a quick sensibility to all healthy sympathies with his country and mankind. His plan of life has been kept inviolate: his home is still among the mountains; his heart is with humanity the wide world over:—

"He murmurs near the running brooks
A music sweeter than their own.
He is retired as noontide dew,
Or fountain in a noonday grove:
And you must love him, ere to you
He will seem worthy of your love.
The outward shows of sky and earth,
Of hill and valley, he has viewed,
And impulses of deeper birth
Have come to him in solitude."

Wordsworth has been fortunate in the cordial communion with Coleridge and Southey and Lamb, and in the friendship of Sir Walter Scott and the patriarch of contemporary poets,—Rogers. He has been happy, too, in the intellectual female sympathy he has enjoyed in the bosom of his own family. This appears not only in his delicate allusions to the members of his household, but from a passage in Mr. Southey's Life of Cowper, plainly alluding to Wordsworth. After speaking of the valuable influence on Cowper's mind of his intimacy with Mrs. Unwin and Lady Austin, Southey adds, "Were I to say that a poet finds his best advisers among his female friends, it would be speaking from my own experience, and the greatest poet of the age would confirm it by his."

The aim of all Wordsworth's endeavours in poetry, as he has stated it, has been that they should be fitted for filling permanently a station, however humble, in the literature of his country. It is remarkable that in not a line can be detected any lowering of that aim to the secondary objects of authorship: no trace of mercenary motive, no paltering with artificial tastes, no sacrifice of truth and nature for the gain of notoriety, no dallying with fashion, betray a faltering in the purpose to which he devoted himself. This demanded extraordinary self-possession—all the fortitude, the magnanimity of genius—to preserve its composure. He moved on fearlessly, following the call of his own imagination; and it is a grand thing now to behold the young and ingenuous, the older and thoughtful, vying with each other in rendering to him the tribute of a grateful admiration.

On the poet's return from the Continent, the love of nature, which had been coeval with his early consciousness, was undiminished. He carried it along with him in his inmost heart, amid all the uncongenial scenes he had been a witness to. There are some admirable lines of his, familiar to every student of Wordsworth's poetry, composed in the neighbourhood of Tintern Abbey, on revisiting the banks of the river Wye: they finely represent the change from the passionate to the meditative love of nature,—the maturing of the emotion of sentient boyhood to that of thoughtful manhood. But I refer to them because they show how the beauteous forms of the external world revisited his memory and his feelings even in unpropitious circumstances,—doubtless amid the tumultuous agitations of the Parisian mobs, the frenzy of the factions, the waves of a ruthless multitude beating against the ancient palace of their kings, the convulsion of every resting-place of society, the unnatural ferocity of revolutionary women, and the boundless vengeance of the metropolis, with the sympathetic restlessness of the provinces. Amid all this, the poet's heart was gladdened by a return of a memory of the emotion which some placid scene had inspired him with:—

"Oh! how oft,
In darkness, and amid the many shapes
Of joyless daylight, when the fretful stir
Unprofitable, and the fever of the world,
Have hung upon the beatings of my heart,—
How oft in spirit have I turned to thee,
O sylvan Wye! Thou wanderer through the woods,
How often has my spirit turned to thee!"

He came forth from amid the cloudy, stormy elements of society to render the unwearied service of a worshipper of nature :—

"I know that nature never did betray
The heart that loved her: 'tis her privilege,
Through all the years of this our life, to lead
From joy to joy; for she can so inform
The mind that is within us, so impress
With quietness and beauty, and so feed
With lofty thoughts, that neither evil tongues,
Rash judgments, nor the sneers of selfish men,
Nor greetings where no kindness is, nor all
The dreary intercourse of daily life,
Shall e'er prevail against us, or disturb
Our cheerful faith that all which we behold
Is full of blessings."

No poet has ever yet so devoted his imagination to the study of the face of nature as Wordsworth. He has communed with her in all her moods, and contemplated the ever-varying expression of her countenance. It would transcend even the expansive limits of these lectures to illustrate his descriptive poetry, and I can only endeavour to give some idea of the spirit of it. In the last lecture I had occasion to show how dangerous the love of nature may become if perverted into a sentimental and insidious materialism. In the heart of Wordsworth the passionate love of nature has not been so betrayed. It is coupled with the faith that infinite wisdom has so formed the earth, the elements, and the physical heavens, that the soul, during its abode in its mortal tenement, can gather, from all that meets the senses, food for its noble faculties :—

> "The glorious habit by which sense is made
> Subservient still to moral purposes,
> Auxiliar to divine."

Deep and habitual as is Wordsworth's devotion to nature, it is no idolatry of what is material. The worlds of the eye and the ear, like the senses that observe them, are subject to decay; and it is not the character of his genius to pause upon what is perishable. He never fails to impress on us that the forms of nature, loved as they are, are fugitive, valueless, except when contemplated in their relation to man and to his Maker; that the earth—the dear, green earth—will darken in the absence of imagination. Nay, more: rising to the height of as lofty aspiration as ever was conceived, either in poetry or philosophy, he proclaims the awful truth that the universe itself—the material universe—is a hollow shell, from which the ear of faith alone can hear mysterious murmurings of eternity. This moral is expounded by means of one of the finest images that ever entered into the heart of poet to conceive,—beautiful in itself and sublime in its application :—

> "I have seen
> A curious child, who dwelt upon a tract
> Of inland ground, applying to his ear
> The convolutions of a smooth-lipped shell,
> To which, in silence hushed, his very soul
> Listened intensely, and his countenance soon
> Brightened with joy; for, murmuring from within,
> Were heard sonorous cadences, whereby
> To his belief the monitor expressed
> Mysterious union with its native sea.
> Even such a shell the universe itself
> Is to the ear of Faith."

There is another passage in the "Excursion," bearing on this subject,—one of those sublime strains with which that poem abounds, and loftier than aught that English poetry has known since the age of Milton. It is an apostrophe to the Deity, and, while it tells that the universe shall perish, also tells the one great element of its glory:—

" Thou who didst wrap the cloud
Of infancy around us, that thyself
Therein, with our simplicity, a while
Might'st hold on earth communion undisturbed,
Who, from the anarchy of dreaming sleep,
Or from its deathlike void, with punctual care
And touch as gentle as the morning light,
Restor'st us daily to the powers of sense
And reason's steadfast rule,—thou, thou alone
Art everlasting, and the blessed Spirits
Which thou includest, as the Sea her Waves,
For adoration thou endurest
This universe shall pass away,—a work
Glorious! because the shadow of thy might,
A step, or link, for intercourse with thee!"

I cite these passages to show the principles of Wordsworth's descriptive poetry,—his love of nature how spiritual; for, amid all his admiration of the world of sense, the undying incorporeal power, the soul, preserves its undaunted sovereignty. So far from suffering his profound sense of the beauty of the material world to entangle his genius in the meshes of materialism, his rapt imagination looks on all the glories of the universe as but a poor substitute for what the soul may know in the imperial palace of its home with God. In the mighty effort of his imagination, the greatest ode in the English language, the ode on the intimations of immortality, dwelling upon the heavenly innocence of childhood,—a feeling in harmony with the Saviour's words; and then, raising the human soul above its material life, he has cast a ray of poetry upon that the most impenetrable of all mysteries,—the origin of the soul before its lodgment in the body. Thus, sublimely asserting our immortality, he heeds this earth as no more than ministering to the spirit that has wandered from some better home into this mortal life:—

"Our birth is but a sleep and a forgetting:
The soul that rises with us, our life's star,
Hath had elsewhere its setting,
And cometh from afar.
Not in entire forgetfulness,
And not in utter nakedness,
But trailing clouds of glory, do we come
From God, who is our home.
Heaven lies about us in our infancy!
Shades of the prison-house begin to close
Upon the growing *boy;*
But he beholds the light, and whence it flows;
He sees it in his joy.
The *youth* who daily farther from the east
Must travel still is nature's priest,
And by the vision splendid
Is on the way attended.
At length the *man* perceives it die away
And fade into the light of coming day.
Earth fills her lap with pleasures of her own;
Yearnings she hath in her own natural kind,
And even with something of a mother's mind,
And no unworthy aim,
The homely nurse doth all she can
To make her foster-child—her inmate, man—
Forget the glories he hath known,
And that imperial palace whence he came."

The purpose which the poet proposes to himself, in his descriptive poetry, was to show how the mind and the external world are fitted to each other, and to accomplish this by rescuing from neglect the unheeded impressions perpetually made upon us, and giving us a distinct consciousness of them when shaped by poetic imagination. Wordsworth's poetry abounds with manifestations of the deep impressions he receives from slight hints, such as occur to any of us in daily life; and it is this which makes a genial admiration of his writings so precious an acquisition. It is a companionship which clings to humanity in all its paths. Once open your heart to it, and its benignant light will be shed on your domestic hearth, upon all your intercourse with your fellow-men, upon your civic responsibilities to your country, and the sublimer relations in which man is placed. Feelings that are apt to run to waste ripen beneath the influence of his imagination, hope is cherished, and the best impulses confirmed, the noblest aspirations sustained. Hence comes that ardent affectionate gratitude for moral and intellectual obligations which, from so many hearts, is the silent tribute to the aged poet:—

"Beauty—a living Presence of the earth,
Surpassing the most fair ideal Forms
Which craft of delicate Spirits hath composed
From earth's materials—waits upon my steps;
Pitches her tents before me as I move,
An hourly neighbour. Paradise, and groves
Elysian, Fortunate Fields,—like those of old,
Sought in the Atlantic main :—why should they be
A history only of departed things,
Or a mere fiction of what never was?
For the discerning intellect of Man,
When wedded to this goodly universe

In love and holy passion, shall find these
A simple produce of the common day.
By words
Which speak of nothing more than what we are
Would I arouse the sensual from their sleep
Of death, and win the vacant and the vain
To nobler raptures."

It is this purpose which has led Wordsworth to consecrate by his imagination things which poetry never shone upon before. You will find in this way a dignity and grace given to feelings which before were perhaps deemed unworthy a second thought. For instance, it is hardly possible for any one to pass along the vacant, noiseless streets of a city at very early morn, before the population is stirring,—to move amid the sleeping power of a large city,—without a sense of the tranquillity of the moment. The emotion is a natural, a common, and a simple one, but it is indefinite and evanescent, and therefore needs the imaginative power of a true poet to give it impressiveness without spoiling its simplicity. Wordsworth once gazed upon sleeping London, and the feeling I have just been speaking of is now a thing registered forever in poetry, in the exquisite expression of deep repose which he has given in his famous sonnet on Westminster Bridge:—

"Earth has not any thing to show more fair.
Dull would he be of soul who could pass by
A sight so touchiug in its majesty;
This city now doth like a garment wear
The beauty of the morning; silent, bare,
Ships, towers, domes, theatres, and temples lie
Open unto the fields and to the sky,
All bright and glittering in the smokeless air.

Never did sun more beautifully steep,
In his first splendour, valley, rock, or hill;
Ne'er saw I, never felt, a calm so deep.
The river glideth at his own sweet will;
Dear God! the very houses seem asleep,
And all that mighty heart is lying still."

To take one other illustration: most persons have, I imagine, on looking on the placid surface of a pure and transparent sheet of water, felt a sort of thoughtless impulse, often uttering a sportive wish, to plunge into it. It would hardly be supposed that this blind impulse was susceptible of poetry or of an imaginative solution:—

"Why stand we gazing on the sparkling brine
With wonder, smit with its transparency,
And all enraptured with its purity?
Because the unstained, the clear, the crystalline,
Have ever in them something of benign;
Whether in gem, in water, or in sky,
A sleeping infant's brow, or wakeful eye
Of a young maiden, only not divine:
Scarcely the hand forbears to dip its palm
For beverage drawn as from a mountain well;
Temptation centres in the liquid calm;
Our daily raiment seems no obstacle
To instantaneous plunging in deep sea
And revelling in long embrace with thee."

Another form of poetic communion with nature is that which discovers a sympathy between the appearances of the outer world and emotions stirring in the heart. This is another great element of Wordsworth's poetry. On one occasion, having just read that the death of a celebrated and very popular British statesman was hourly looked for, he walks forth in the evening of a stormy day, and what he beholds and feels is a type of both the agitated spirit of the poet and his countrymen and of the steady placid light of a meditative resignation:—

"Loud is the vale: the voice is up
With which she speaks when storms are gone,—
A mighty unison of streams!
Of all her voices one!

"Loud is the vale: this inland depth
In peace is roaring like the sea;
Yon star upon the mountain-top
Is listening quietly.

"Sad was I, even to pain depressed;
Importunate and heavy load!
The comforter hath found me here
Upon this lonely road;

"And many thousands now are sad,
Wait the fulfilment of their fear;
For he must die who was their stay,
Their glory disappear.

"A power is passing from the earth
To breathless nature's dark abyss;
But, when the great and good depart,
What is it more than this?—

"That man, who is from God sent forth,
Doth yet again to God return?
Such ebb and flow must ever be:
Then wherefore should we mourn?"

Passing from inanimate nature, I must hasten rapidly along the far-reaching line of Wordsworth's poetic sympathies, entering next into the range of the lower orders of animal life. The tenderness of the human heart for the dumb creatures which surround us is a sentiment as pure as it is appropriate. Neglected, it leads to cruelty worse than brutish; but, on the other hand, it may be overwrought into a species of sentimental misanthropy. When one of Sir Walter Scott's dearest pet dogs died, he caused it to be buried in his garden,—his children weeping over the remains of their mute playmate, and he, as Mrs. Lockhart remembered, smoothing down the turf with one of the saddest expressions she had ever seen on his face. When afterwards the noblest and most celebrated of his favourites died, he caused a stone and inscription to be placed, near the gate of Abbotsford, over the dog's grave. When Lord Byron's dog expired, he set up a conspicuous monument in the garden at Newstead Abbey, with an elaborate poetic inscription, recording the virtues of the dead dog in an affected strain of abuse and hatred of living men. The poet, moreover, by his will, directed his own body to be buried near his faithful favourite. Now, every one must feel that this is a gross perversion of a feeling which might be chastened to better uses. The moment you find appropriated to the brute creation the obsequies which the heart hallows for man alone, you recoil instinctively from it, as either involving a heartless mockery or as degrading to humanity. The affection towards the creatures beneath us in the scale of being may be made to flow in a deep and true channel, as this tribute to a favourite dog well shows:—

"Lie here, without a record of thy worth,
Beneath a covering of the common earth!
It is not from unwillingness to praise,
Or want of love, that here no stone we raise.
More thou deservest; but *this* man gives to man,
Brother to brother:—*this* is all we can.
Yet they to whom thy virtues made thee dear
Shall find thee through all changes of the year:

This oak points out thy grave: the silent tree
Will gladly stand a monument of thee.
I grieved for thee, and wished thy end were past,
And willingly have laid thee here at last:
For thou hadst lived till every thing that cheers,
In thee, had yielded to the weight of years;
Extreme old age had wasted thee away
And left thee but the glimmering of the day.
Thy ears were deaf, and feeble were thy knees;
I saw thee stagger in the summer breeze,
Too weak to stand against its sportive breath,
And ready for the gentlest stroke of death.
It came, and we were glad: yet tears were shed;
Both man and woman wept when thou wert dead;—
Not only for a thousand thoughts, that were
Old household thoughts, in which thou hadst thy share,
But for some precious boons vouchsafed to thee,
Found scarcely anywhere in like degree!
For love that comes to all—the holy sense,
Best gift of God—in thee was most intense.
A chain of heart, a feeling of the mind,
A tender sympathy, which did thee bind
Not only to us men, but to thy kind.
Yea, for thy fellow-brutes in thee we saw
The soul of love, love's intellectual law:
Hence, if we wept, it was not done in shame;
Our tears from passion and from reason came,
And therefore shalt thou be an honoured name."

There is a beautiful expression of Wordsworth's meditative fancy inspired by musing over some gold and silver fishes in a vase, which I allude to, however, rather because of a higher inspiration prompted by the slight hint,—the restoration of them to freedom. It tells his deep sympathy with the liberty of all the mere animal creation:—

"Who can divine what impulses from God
Reach the caged lark, within a town-abode,
From his poor inch or two of daisied sod?

Oh, yield him back his privilege! No sea
Swells like the bosom of a man set free;
A wilderness is rich with liberty.
Roll on, ye spouting whales, who die or keep
Your independence in the fathomless deep!
Spread, tiny nautilus, the living sail;
Dive at thy choice, or brave the freshening gale.
If unreproved the ambitious eagle mount
Sunward to seek the daylight in its fount,
Bays, gulfs, and oceans, Indian width, shall be,
Till the world perishes, a field for thee."

But the noblest dedication of Wordsworth's genius has been in his communion with his fellow-men,—a sympathy as expanded as ever filled the human heart, comprehensive of the highest and the lowliest of the race, and shedding a glory on all conditions of humanity:—

"'Tis nature's law
That none, the meanest of created things,
Of forms created the most vile and brute,
The dullest or most noxious, should exist
Divorced from good,—a spirit and pulse of good,—
A life and soul to every mode of being
Inseparably linked. Then be assured
That least of all can aught that ever owned
The heaven-regarding eye and front sublime
Which man is born to, sink, howe'er depressed,
So low as to be scorned without a sin,
Without offence to God, cast out of view,
Like the dry remnant of a garden-flower
Whose seeds are shed, or as an implement
Worn out and useless.
No! man is dear to man; the poorest poor
Long for some moments in a weary life
When they can know and feel that they have been
Themselves the fathers and the dealers out
Of some small blessings, have been kind to such

As needed kindness, for this single cause :—
That we have all of us one human heart."

This principle is the great moral element of Wordsworth's poetry,—the sameness of the human heart. I am painfully conscious of the injury I am doing to it by these hurried comments. He has vindicated the sensibilities of mankind in humble life, and, by showing their susceptibility to kindness, has fostered the natural love between man and man. He thus silences a common plea of selfishness, in treating the story of the ingratitude of the poor as a thing only heard of at a distance. This is the fine moral of the little ballad of Simon Lee, closing with these stanzas :—

"My gentle reader, I perceive
How patiently you've waited;
And now I fear that you expect
Some tale will be related.

"O reader! had you in your mind
Such stores as silent thought can bring,—
O gentle reader! you would find
A tale in every thing.

"What more I have to say is short,
And you must kindly take it:
It is no tale; but, should you think,
Perhaps a tale you'll make it.

"One summer day I chanced to see
This old man, doing all he could
To unearth the root of an old tree,—
A stump of rotten wood.

"The mattock tottered in his hand;
So vain was his endeavour,
That at the root of the old tree
He might have worked forever.

"'You're overtasked, good Simon Lee;
Give me your tool,' to him I said;
And, at the word, right gladly he
Received my proffered aid.

"I struck, and with a single blow
The tangled root I severed
At which the poor old man so long
And vainly had endeavoured.

"The tears into his eyes were brought,
And thanks and praises seemed to run
So fast out of his heart, I thought
They never would have done.

"I've heard of hearts unkind, kind deeds
With coldness still returning:
Alas! the gratitude of men
Hath oftener left me mourning."

In Wordsworth's highly-cultivated affection for human nature, of course, is comprehended that reverence of womanly nature which we have observed as an element in the genius of all the great English poets. It is part of his comprehensive scheme for elevating and purifying humanity, to throw the light of his imagination upon the meek majesty of the female heart, its faithfulness, its fortitude, its heroism. What can be more touchingly beautiful than the account of a woman's slowly-wasting spirit, in the story of the "Deserted Cottage," in the first book of the "Excursion"? The sanity of Wordsworth's genius admits of no romantic exaggeration or vapid sentimentality on this subject. While it is his delight to show how divine a thing a woman may be made, he regards her moving in the orbit of domestic life, not as enshrined by a superstitious chivalry, but the being that God gave because it was not good for man to be alone. It is a worthy and no light effort of poetic genius to take from the extravagances of romance all that is attractive, and to blend it with the daily household worth of woman, and, thus preserving its beauty, to reveal the spiritual and the practical which in their harmony make up the perfection of female loveliness.

I had it much at heart to treat of Wordsworth's political poems, and to show how valuable a use they might subserve in elevating and chastening public sentiment. But the subject is too fine a one to be injured by such hurried discussion as I would now be compelled to give it. Let me only, in evidence of his large-hearted sympathy with our institutions, repeat an unpublished sonnet, composed on reading an account of what he charitably calls some misdoings in our land:—

"Men of the Western World! in Fate's dark book
Whence this opprobrious leaf of dire portent?
Think ye your British ancestors forsook
Their narrow isle, for outrage provident?
Think ye they fled restraint they ill could brook,
To give in their descendants freer vent
And wider range to passions turbulent,
To mutual tyranny a deadlier look?
'Nay,' said a voice more soft than zephyr's breath;
'Dive through the stormy surface of the flood
To the great current flowing underneath;
Think on the countless springs of silent good;
So shall the truth be known and understood,
And thy grieved spirit brighten strong in faith.'"

I had hoped to present the subject of this lecture with all the care due to a poet whose fame, not yet sanctioned by time, is therefore vaguely appreciated. But circumstances far beyond my control have so embarrassed the requisite preparation, that I have been constrained to presume upon your indulgence in the hasty and very inadequate suggestions which have constituted this evening's lecture.

It has been my unaffected desire that this course of lectures should be conducted with as little obtrusion of the lecturer personally as possible. It is the *cause* which I have been anxious to impress you with, leaving him to whom you have listened to be recognised as scarce more than a mere voice. A few words were given to personal considerations in first meeting you; a few more may be indulged in now parting from you. I then stated the principles on which this literary enterprise was undertaken,—a duty to this community arising from my position in it. It was not consistent with either that duty or my inclination to court a reluctant attendance or solicit it as a favour. Taking no step of that sort, and, in these times of indiscriminate and exaggerated puffing, avoiding all the machinery of extrinsic influences, it was my resolution that the fate of this course, be it what it might, should be its real fate. I thought it no more than my right distinctly to say so, believing that so we would understand each other the better. It is my wish now to say that the feeling then asserted, so far from hindering, has best promoted, a deep sense of gratefulness for the kindness I have met with. It never entered into my thoughts that my duty to offer this course brought the least obligation upon you to attend it. What claims had I upon that patience which has been so bountifully bestowed on me? What assurance was there that these lectures could or would be conducted in a way that would be satisfactory to you? I well know the inconvenience, the restraint, the interference with other engagements and habits, which your attendance here must have subjected you to; and, when I look back and think that this has been so for sixteen successive weeks, my heart leaps up with pride that a subject so purely imaginative should have thus won your attention, and with gratitude for the kind, friendly, and indulgent feelings which the interest of that subject has been the means of extending to me personally. This course has been protracted longer than appears to me desirable; each lecture, too, has exceeded its due limits. Conscious of this, it has been the more gratifying to experience your consideration for me in restraining all symptoms of impatience. No one can be more sensible than I am of the deficiencies of the course, resulting from two very ample though widely-different causes—the superabundance of the materials and the inability to do the subject the justice which is its due. It is unavailing, however, now to dwell upon those deficiencies, and I would rather turn to the hope suggested by them—necessarily an indefinite hope—of entering with you, on some future occasion, into some of those regions of our literature of which thus far we have in not a few instances only touched upon the frontiers. In the mean time I can bear away the happy recollection of having witnessed the power which true poetry exerts over the best of our intellectual and moral sympathies, for I know that the hearts of young and old have kindled here with the sound of the noble strains uttered by our English imagination. All that has reached me respecting these lectures has been kindness—unqualified kindness,—inspiring this feeling above all others:—an anxiety to bring them far nearer than has been done to the ideal of what might merit such acknowledgments. It is, therefore, with entire sincerity that for the last words to pass between us I appropriate that simple stanza, the very voice of gratefulness, repeated once already this evening:—

> "I've heard of hearts unkind, kind deeds
>   With coldness still returning:
> Alas! the gratitude of men
>   Hath oftener left me mourning."

Miscellaneous Essays

ON

ENGLISH POETRY.

MISCELLANEOUS ESSAYS

ON

ENGLISH POETRY.

ESSAY I.

English Sonnets.

It is matter of familiar observation, that the success of literary productions is sensibly dependent on the forms in which they are presented. In the domain of English poetry, there is a section to which justice has not been done: its quality is not held in very high repute, and the title to it is regarded as somewhat doubtful. I refer to that form of metrical composition which is denominated the Sonnet. To prove that it has not found favour always even in the eyes of those who have cultivated a taste for other forms of poetry, I would ask them whether, when they have met with its modest structure, they have not generally passed it carelessly by. Besides, in the minds of those who do not entirely neglect it, there may be detected a peculiar feeling, aptly to be described as unkindly; they regard it not with the look that a man gives to his own kin and countrymen, but with that which is cast coldly and doubtingly upon a stranger or foreigner. While the sonnet is read, an *un-English* feeling is found to be creeping about the heart, and the fancy is filled unconsciously with thoughts of Petrarch and images of Laura and the Vaucluse. While its melody is falling on the ear, we are too often overtaken with a kind of misgiving that we are listening to the rich music of, indeed, our own mother-tongue, but tuned to a strange note; that we hear its glorious words uttered through a foreign instrument. This is not as it should be. The Muse of England should not stand a suppliant or a vassal anywhere. She holds in her own right, or she holds not at all. So far as literature is concerned, we are, by our calling, guardsmen of English rights and English merits; and, as the form of poetry in question seems to be regarded as not having yet worked out its independence, I mean to try to undertake its vindication. I proclaim at the outset that we acknowledge no allegiance—own no homage—to the Italian. Our literary territory is held absolutely, or it had better be relinquished entirely. There is too much Saxon blood in our veins to bide content on a divided soil or under a feudal tenure. It may be shown that the sonnet is a form of poetry fairly introduced into the literature of England, fully sustained, and now, without reserve or qualification, by the law of letters it is our own. I propose, therefore, to say a word for our English title and our English fame in this province of poesy.

Before advancing further, the looseness in the acceptation of the term "sonnet," in consequence of its application to several different forms of poetry, demands some attempt to ascertain its true use, or, at least, to give it some precision. The most obvious property, which is common to the sonnets of all countries, is its limitation to fourteen lines. With the exception of some of the earliest English sonnets, and those of not much merit, which extended to eighteen lines, this may be said to be universally true. It is composed of four parts, two quadrains and two terzines, which are usually indicated by the typography in the foreign sonnets, but not in the English. Rhyme is also an essential property, and it is to it that the different varieties of the sonnet have reference: the lines are of equal length and the measure iambic. The form which is considered as especially entitled to the name is that which is framed after the Italian sonnet,—the Petrarcan model. In this the rhymes are repeated at certain intervals so as to produce a recurrence of the same closing sound; and it is this property which seems to suggest the origin of the name itself. The arrangement is such that, in fourteen lines, there are but five, and sometimes not more than four, several rhymes. I am a little fearful I am making myself disagreeable by the technicalities of prosody. By means of a specimen, I may accomplish my wish of conveying an idea of the general structure of this variety of the sonnet much better and certainly more agreeably. In quoting, with this view, Mr. Wordsworth's sonnet composed upon Westminster Bridge, I did not intend to be diverted from the mere consideration of its metrical character. I cannot, however, refrain from asking the reader to recall his feelings when he has happened to pass along the streets of a city yet in its slumbers; and, unless our own deceive us, he will find, we think, an echo to them in the following specimen of the metre of the sonnet:—

> "Earth has not any thing to show more fair:
> Dull would he be of soul who could pass by
> A sight so touching in its majesty.
> This city now doth like a garment wear
> The beauty of the morning; silent, bare,
> Ships, towers, domes, theatres, and temples lie
> Open unto the fields and to the sky,
> All bright and glittering in the smokeless air.
> Never did sun more beautifully steep,
> In his first splendour, valley, rock, or hill;
> Ne'er saw I, never felt, a calm so deep!
> The river glideth at his own sweet will:
> Dear God! the very houses seem asleep,
> And all that mighty heart is lying still!"

In this form the poem is cast by those who have implicitly revered the ancient landmarks. It is the most usual form of the Spanish and Portuguese as well as the Italian sonnet. The English poets, with Shakspeare as a leader, have, with a characteristic temper, claimed greater freedom. This appears in several different structures of the poem, in which the variety is effected in some by a different distribution of the rhymes, and in others by increasing the number of them to six and seven, but not attaching them throughout to consecutive lines. The following, selected from the same poet in order to avoid distracting attention to other points of comparison, may serve as specimens of some of these varieties:—

"The shepherd, looking eastward, softly said,
'Bright is thy veil, O moon, as thou art bright!'
Forthwith that little cloud, in ether spread
And penetrated all with tender light,
She cast away, and showed her fulgent head
Uncovered,—dazzling the beholder's sight,
As if to vindicate her beauty's right,—
Her beauty thoughtlessly disparaged.
Meanwhile that veil, removed or thrown aside,
Went floating from her, darkening as it went;
And a huge mass, to bury or to hide,
Approached this glory of the firmament,
Who meekly yields and is obscured,—content
With one calm triumph of a modest pride."

The following specimen may be noticed, by-the-way, as presenting a striking instance of the combined action of reflective and imaginative power:—

"In my mind's eye a temple, like a cloud,
Slowly surmounting some invidious hill,
Rose out of darkness: the bright work stood still,
And might of its own beauty have been proud.
But it was fashioned and to God was vowed
By virtues that diffused, in every part,
Spirit divine through forms of human art:
Faith had her arch,—her arch, when winds blow loud,
Into the consciousness of safety thrilled;
And Love her towers of dread foundation laid
Under the grave of things; Hope had her spire
Star-high, and pointing still to something higher.
Trembling I gazed, but heard a voice: it said,
Hell-gates are powerless phantoms when we build."

The recently-published volume of poems by Mr. Wordsworth contains a number of sonnets showing his talent in unabated vigour:—

"TO THE PLANET VENUS, AN EVENING STAR.

COMPOSED AT LOCH-LOMOND.

"Though joy attend thee, orient, at the birth
Of dawn, it cheers the lofty spirit most
To watch thy course when daylight, fled from earth,
In the gray sky hath left his lingering ghost
Perplexed, as if between a splendour lost
And splendour slowly mustering. Since the sun,
The absolute, the world-absorbing One,
Relinquished half his empire to the host,
Emboldened by thy guidance, holy star,
Holy as princely, who that looks on thee,
Touching, as now, in thy humility
The mountain-borders of this seat of care,
Can question that thy countenance is bright,
Celestial Power! as much with love as light?"

One word more on this subject of definition before I leave it. Some one perhaps may seek to resolve his doubts on the acceptation of the term "sonnet," by that innocent-hearted method of looking into the dictionary. In the folio edition of Johnson's he will find the following definition:—"*Sonnet*, a short poem consisting of fourteen lines, of which the rhymes are adjusted by a particular rule. It is not very suitable to the English language, and has not been used by any man of eminence since Milton." And then, in evidence of the lexicographer's conception of the character of the poem in question, inserted at length is Milton's sonnet, written on the detraction which followed his "Tetrachordon" and other of his prose treatises. It was a piece of scoff at his political foes; and the humour of it, such as it is, seems to consist in the introduction of as many rugged proper names as the poet could manage in the space of fourteen metrical lines. The smile of the great republican poet, at least as far as we trace it in his prose writings, was certainly not his most agreeable expression: it was tinctured with bitterness. If Dr. Johnson meant, as no doubt he did, to cite that sonnet as a fair specimen, it either evinces a lamentable want of taste, or is additional proof how completely his vision was sealed to the wealth of the best periods of English poetry. The definition which succeeds to the above is "*Sonnetteer*, a small poet; in contempt." Let us see who they are. To say nothing of the worthy train of early poets who were small only by comparison with their great contemporaries, the sonnet was a favourite form of composition with each one of that glorious triumvirate who kindled the flame of poetry higher than ever since the creation it flamed by mere human kindling, and kept it burning at its brightest for a century:—EDMUND SPENSER, WILLIAM SHAKSPEARE, JOHN MILTON,—sonnetteers all,—"small poets, in contempt!" Samuel Johnson! in charity I hope that you are forgiven!

My principal object, thus far, has been merely to illustrate what form of English poetry it is which is designated by the name of the sonnet, and incidentally to call attention to the true conception and exquisite finish of the specimens, selected with no very great pains, from the pages of a living poet. Let it now be distinctly understood that I do not, of course, claim for England the invention of the sonnet. It had its birth under a Southern sky. Whether Italian or Provençal in its origin would not be pertinent at present to discuss. Its date is anterior to Petrarch, though, from the fact that it was developed and rendered more popular by him, it is identified so intimately with his name. There is a theory suggested by Ginguené or Sismondi, which traces to the poetry of the Arabs the fashion of continuing and intermingling the metrical sounds in their verses. Now, this is one of the distinguishing features of the sonnet; and the use of rhyme, which is another, is a Gothic fashion, —a northern barbarism, as it was regarded by all who, like old Roger Ascham, fed in their hearts the hope of living to see their vernacular dialects set to the tune of hexameters. May it not be, then, that the wealth of several different quarters of the globe was laid under contribution to be coined in the diminutive mould of the sonnet? It would be a singular boast for any thing so humble and unassuming. It is easy, we are aware, to weave theories, and, upon this subject, to extract much plausibility from the fact of the singular fusing of the European and Saracenic races together in the South of Europe during a part of the Middle Ages. History presents, probably, no more extraordinary instance of the kind than the intermingling of three distinct races in a very limited territory at the time of the Norman establishment in Sicily: there was the remnant of the old Sicilian race—their conquerors, the Arabs—and the final victor, the Norman. Well might their music blend together, where they were girt in by the ocean in this little plot. In all diffidence we offer our fancy—we will not dignify it with the title of theory—that one graft was brought by the Arab from the East, and another from the region of the Goth, and that these grew into one growth under the genial influence of an Italian or Sicilian sun.

How is a nation's claim to any form of composition, whether metrical or not, to be established? Not by discovery or preoccupation. Parnassus is as free and illimitable as the ocean or the wind. If there be any method of taking a ceremonious possession, as territory is acquired by planting a standard or erecting a pile of stones, I have yet to learn what it is. It would not be more presumptuous and irrational to attempt to check the free current of a breeze that has wafted over Italy, than to contend that a certain arrangement of poetic melodies first uttered there must, therefore, remain Italian to the end of time. The domain of letters is no more susceptible of private exclusive dominion than is the open sea. If there should be perceived a disposition on the one hand to assert, and on the other to yield to such a claim, it would be time for some one, invoking the spirit of old Grotius to his aid, to compile a *Helicon Liberum*. What would it be but reviving the principle of the old Portuguese claim? Petrarch, like De Gama, may have all the fame of discovery, but we yield nothing of long-maintained possession and of present title. We claim our ancient English rights of sailing on the wide sea wherever the winds may carry us, and of tuning our language to any note to which it will answer.

Any form of writing, no matter how artificial in its structure or how remote in its origin, may be naturalized into a language, if it is adapted to the character of that language, and if writers can be found who have shown this by actual experiment. In reference simply to origin, the sonnet is an exotic; but so is the epic or the ode. I cheerfully admit as much in one case as in the other, but nothing more; and this admission is but equivalent to the acknowledgment that Homer came into the world before Milton, Pindar before Dryden and Gray, and Petrarch before Surrey. A seed from this Southern plant has been sown in the soil of English literature, and, exposed to all the inclemency of a Northern climate, it has been followed by a growth as vigorous and flourishing as the parent-stock. What I take exception to is the propensity still to regard it as an unnatural transplantation, or a forced and artificial growth. When we dwell with an exulting national pride upon the pages of the "Paradise Lost,"—our own English epic,—we are never rebuked by being reminded of the claims of Homer. And when we read the English sonnet, able as we are to cite hundreds of them which would adorn the literature of any country, we cannot consent to stand always cap-in-hand to the shade of Petrarch. A brief reference to a few of the English sonnet-writers of different periods will firmly establish our claim, and serve at the same time to correct the prejudices against the form itself.

The most obvious of these prejudices is directed against the narrow and precise limits of the sonnet. How, it is asked, can the free spirit of poetry breathe in such bondage,—the certain bounds of fourteen lines, never to be passed over yet always to be reached? How can fancy or imagination survive? If the sentiment be expansive or the imagery abundant, all must be cramped or curtailed. If, on the other hand, it can touch the reader's heart in an expression more brief, it must, notwithstanding, be stretched out to the standard. Such is the argument; and, as a matter of course, Procrustes' bed is usually rolled in by way of illustration. Richness of thought and fancy must be reduced, and poverty must be eked out. Now, all of this, if true, is very objectionable, and that it is often true there is many a luckless sonnet on record to testify. But what does it prove? Not that the sonnet is an inappropriate form of poetry, but only that it is often employed upon subjects that are not adapted to it, and by writers who are unequal to it. The objection establishes nothing more than that there may be an incompetent poet or an injudicious selection of the topic,—an objection surely not peculiar, but which would form an equally reasonable prejudice against the ode, the drama, or the epic. But the complaint does not stop here. One fault, it is alleged, leads to another,—violations of literary propriety, like breaches of veracity, being of a very social tendency. Unnatural forms of expression are traced as a necessary consequence of an unnatural form of composition. The poet, unable, by reason of his artificial restraints, to give sufficient development to his feeling or his imagery, finds himself obliged to produce his impression by resorting to points and antitheses, and all the devices of artificial expression. Hence, it is said, the conceits for which the Italian sonnet is signally noted, and which may be observed also in no inconsiderable degree in so many of those of other nations. Again, we might resist this attack by charging the fault upon the individual poet: it proves his weakness and nothing else. But we are willing to take the burden of proof upon ourselves. We maintain that these faults are not naturally or necessarily inherent in the sonnet; and how can the question be better settled than by reference to what has actually been accomplished by it? Let us conceive, proposed as a topic for a sonnet, a vindication of the form of poetry itself, to be effected by an enumeration of the famed poets of various countries who have made use of it, with allusions to their general character, the prominent circumstances of their lives, and their several purposes in writing; this to be done adequately, without restraint or prolixity, in language at once poetical and natural, and with a strict regard to the requisitions of versification. The conception would be surely ample enough for a poem of fourteen lines, under peculiar metrical laws. Whether the sonnet be equal to it may be best ascertained by the perusal of another of Wordsworth's, in which the reader will recognise the execution of the conception which we have just sketched in a very lifeless paraphrase :—

"Scorn not the sonnet; critic, you have frowned,
Mindless of its just honours: with this key
Shakspeare unlocked his heart; the melody
Of this small lute gave ease to Petrarch's wound;
A thousand times this pipe did Tasso sound;
Camoens soothed with it an exile's grief;
The sonnet glittered a gay myrtle-leaf
Amid the cypress with which Dante crowned
His visionary brow; a glowworm lamp,
It cheered mild Spenser, called from faery-land
To struggle through dark ways; and when a damp
Fell round the path of Milton, in his hand
The thing became a trumpet, whence he blew
Soul-animating strains,—alas, too few!"

What could be more finished, more perfect, whether you regard it for its mere fancy, or as a piece of eulogy or criticism? What more natural in the expression, more free from every thing like false effect, more varied in its harmonies? What melody could be sweeter than the fall of its close? Is there a word that could be taken away, or one that could be added? Well would it alone sustain the fine illustration which has been given of Wordsworth's sonnets, and which is also in a great measure applicable to all the best sonnets in the language:—"Wordsworth's sonnet never goes off, as it were, with a clap or repercussion at the close; but is thrown up like a rocket, breaks into light, and falls in a soft shower of brightness." Another, very characteristic of his general manner, may serve to show that a very simple sentiment—that of local association—may be gracefully amplified to the space of the sonnet, without any of the insipid dilution which distinguishes so many of them:—

"There is a little unpretending rill
Of limpid water, humbler far than aught
That ever among men or naiads sought
Notice or name! It quivers down the hill,
Furrowing its shallow way with dubious will;
Yet to my mind this scanty stream is brought
Oftener than Ganges or the Nile; a thought
Of private recollection sweet and still!
Months perish with their moons; year treads on year;
But, faithful Emma, thou with me canst say
That, while ten thousand pleasures disappear,
And flies their memory fast almost as they,
The immortal spirit of one happy day
Lingers beside that rill, in vision clear."

I am tempted to add another sonnet, as a happy specimen of art,—a singular instance of secondary description, illustrating clearly the frequent analogy between poetry and painting, or, to describe it more philosophically, between fancy and the bodily eye:—

"UPON THE SIGHT OF A BEAUTIFUL PICTURE,

PAINTED BY SIR G. H. BEAUMONT, BART.

"Praised be the art whose subtle power could stay
Yon cloud, and fix it in that glorious shape,
Nor would permit the thin smoke to escape,
Nor those bright sunbeams to forsake the day;
Which stopped that band of travellers on their way,
Ere they were lost within the shady wood;
And showed the bark upon the glassy flood
Forever anchored in her sheltering bay.
Soul-soothing art! which morning, noontide, even,
Do serve with all their changeful pageantry;
Thou, with ambition modest yet sublime,
Here, for the sight of mortal man, hast given
To one brief moment caught from fleeting time
The appropriate calm of blest eternity."

There is also great merit in the following as a piece of landscape description, illuminated with a very rich moral light, the imagery of the closing lines, especially, evincing admirable taste:—

"A PARSONAGE IN OXFORDSHIRE.

"Where holy ground begins, unhallowed ends,
Is marked by no distinguishable line;
The turf unites, the pathways intertwine;
And, wheresoe'er the stealing footstep tends,
Garden, and that domain where kindred, friends,
And neighbours rest together, here confound
Their several features, mingled like the sound
Of many waters, or as evening blends

> With shady night. Soft airs from shrub and flower
> Waft fragrant greetings to each silent grave;
> And, while those lofty poplars gently wave
> Their tops, between them comes and goes a sky
> Bright as the glimpses of eternity
> To saints accorded in their mortal hour."

The complaint of the narrowness of the limits of the sonnet appears indicative more of the character of the mind of him who makes it than of any thing else. Writers vary wonderfully in the room they require: some can breathe freely in no space narrower than a modern state paper, while others are more considerate. The former are not the men to write sonnets: we commend them to the epic. But is there not in this craving for space something that does not accord very well with true poetic temperament? If a writer be indeed worthy of his calling, if he do indeed belong to that creative class who make the world they inhabit, what need has he of calling for more ground? Is it not enough that he has a spot to rise from? The peak of a broken crag, or the point of a blasted branch, would be sorry quarters indeed for a bear or a buffalo; but the majesty of the eagle claims no wider sovereignty for his footing, when he is springing from the earth to bathe his wings in the floods of the sun. Or, when the lark soars, like a sick-man's hope, to meet the coming dawn, the home he leaves is wrapped in the little circumference of a tuft of grass. To these the spirit of true poetry is kindred. The insatiate demand for room is the symptom of a restless and licentious intellect,—of feelings undisciplined. If we should hear it from the lips of one in whom we could discern a trace of poetic promise, we would address him in the language of affectionate entreaty:—Get thee to thy study, and there, seeking the writings of those who adorned our literature in that happy age when authors had not yet become part of a printer's stock in trade,—when men wrote from the fulness of the heart and not the emptiness of the purse,—and, communing with their pages, chasten thine own heart. There are doubtless many who are unable, and many who are unwilling, to brook the restraints of the sonnet; but that proves only that there are many faint-hearted and many false-hearted poets. All that we contend for is that the difficulty, the existence of which we freely admit, is not insuperable; that there is no quality of poetry which may not be brought within its bounds. When a poet repudiates it, he is the unconscious witness to convict himself of a licentiousness which he mistakes for the indignant spirit of true freedom. But, again, let the sonnet speak its own vindication:—

"Nuns fret not at their convents' narrow room;
And hermits are contented with their cells;
And students with their pensive citadels;
Maids at the wheel, the weaver at his loom,
Sit blithe and happy; bees, that soar for bloom
High as the highest peak of Furness Fells,
Will murmur by the hour in foxglove-bells:
In truth, the prison unto which we doom
Ourselves no prison is: and hence to me,
In sundry moods, 'twas pastime to be bound
Within the sonnet's scanty plot of ground:
Pleased if some souls (for such there needs must be)
Who have felt the weight of too much liberty
Should find brief solace there, as I have found."

It is to the narrow bounds of the sonnet that we may safely ascribe its frequent want of popularity, and the countless failures of many who have attempted it. For its most perfect conception and execution, it demands, I have little hesitation in saying, powers as great and varied as the epic itself. In addition to the qualifications for the usual forms of poetry, the poet must bring to the sonnet a profound judgment and a command of language that never fails; his power for condensation of thought must be irresistible; he must possess that suggestive talent in writing, by no means a common one, by which the reader may be set upon trains of thought or feeling. His heart must be under equal discipline. On the part of the reader, too, much is required. There is, as we all know, one state of mind for prose, and another for poetry. The former may correspond with many of the states of feeling in which men happen to be; the latter differs essentially from most of them. It varies with the constitution; it may be felt in different degrees at different times; often it requires a process of preparation. It was one of Charles Lamb's observations—deep-dyed as they all were in truth and the tints of his own peculiar humour—that "Milton almost requires a solemn service of music to be played before you enter upon him. But he brings his music, to which who listens had need bring docile thoughts and purged ears." It was a fine philosophical thought, entitled to more consideration, as coming from one whose heart, if ever the heart of man was, was in a state of perpetual susceptibility to all that is true and beautiful in nature. Now, this process of preparation is usually part of the poet's own work: much of every poem of any length may be devoted to the mere purpose of elevating the reader's feelings to the required pitch: the world is too much with us for us to dispense with the poet's chastening. But the brevity of the sonnet precludes it. The consequence is, that the reader, perusing it with feelings not sympathetic or not susceptible enough, may, with great injustice, impute to the poem a want of impression which really is the result only of his own mood. Every reflective reader of poetry must have noticed how differently he has been affected at different times by the same piece. The sonnet, therefore, while it requires a writer of peculiar ability, needs a reader of somewhat more than ordinary reading-capabilities. These are causes abundantly sufficient to account for frequent failures in sonnet-writing and frequent want of popularity when successful. But we greatly err if the sonnet be not a favourite abiding-place for him who, whether as a writer or a reader, joins to an intellect well disciplined a heart nursed in the spirit of genuine freedom. His feelings will be congenial with those of the gallant cavalier who kept the liberty of his soul unbroken by the durance of his body; and, in answer to the reproach of restraint, we can fancy him breaking out in the same exulting strains:—

"Th' enlargéd windes, that curle the flood,
Know no such libertie.
Stone walls do not a prison make
Nor iron barres a cage;
Mindes innocent and quiet take
That for an hermitage.
If I have freedom in my love
And in my soul am free,

Angels alone, that soare above,
Enjoy such libertie."*

If further proof be required of the capabilities of the sonnet, an argument of no mean authority may be found in the fact that it was not too narrow for the spirit of Shakspeare. If any one still believes that the loftiest poetic temperament should not brook its bondage, let him stand up and say so after reading the following, one of the least-neglected, perhaps, of the collection of Shakspeare's sonnets:—

"Let me not to the marriage of true minds
Admit impediments. Love is not love
Which alters when it alteration finds,
Or bends with the remover to remove:
Oh, no; it is an ever-fixèd mark,
That looks on tempests and is never shaken;
It is the star to every wandering bark,
Whose worth's unknown, although his height be taken.
Love's not Time's fool, though rosy lips and cheeks
Within his bending sickle's compass come;
Love alters not with his brief hours and weeks,
But bears it out even to the edge of doom.
If this be error and upon me proved,
I never writ, nor no man ever loved."

It would be difficult to cite a finer passage of moral poetry than this description of the master-passion.†

---

* Lovelace, 1642.

† The fame of having composed the finest *prose* delineation of the passion of Love may be claimed for Coleridge: it may be found in a piece entitled "The Improvisatore," included in his poetical works. For philosophical analysis and for beauty of expression it is unequalled by any single passage on the subject. As a piece of abstract description or definition it is not surpassed by the celebrated definition of wit in Barrow's Sermons.

How true and how ennobling to our nature! We at once recognise in it the abstraction of that conception which has found a dwelling and a name in the familiar forms of Desdemona, Juliet, Imogen, Cordelia,—of Romeo, and of Othello too, if that character be correctly understood. If this sonnet was written before his dramas, then it was the pregnant thought from which were destined to spring those inimitable creations of female character that have been loved, as if they were living beings, by thousands. If, as is most probable, it was written afterwards, it is Shakspeare's own comment, and might be prefixed as a most apposite motto to those dramas in which he has given life and motion to the conception. The gladdening influences of a lover's thoughts—the cheering light of a pure affection—were never depicted with truer feeling than in the following sonnet:—

"When, in disgrace with fortune and men's eyes,
I all alone beweep my outcast state,
And trouble deaf heaven with my bootless cries,
And look upon myself, and curse my fate,
Wishing me like to one more rich in hope,
Featured like him, like him with friends possessed,
Desiring this man's art and that man's scope,
With what I most enjoy contented least;
Yet in these thoughts, myself almost despising,
Haply I think on thee. And then my state
(Like to the lark at break of day arising
From sullen earth) sings hymns at heaven's gate;
For thy sweet love, remembered, such wealth brings,
That then I scorn to change my state with kings."

I make no apology for quoting from the same collection another specimen, in which the reader cannot fail to observe an abundant measure of that exquisite but uncloying sweetness which distinguishes so much of the old English poetry. This sonnet would have been a meet melody to be chanted, with the songs of Herbert and Herrick, by the honoured lips of old Izaak Walton:—

"Oh, how much more doth beauty beauteous seem
By that sweet ornament which truth doth give!
The rose looks fair, but fairer we it deem
For that sweet odour which doth in it live.
The canker-blooms have full as deep a dye
As the perfumèd tincture of the roses,
Hang on such thorns, and play as wantonly
When summer's breath their maskèd buds discloses:
But, for their virtue only is their show,
They lived unwooed, and unrespected fade;
Die to themselves. Sweet roses do not so;
Of their sweet deaths are sweetest odours made:
And so of you, beauteous and lovely youth,
When that shall fade, by verse distils your truth."

Besides these objections, which are equally applicable to the sonnets of all nations, the English sonnet is charged with faults of its own. Dr. Johnson's opinion has been already adverted to. Lord Byron, in one of the very few sonnets he wrote, makes the same admission,—that it is a form of poetry not suited to our language; and, though some allowance is to be made for the language of compliment which he was addressing to an Italian lady, yet the fact that the noble poet, with all his Italian promptings, so rarely made use of the sonnet, is proof enough of his sentiments. I have thus frankly referred to the opinions of Dr. Johnson and Lord Byron, (odd company indeed!) both strong names and witnesses against our cause. I must be allowed to speak of them with equal freedom. There will be no novelty in the expression of an opinion derogatory to Dr. Johnson's character as a critic of poetry, nor will it be necessary, I presume, to remind the reader of the errors, both of judgment and taste, in his principal critical work. Dr. Johnson had, in fact, a hearty love for only one period of English poetry, and that not its best period. His affection was given to the poetry of that time when the native vigour of the poetry of England was enfeebled by the introduction of Gallic refinements,—when the healthy, sanguine English Muse was miserably depleted. To say that he was little better than blind and deaf to all else would scarcely be using language too strong. Out of the limits of the period referred to, he praised only by compulsion, as is apparent from his reluctance, such as is manifested in his criticisms on the minor poems of Milton. There is no instance on record in which the guilt of literary omission attaches more strongly and has done more injury than in Dr. Johnson's "Lives of the English Poets." For aught that appears there, Chaucer, and Spenser, and Shakspeare, (as a poet apart altogether from the dramatist,) and Drayton, Daniel, Sir Philip Sidney, and others of the age of Queen Elizabeth, —the chief of the poets of England,—might never have breathed a verse. And, in the dreary absence of these, after what names is the misguided reader led in chase? Stepney, Mallet, Granville and Pomfret, Hughes and Yalden and Sprat,—"rats and mice and such small deer." Now, the school of poetry which was favourite with Dr. Johnson was exactly that by which the sonnet was completely repudiated; it demands too much of the substance of poetry to have found favour in the eyes of the Charles II. and Queen Anne's men.* It is a fact of considerable interest as bearing on our subject, and one which will be appreciated by those who are familiar with the different ages of English poetry, that during the most artificial period the sonnet was neglected almost universally; and that it revives with the taste for the earlier models, which is one of the best features in the literature of our day, and from which we may infer that poetry at least is completing a cycle by a return to primitive power and simplicity. To invalidate the authority of Lord Byron's name may be a more delicate task than that we have just attempted. Conceding all the vigour of imagination that may be claimed for him by that large but decreasing class, his zealous admirers, I cannot but believe that he greatly wanted the qualities essential to success in the severer forms of poetry. This would have been especially felt in the sonnet. Neither his habits of thought nor his modes of feeling were adapted to it, nor had he sufficient command of expression. His head and his heart and his tongue were all undisciplined. The time has gone by, I hope, for the misplaced sympathy with what are called the eccentricities of genius, and for the fallacy which recognises the right of any mortal to claim exemption from the laws which universally control the intellectual as well as moral being of man-

* We may be reminded that the selection for the lives was made by the publishers. We are aware of that fact, but it is an inadequate apology. Dr. Johnson himself suggested names,—some of those we have referred to in the text. He might have controlled and extended the selection; or, if not, he might at least have proclaimed the existence of other treasures, if his taste had prompted him to an acquaintance with the earlier poetry of England.

kind. How much is it to be deplored that Lord Byron was too disdainful habitually to lay his restless head in the lap of nature! His conceptions, lofty as they unquestionably often were, were not distinct enough for a poem of limited size; his emotions, deep as they were, unhappily were not chastened. Language did not sit upon him as a garment, but girt him like harness, as his more discriminating admirer often, to his own discomfiture, perceives. When we hear Lord Byron's doubts as to the capabilities of the English language for the sonnet, we should recollect that he was far from being well read in English poetry, and that he was not well inclined to believe that what he himself was unequal to could be accomplished by any of his contemporaries.

But, leaving the witnesses, let us look to the charge. The sonnet is not suited to the English language. In what respect does the language fail? Surely not in expression; for no one will venture to deny that a certain number of English words will convey as much thought as an equal number of the words of any language, living or dead. The alleged defect refers, we may fairly presume, to considerations of versification. A poverty of rhyme and a deficiency of harmony are imputed to the language, which, if merited, would indeed disqualify it for the continuous melody of the sonnet. I regard the charge as an idle prejudice. To complain of language is a hackneyed device to conceal ignorance or incompetency. Let any one reflect on what has been accomplished by the English tongue, let him muse a while on the achievements of English prose or English verse, and he may well be impatient of these disloyal repinings.

Whoever undertakes to bring down Sir Thomas Brown's record to our own times, to be the historian of vulgar errors, of men's follies and mistakes, should place this in the foremost rank,—the opinion which ascribes a narrowness to that glorious way over which Shakspeare and Milton, Taylor and Barrow, Baxter and Bunyan, Burke, Coleridge, and Wordsworth, have passed into the hearts and minds of the British race on both sides of the Atlantic.

The sonnet has been successfully naturalized into English literature. Its first introduction was contemporary with the early improvement in our poetry by which metrical forms of versification were substituted for the old rhythmical mode. Its prescriptive title is, therefore, as good as that of any other form. The first English sonnets were written by Henry Howard, the gallant but unfortunate Earl of Surrey. The melodies of strange languages had fallen on his ear; yet he neither remained abroad to renounce his own home, nor did he return with a heart corrupted by foreign travel, but, in a spirit of pure and lofty patriotism, he sought his native land, to call up the yet-buried harmonies of his mother-tongue. This honour is shared with him by his contemporary and friend, Sir Thomas Wyat. I have already shown that the sonnet has been employed with honour by others,—the chief of English poets. In the hands of Shakspeare its form was modified; and, as we are much more disposed to regard him as a lawmaker than as an outlaw, we cannot but think that there is too dainty a preciseness in the hesitation which is felt in applying the name to other forms than the original model. We are ready to adopt Shakspeare's enlargement of the meaning of the word, because no essential principle whatever of the poem is sacrificed by the variety. But to avoid the appearance of a mere verbal dispute, if we adopt the stricter sense of the term, the severer form of the poem, the legitimate sonnet, as it is called, the poets of England have abundantly vindicated the powers of the language. It is to a living poet that the glory of consummating this victory over a wide-spread prejudice is due. The notes that proclaim this triumph of the English Muse are uttered by the sonnets of William Wordsworth. From these alone we might readily show the abundant richness of the language in rhymes, its power of expression, and its flexibility of metre. With those, indeed, who are accustomed only to the more prominent rhymes and the more marked forms of verse, the melody of the sonnet may often fall as on a deaf ear. But to a cultivated taste, and to the secret sense of hearing, apt for the music of poetry, we would cheerfully commit almost any one of Wordsworth's sonnets, without an apprehension that the sweetness and variety of its harmony would pass unheeded. The following may be taken after little more than a moment's selection :—

"It is a beauteous evening, calm and free:
The holy time is quiet as a nun
Breathless with adoration; the broad sun
Is sinking down in its tranquillity;
The gentleness of heaven is on the sea.
Listen! the mighty Being is awake,
And doth, with his eternal motion, make
A sound like thunder—everlastingly.
Dear child! dear girl! that walkest with me here,
If thou appearest untouched by solemn thought,

> Thy nature is not therefore less divine:
> Thou liest in Abraham's bosom all the year,
> And worshippest at the Temple's inner shrine,
> God being with thee when we know it not."

Another prejudice, perhaps the most deeply seated, against the sonnet, results from an impression that it always treats a subject exclusively with reference to the feelings of the poet. Hence it is censured as egotistical, and is looked upon as the vent of moping and discontented humours, and of insipid sentimentality. That there are very many sonnets justly obnoxious to these reproaches may be freely admitted; and, also, that a bad sonnet is, for reasons that might readily be stated, one of the worst of failures. Of those who have been able to find none other, I can only say that they have been indeed unfortunate in their selection. But I protest against this indiscriminate grouping of the good and bad. If the sonnet be judged on that principle, how will the epic abide it? A bad epic is very bad, too, and a great deal more of it. It is one of the merits of the English sonnet-writers that they have qualified the *subjective* character of the poem; the feelings of the poet are not necessarily most prominent: many of the best of the English sonnets may be read without recognising him as any thing more than a voice.

That the sonnet is egotistical is obviously only a comparative censure. Whether this is to be imputed to it for its reproach or its repute will manifestly depend upon whose egotism it is. If it express the feelings of a hollow heart or the thought of an empty head, nothing can be more valueless. But has it not been the key to open the secret cabinet of spirits whose stores were precious? When Shakspeare meditated upon his theatrical profession, it was in the sonnet that he breathed out his sense of degradation in that beautiful lament, of which the tone is a little louder than a sigh and yet not so harsh as a murmur. It is here that his genius, no longer embodied in its creations, appears to us in its individual nature;—he walks upon the earth in his own personal form. What poem can boast of greater interest?—

"Alas! 'tis true, I have gone here and there,
And made myself a motley to the view,
Gored mine own thoughts, sold cheap what is most dear,
Made old offences of affections new.
Most true it is that I have looked on truth
Askance and strangely; but, by all above,
These blenches gave my heart another youth,
And worse essays proved thee my best of love.
Now all is done, save what shall have no end:
Mine appetite I never more will grind
On newer proof, to try an older friend,—
A God in love, to whom I am confined.
Then give me welcome, next my heaven the best,
Even to thy pure and most most loving breast."

Again, in reference to the same topic:—

"Oh, for my sake do you with Fortune chide,
The guilty goddess of my harmful deeds,
That did not better for my life provide
Than public means, which public manners breeds.
Thence comes it that my name receives a brand,
And almost thence my nature is subdued
To what it works in, like the dyer's hand:
Pity me, then, and wish I were renewed;
Whilst, like a willing patient, I will drink
Potions of eysell, 'gainst my strong infection;

No bitterness that I will bitter think,
No double penance, to correct correction.
Pity me, then, dear friend, and I assure ye
Even that your pity is enough to cure me."

This would be sweet language from any lips; but what can be deeper than the pathos of it, when you reflect that it is the grief of one whose wisdom, for more than two centuries, has been reverently quoted by statesmen, philosophers, and divines, whose plots have wound round so many hearts and moistened so many eyes, whose pictures of passions have moved such sympathies, and whose wit has gladdened so many faces? It is in his sonnets that you find the conclusive proof that he was "the *gentle* Shakspeare."* It will be recollected that he retired to Stratford to pass the evening of his days. We quote the following sonnet, which appears to refer to that period, partly for the fine amplification it contains of a well-known phrase in Macbeth, and chiefly for the sur-

* Of all the epithets that are attached to the name of Shakspeare, there are but two or three that are to be tolerated. You can scarcely, by means of any term, add to the conception of genius which is suggested by the single word "Shakspeare." The phrase, "the gentle Shakspeare," deserves to be a favourite one, because it teaches a truth of deep moral interest: it tells of the blessed union of genius and gentleness,—that there is a natural alliance between the highest powers of intellect and tenderest emotions of the heart. There might, perhaps, be no other objection than the appearance of quaintness to his sharing Hooker's epithet, "the judicious Shakspeare," as indicating those faculties which, combined with imagination, are found only in poets of the first order. Mr. Coleridge applied to Shakspeare the expression "the myriad-minded," ανηρ μυριονους, having *reclaimed* it from a Greek monk, by whom it had been used in reference to a patriarch of Constantinople. As to most other epithets for him, they are as tinkling cymbals.

passing beauty of the images illustrative of a poet's silent old age. We challenge the poetry of the world against that one line:—

"That time of year thou mayest in me behold,
When yellow leaves, or none, or few, do hang
Upon those boughs which shake against the cold,
Bare, ruined choirs where late the sweet birds sang.
In me thou seest the twilight of such day
As after sunset fadeth in the west,
Which by-and-by black night doth take away,—
Death's second self, that seals up all in rest.
In me thou seest the glowing of such fire,
That on the ashes of his youth doth lie,
As the death-bed whereon it must expire,
Consumed with that which it was nourished by.
This thou perceivest, which makes thy love more strong,
To love that well which thou must leave ere long."

One other instance may be cited by way of refutation of the charge of insipidity brought against the sonnet. When Milton addressed the grave appeal of patriotism to his contemporaries, Cromwell and Fairfax and Vane, he chose this form. When he invoked a higher power, it was the sonnet by which he uttered the prayer, "Avenge, O Lord, thy slaughtered hosts,"—a note so fearful and so loud that we can almost fancy it echoing over the valleys in which the bones of the martyrs lay covered with snow. And when, at last, no longer able to resist the belief that he had been labouring for an unworthy age, that he had been prompting to freedom a race that was sluggish and sensual, it was in the sonnet that he expressed his solemn resignation. It was a fitting close for his eventful career. The storm that had risen on the meridian of his life had slowly abated, and, while the fragments of it were yet strewn on every side and the thunders of his controversial voice were echoing in the distant sky, there broke forth, at sunset, a placid gleam of that light which had beamed upon his youth. His sight extinguished, a hostile dynasty restored,—"Darkness before and Danger's voice behind,"—he bowed his head with the unsoured cheerfulness of his early days. In that spirit we find him in the sonnets communing with a few chosen friends and with his God. To appreciate Milton's sonnets fully, we should refresh our recollections of some of his prose-writings; we should recall the fierce indignation and the bitter scorn hurled against Salmasius; we should recur to the closing passages of his tract of "Reformation in England,"—the most awful imprecation ever uttered by the voice of man, save when it has been prophetic of the vengeance of the Almighty. Then let either of the sonnets addressed to Cyriac Skinner be read:—

"Cyriac, this three years day these eyes, though clear
To outward view of blemish or of spot,
Bereft of light their seeing have forgot,
Nor to their idle orbs doth sight appear
Of sun, or moon, or star, throughout the year,
Or man or woman. Yet I argue not
Against Heaven's hand or will, nor bate a jot
Of heart or hope; but still bear up and steer
Right onward. What supports me, dost thou ask?
The conscience, friend, to have lost them overplied
In liberty's defence, my noble task,
Of which all Europe talks from side to side.
This thought might lead me through the world's vain mask,
Content, though blind, had I no better guide."

Can it be that the torrent which before leaped so madly and so loudly from rock to rock has passed into this gentle current? How full, how tranquil, is its flow!

Spenser's sonnets are of secondary merit. Inferior to his other minor poems, they are unimpassioned productions, of a character which seems to be suggested by the title "*Amoretti*" prefixed to them. The poet who, as a sonnet-writer, has gained a place by the side of Shakspeare and Milton, is Wordsworth. And when it is considered that all of these have given to the world works of a more enlarged form and of the highest order of poems, it would seem that the sonnet was used as a kind of private tablet to preserve the detached and passing thoughts which must ever be rising in the ceaseless fountain of a great poet's heart. It is the record of

"The sessions of sweet, silent thought,"

to borrow from a sonnet of Shakspeare one of those exquisite phrases which fell so naturally and so gracefully from his tongue, and which justify us in saying (not irreverently, we trust) that he spake as never man spake. Let no one look upon the little poem with a hasty superciliousness. I have shown that it has been the retreat of poetic genius of the first rank,—an oratory for those who have worthily ministered in the solemnities of cathedral service.

The sonnets of Wordsworth would richly deserve a separate examination. He, more than any other poet, has shown its adaptation to a very great variety of subject and of feeling. If there were none other in the language, there would be reason enough to claim the sonnet as a form of poetry completely naturalized into English literature. The public is at last rendering him justice; the sound of the war that was waged against him has died away. It is his singularly-happy fortune, in which his early admirers especially sympathize, to witness the beginning of the maturity of his fame. It will be completed by the reputation of his sonnets, which will probably be the last of his works to gain very general favour. For this reason we have quoted from them freely, and if the reader desire the eloquence, the pathos, and the philosophy of poetry, with all its harmonies, we commend him to the several collections of sonnets among the poems of Wordsworth.

In adverting to contemporary poetry, we cannot suppress a regret that Coleridge — that other great light, but recently extinguished—did not, in the later periods of his life, revive his early attachment to the sonnet. In expressing this regret, I would not be understood as participating in the charge of inactivity that has so inconsiderately been brought against him. Of that injustice we wash our hands, for we entertain too deep a gratitude for what he has done, and too firm conviction that few writers have contributed more to the thoughts of their fellow-beings. Coleridge has been our friend,— our companion, our guide, our own familiar friend. We could not lay upon the grass that grows on his grave the weight of the lightest complaint. I merely regret that in his old age he did not renew the series of his youthful sonnets, because his constitutional habits of reflection and his singular powers of versification pre-eminently qualified him for this form of poetry. I could readily point out many a passage in Mr. Coleridge's prose-works, in which some noble thought is illuminated by a richly-imaginative illustration, and which would need only the metrical arrangement to constitute a sonnet of the first order. His son, Hartley Coleridge, who has given proof that the genius of the family has not been buried in the father's grave, might find in such a process of transformation a task affectionate to the memory of his parent and worthy of his own powers.*

It is irksome, we are aware, to write from other men's suggestions, and the best efforts of mind are those which are purely self-evolved. The mere difficulty of any undertaking would be no obstacle to the intellect that could conceive a sonnet in all respects so adequate to its

* If our voice could reach him, we would commend such passages as the following as suitable material for a sonnet: the fine comparison in the "Friend,"—"Human experience, like the stern-lights of a ship at sea, illumines only the path we have passed over:"—or Coleridge's impassioned wish respecting the reception of his works:—"Would to Heaven that the verdict to be passed on my labours depended on those who least needed them! The water-lily, in the midst of the waters, lifts up its broad leaves and expands its petals at the first pattering of the shower, and rejoices in the rain with a quicker sympathy than the parched shrub in the sandy desert:"—or his bold conception respecting the design of miracles, in the "Statesman's Manual:"—"It was only to overthrow the usurpation exercised in and through the senses, that the senses were miraculously appealed to. Reason and revelation are their own evidence. The natural sun is, in this respect, a symbol of the spiritual. Ere he is fully arisen, and while his glories are still under veil, he calls up the breeze to chase away the usurping vapours of the night-season, and thus converts the air itself into the minister of its own purification; not, surely, in proof or elucidation of the light from heaven, but to prevent its interception."

high theme as the following from the poems of Hartley Coleridge :—

"TO SHAKSPEARE.

"The soul of man is larger than the sky,—
Deeper than ocean, or abysmal dark
Of the unfathomed centre. Like that ark
Which in its sacred hold uplifted high,
O'er the drowned hills, the human family,
And stock reserved of every living kind,
So, in the compass of the single mind,
The seeds and pregnant forms in essence lie
That make all worlds. Great poet! 'twas thy art
To know thyself, and in thyself to be
Whate'er Love, Hate, Ambition, Destiny,
Or the firm fatal Purpose of the Heart,
Can make of Man. Yet thou wert still the same,
Serene of thought, unhurt by thy own flame."

In closing my enumeration of the capabilities of the sonnet, there is one other purpose to which it was equal. It could express the feelings of Charles Lamb. Why of Charles Lamb more than of any one else? Reader, if you ask that question you have not yet learned the dear mystery of those two monosyllables, "*Charles Lamb.*" But if you have been more fortunate, how much of the spirit of "Elia" will you not recognise in these two brief poems!—

"WORK.

"Who first invented Work, and bound the free
And holiday-rejoicing spirit down
To the ever-haunting importunity
Of business in the green fields, and the town,—
To plough, loom, anvil, spade,—and, oh! most sad,
To that dry drudgery at the desk's dead wood?—

Who but the being unblest, alien from good,—
Sabbathless Satan! he who his unglad
Task ever plies 'mid rotatory burnings,
That round and round incalculably reel—
For wrath divine hath made him like a wheel—
In that red realm from which are no returnings;
Where, toiling and turmoiling, ever and aye,
He and his thoughts keep pensive working-day.

"LEISURE.

"They talk of time, and of time's galling yoke,
That like a millstone on man's mind doth press,
Which only works and business can redress;
Of divine Leisure such foul lies are spoke,
Wounding her fair gifts with calumnious stroke.
But might I, fed with silent meditation,
Assoilèd live from that fiend, Occupation,—
Improbus labor, which hath my spirit broke,—
I'd drink of time's rich cup, and never surfeit;
Fling in more days than went to make the gem
That crowned the white top of Methusalem;
Yea, on my weak neck take, and never forfeit,
Like Atlas bearing up the dainty sky,
The heaven-sweet burden of eternity."

I have thus endeavoured, not very systematically, to vindicate a neglected department of English poetry. I never engage in an investigation of the kind, involving a recurrence to the early periods of English literature, without feeling disposed, on closing it, to give way to a thanksgiving that "the lines have fallen to us in such pleasant places; that we have so goodly a heritage." To the student of poetry—we hope a distinction is drawn between such and many of the ordinary readers of poetry—we commend the sonnet as worthy of his regard and as one of the best tests of a cultivated taste.

The public taste for the sonnet is reviving, and it would not be a difficult task to give it a true tone. Let a selection be made from the sonnets of Shakspeare, Milton, Spenser, Sir Philip Sidney, and other of the earlier poets, and from those of Warton, Bowles, Wordsworth, Southey, Coleridge, and others, illustrated with occasional critical notices. A volume might be formed into which none but the best English sonnets should be admitted. Besides its intrinsic merit, such a book would possess much of the charm of novelty, and, what would distinguish it most favourably from all books of selections, each selection would be a complete and perfect poem in itself. I can scarcely imagine a more agreeable volume for the study or for the parlour-table. I recommend the suggestion to some enterprising publisher, as one likely to be successful, and which would certainly render a service to the cause of English letters.

ESSAY II.

Poems of Hartley Coleridge.

We love to meet occasionally with a new name in the annals of literature. For, though there is a sovereign company to whom we never falter in our allegiance, yet, for the honour of time present, and for the satisfaction of knowing that the best portion of the world is not standing still, we rejoice now and then to hail a new author. Under this designation we desire to be distinctly understood as not including that growing class of handicraftsmen who are engaged in the manufacture of what by courtesy are called books. When we speak of authorship, we mean that occupation which gives to a name an abiding-place in the history of letters. It is one of the evils of the accumulation of modern publications, that a man, unless gifted with supernatural reading-powers, is compelled to be somewhat reserved in forming new literary acquaintances. He contents himself with his old friends; he retreats to the shelf of his library that has become endeared to him; he finds his security among the familiar volumes that he could lay his hand upon in the dark; he is shy of new-made gentry. Yet these very feelings probably enhance the pleasure of meeting with a volume which bears the stamp of something above the mere mechanism of bookmaking.

It is an added pleasure to be able to greet a new *poet.* The world, we are apprehensive, is growing too *prosy.* We are haunted with a vague sort of alarm — more like a dream, or a nightmare, than a waking thought — that hosts of the tenants of this goodly green globe will turn into brokers and money-dealers. The hearts of men, we fear, will be in the stocks. It is one of the characteristics of the times, that whole communities are alarmingly utilitarian. Nothing is secure from the base uses of economists and calculators; no spot or edifice, however hallowed, is assured in its moral associations; no spectacle, however glorious by the work of nature, is safe from the rude touch of heartless speculation. Men have been found bold enough to lay their impious hands upon scenes the most awful in creation. The cataract and the cascade are measured for water-power; the mountain-torrent is a feeder. A traveller, revisiting a district of country after a few years' absence, inquires after a waterfall as he does after an old inhabitant, and is no more surprised at finding that one has gone to his rest than that the other has been turned to its work. Niagara has scarcely been secure. Presumptuous as modern "improvement" is, there need not, we suppose, be a rational fear that the ceaseless discharge of more than five inland seas might be perceptibly diminished; but that the matchless sublimity of that spot may be grievously impaired, we have greatly feared. Our last pilgrimage to that place of worship — that shrine of the Almighty—was hastened by this apprehension.

As we approached it, we heard of railroads to the Falls, —of the "City of the Falls,"—of town-lots, and of water-power. We saw, with a heavy heart, the actual plan of these devices. Alas! thought we, shall that voice of the Creator be silenced?—shall the deep that there crieth unto deep be hushed? But there came glad tidings that nature was avenged. The bold mortal —the Titan of the land-jobbers—who had dared to traffic with her glories was laid prostrate in the very deed. We turned pagan for the nonce, and gave thanks to the spirit of the cataract, whom, in fancy, we beheld triumphing over the prostrate evil genius of Speculation. It will, we fondly trust, prove a lesson against future presumption. We have no fear that man, with all the pomp and power and pride of mechanism, can draw more than a drop from that flow; yet he may most vexatiously intrude: the shrill accents of art may be mingled with the solemn tones of nature,—a harsh accompaniment to the unison of voices of the great waters. The surrounding scenery may be sadly defaced, if touched by any hand which is not restrained by a sense of the sublimities of the place. As we wandered about the neighbourhood, a group of Indians glided across our path,—a young Tuscarora, with a very unabated look, and his squaw with her infant peering out of its cradle on its mother's back. By-the-by, an Indian mother's love should be exceeding deep, we surmise, for her dear little savage is borne so much more than the infants of the sophisticated matrons in civilized communities. As we looked at them, a thought came into our mind that the traces of the world as it has been were not yet quite effaced,—that something was still left untouched by the restless, feverish hand of coveteousness. We gazed upon the savages as the Ancient Mariner did upon the bright water-snakes :—

> "A spring of love gushed from my heart,
> And I blessed them unaware;
> Sure my kind saint took pity on me,
> And I blessed them unaware."

We have no ambition to be sentimentally conservative; but we do lament that the spirit of change is restrained by no higher consideration than a distrust of investment, and that it has no fear of assaulting the bounds set by nature or by moral association. It is only when it trangresses its lawful limits—as in the glaring instance we have adverted to—that we deplore the progress of improvement so called. The world would be all the better, we fancy, if the practical fit which is on it were somewhat abated. A factitious standard has been introduced by the self-sufficient wisdom of the day, which tests all things by what is called a practical character,—which means, we believe, the quality of teaching men to make money, or to increase the crops, or to multiply the fabric of "stuffs," under which latter denomination may be included a large proportion of the products of the press. Books are valued according to the same standard. Now, we most thankfully greet any literary effort which recognises a higher aim and a nobler end. Surely there is a practical character of a better kind than that which is indicated by the ordinary acceptation of the term; surely something more is to be *done* than to administer to man's physical wants; he is to be supplied with something more than food, and clothing, and the trash called "light reading" by those who look upon books as mere allies against time. A writer elevating himself above the lower spheres of authorship is worthy of a more than ordinary welcome. We delight, therefore, we repeat, to meet with a new *poet.*

The name of Hartley Coleridge will probably be new to many of our readers. He is the son—the first-born—of the late Samuel Taylor Coleridge, the poet and philosopher: we always hesitate which to call him, and regret that the language supplies no word comprehensive of both titles. Mr. Hartley Coleridge has therefore a patrimonial reputation. How far, however, that species of inheritance may be available to a man's own reputation, is, we think, somewhat questionable; for it is quite as apt to induce an invidious comparison as a willingness to trace the ancestral power. It has the effect of interesting public curiosity, but beyond that the heir's own fame must be earned by his own efforts.

It is pleasing to find any instance in which the strength and qualities of the mind have descended from father or mother to the offspring. The likeness has much greater interest than those physical similitudes in which there is often so carefully transmitted the shape of a nose or a mouth, or the twist of an eyebrow, or that most imperishable of all traits, which is rarely quenched by the lapse of less than three or four generations,—a head of red hair. A case of intellectual inheritance is an agreeable exception to the general tendency to degeneracy. The necessity of crossing the breed seems to make such brutes of us that it is not a pleasing theory. The instances of hereditary talent in literature are, however, we are obliged to acknowledge, of rare occurrence. After a few minutes' labour of recollection, the only examples we are able to call to mind are Kings David and Solomon, and the two Drs. Sherlock. The latter of these cases is not of sufficient note, and the circumstance of inspiration obviously puts the former out of the question, for it might probably be regarded as an exception to a general rule rather than an illustration of it. Poetic genius especially is so delicate a combination, that it is likely to be destroyed by any change in its constitution. Two of Dryden's sons attempted to follow in their father's path; but the spirit of "glorious John" had fled, and what they wrote the world has willingly let die.* Spenser left two sons, —one with a name at least that might well befit a poet, "Sylvanus Spenser,"—the other with a name that would have suited one whose walks were on the highways of prose, "Peregrine Spenser." What, by-the-by, had become of the poet's own beautiful name, "Edmund Spenser"? Perhaps the child was so named that perished in the flames when Spenser's dwelling was fired by the Irish rebels and he driven from the country.†

---

* Perhaps in the constitution of the sons there was too large a proportion of the mother's character. A letter from Dryden's wife—the Lady Elizabeth, as she was styled, from her noble lineage of the Howards—has been preserved, in which the following passage occurs:—"Your father is much at woon as to his health, and his defnese is not wosce, but much as he was when he was heare. Give me a true account how my deare sonn Charlles is head dus."

† This calamity is mentioned by Southey, in his notices of the early British poets, in a manner rather peculiar:—"When Tyrone's

Unless that child, over whose untimely and disastrous fate the poet's broken heart beat its last throbs, inherited some of the parent's spirit, his boundless imagination came not down to others of the name. Milton's son—John Milton, junior—died in his infancy; but, we dare say, had he lived longer, he would have been literally "a mute, inglorious Milton." Certainly his early death is not to be deplored, if we may conjecture what his character would have been from that of Milton's daughters, who grew aweary of their intellectual attendance upon the blind old bard, and longed for the humbler tasks of needlework. It is an ugly page in female history that records how they turned away from their communion with the spirit of their sire. "The irksomeness of their employment could not always be concealed, but broke out more and more into expressions of uneasiness; so that at length they were all sent out to learn some curious and ingenious sorts of manufactures that are proper for women to learn, particularly embroideries in gold or silver."* The glory of Shakspeare's name began and ended with himself,—his own unheritable self. We hope that the name is not desecrated by the wear of any modern mortal, for it has passed above the common uses of men's names. How anomalous would a "Mr. or Mrs. Shakspeare" sound, and what perfect contradictions in terms would "the little Shakspeares" be! When the Rev. Mr. Dyce, one of Shakspeare's biographers, visited Stratford-on-Avon, in 1820, for the purpose of gathering traditions,

---

rebellion broke out, Spenser's house was burnt by the rebels, and *in it his papers and one of his children.*"—Southey's "British Poets."

* Life of Milton, by his nephew, Edward Philips.

he found a woman upwards of eighty years of age, named Mary Hornby, who gained a livelihood by showing the house in which the bard was born. She claimed a descent from Shakspeare, her maiden name being Hart, and had evidently inherited a full share of his love of the drama. Her high ancestral feeling manifested itself by her saying, "I *writes* plays, sir," and producing a tragedy entitled "The Battle of Waterloo." The old woman, who had better been at her prayers, was, we presume, well read in the three parts of Henry VI.; she had assuredly selected a famous theme for "Alarums —Enter English and French, fighting—Exeunt, fighting —Alarums." So far as syntax is concerned, she seems to have been what the French critics in their ignorance are so fond of calling her great progenitor,—"a wild, irregular genius." Such fallings off may well serve to rebuke man's pride. It was one of the trials of the calamitous life of the sainted Jeremy Taylor to witness the debased career of his own children. Who could have thought that the offspring of one whose spirit dwelt so habitually in the regions of an aspiring devotion would have declined to such degenerate ways? One fell in a duel, staining his dying hand with the blood of his antagonist; the other, with a slower but as deep a perfidy, became a favourite companion of Villiers, Duke of Buckingham. One more of these melancholy instances of degeneracy: Izaak Walton, the great piscator, left an only son, bearing too his honoured name. He, an Izaak Walton, turned away from the banks of the sedgy Lea, became a travelled gentleman, studied the Fine Arts in Italy, returned to one of the English universities, and devoted himself to assisting in the compilation of an ecclesiastical history. There is no record of his having ever angled for a single fish. Another of old Izaak's—"honest Mr. Walton's"—descendants, but, fortunately, not bearing the name, which in this instance was spared the degradation, strayed still further from the harmless paths of his forefather, and acquired some notoriety among that craft who after a fashion are fishers of men, by the authorship of the work, doomed to most criminal associations, entitled, "Hawkins's Pleas of the Crown."

But we are loath to dwell longer on this sad topic. The frequent occurrences of such instances of degeneracy as we have adverted to would almost justify a congratulation on those cases where the race of an illustrious individual has become extinct with him. There would seem to be a tendency in nature to transmit the weaknesses and infirmities rather than the nobler parts of our being. Of this there is so much hazard, that, whenever great powers are blended with any defects, we are tempted to rejoice in our hearts on finding that the line of succession is broken. It would be difficult, for instance, to fancy any being more superlatively disagreeable than a young Dr. Johnson would in all probability have been; and surely, if nature had furnished such an individual, she would have been bound to supply a young Boswell to match him. It was wisely ordained, no doubt, that the late Miss Hannah More lived and died an "unwedded maiden old." We must pause a moment to make our acknowledgment to Mr. Wordsworth for that phrase; for, having a profound affection for several of the class in question, we have long felt the need of some term as a substitute for that other one which has become somewhat tinctured with reproach. The lovely piety which adorned the life of Hannah More might, in the second generation, have subsided into a residuum of mere starch; or, if the aberration had been to the opposite extreme, and as wide as in the family of the good Jeremy Taylor, her descendant might have been an opera-singer or a figurante.

We have been led into these trains of reflection by taking up the volume of Mr. Hartley Coleridge's poems. A literary effort by a son of Coleridge was calculated to attract attention. The influence exerted by the father's writings was deeper than that of most authors; the readers that were moved by him were strongly moved, and we could hardly believe that their influence would be inoperative on his own household. We had anticipations, therefore, of Hartley Coleridge before we knew of his literary pursuits. What he has so far accomplished may be considered chiefly as experiment for him and promise to the world. But enough, we think, has been done to show that the Coleridge name has not yet reaped the whole harvest of its fame. Hartley Coleridge has appeared as the author of the volume of poetry which we purpose examining in this article, and of a volume of biography,—"The Lives of Distinguished Northerns,"—a work of very considerable attractions, with a vein of pleasant writing on the surface and of fine philosophy beneath. The compliment has also been paid of throwing upon him suspicions of the authorship of that extraordinary and delightful production, "The Doctor;" and, although the proofs seem to have accumulated more upon Southey than upon any one else, we are very reluctant to give up a belief of ours that

Hartley Coleridge has a hand in it, participating, probably, with the laureate, and thus reviving that fine old custom of joint authorship which was of no uncommon occurrence in the early days of English literature.

Hartley Coleridge is, by a sort of necessity, a poet, and the lovers of his father's melodious imaginings had a right to indulge great hopes of him. His father's prayers and teachings marked him for the high converse of poesy; and the beautiful allusions to him, when yet an infant, have kept a place in the hearts of the admirers of the sire open for the son. We feel towards Hartley Coleridge as if we could say that we knew him when a child. What happier introduction could he have had than by the little incident narrated with such true parental as well as poetic feeling in Coleridge's exquisite poem, "The Nightingale"?—

"Farewell, O warbler! till to-morrow eve.
And you, my friends! farewell, a short farewell!
We have been loitering long and pleasantly;
And now for our dear homes. That strain again!
Full fain it would delay me! My dear babe,
Who, capable of no articulate sound,
Mars all things with his imitative lisp,—
How he would place his hand beside his ear,
His little hand, the small forefinger up,
And bid us listen! And I deem it wise
To make him nature's playmate. He knows well
The evening star; and once, when he awoke
In most distressful mood, (some inward pain
Had made up that strange thing, an infant's dream,)
I hurried with him to our orchard-plot,
And he beheld the moon, and, hushed at once,

Suspends his sobs, and laughs most silently,
While his fair eyes, that swam with undropped tears,
Did glitter in the yellow moonbeam! Well!—
It is a father's tale. But if that Heaven
Should give me life, his childhood shall grow up
Familiar with these songs, that with the night
He may associate joy!—Once more, farewell,
Sweet nightingale! Once more, my friends, farewell!"

And again, in the lines entitled "Frost at Midnight:"—

"Dear babe, that sleepest cradled by my side,
Whose gentle breathings, heard in this deep calm,
Fill up the interspersèd vacancies
And momentary pauses of the thought!
My babe so beautiful! it thrills my heart
With tender gladness thus to look at thee
And think that thou shalt learn far other lore
And in far other scenes! For I was reared
In the great city, pent 'mid cloisters dim,
And saw naught lovely but the sky and stars.
But thou, my babe! shalt wander like a breeze
By lakes and sandy shores, beneath the crags
Of ancient mountain, and beneath the clouds
Which image, in their bulk, both lakes and shores
And mountain-crags: so shalt thou see and hear
The lovely shades and sounds intelligible
Of that eternal language which thy God
Utters, who from eternity doth teach
Himself in all, and all things in himself.
Great universal Teacher! he shall mould
Thy spirit, and by giving make it ask.

"Therefore, all seasons shall be sweet to thee;
Whether the summer clothe the general earth
With greenness, or the redbreast sit and sing
Betwixt the tuft of snow on the bare branch
Of mossy apple-tree, while the nigh thatch
Smokes in the sun-thaw; whether the eave-drops fall

Heard only in the trances of the blast,
Or if the secret ministry of frost
Shall hang them up in silent icicles,
Quietly shining to the quiet moon."

Such aspirations must have shed a prosperous influence upon the expanding spirit of him whose childhood was thus watched over. The interest of this home-story is completed by the sweet response of the son to the aged parent, upon whose ear—soon after sealed by death—it may have sounded as an earnest of his early prayer. It is impossible not to be most favourably prepossessed by the dedication of these poems, not merely for the admirable simplicity of the expression, but for the pure and right-hearted feeling which pervades it:—

"DEDICATORY SONNET,

TO S. T. COLERIDGE.

"Father, and bard, revered! to whom I owe—
Whate'er it be—my little art of numbers,
Thou, in thy night-watch, o'er my cradled slumbers
Didst meditate the verse that lives to show
(And long shall live, when we alike are low)
Thy prayer how ardent, and thy hope how strong,
That I should learn of nature's self the song,
The lore, which none but nature's pupils know.

"The prayer was heard: I 'wandered, like a breeze,'
By mountain-brooks and solitary meres,
And gathered there the shapes and fantasies
Which, mixed with passions of my sadder years,
Compose this book. If good therein there be,
That good, my sire, I dedicate to thee.

"HARTLEY COLERIDGE."

The feeling with which the volume is offered to the public discovers the same good sense and feeling :—

"Of the verses contained in this volume, none, with a single exception, can claim the privilege of juvenile poems. I neither deprecate nor defy the censure of the critics. No man can know, of himself, whether he is, or is not, a poet. The thoughts, the feelings, the images, which are the material of poetry, are accessible to all who seek for them; but the power to express, combine, and modify,—to make a truth of thought,—to earn a sympathy for feeling,—to convey an image to the inward eye, with all its influences and associations,—can only approve itself by experiment; and the result of the experiment may not be known for years. Such an experiment I have ventured to try, and I wait the result with patience. Should it be favourable, the present volume will shortly be followed by another, in which, if no more be accomplished, a higher strain is certainly attempted."*

This is language very appropriate to the modesty of a first effusion; but the time will come, we are inclined to think, when Hartley Coleridge will feel that "a man *can* know of himself whether he is, or is not, a poet." When he rises (as we trust he will) into that promised higher strain, he must rely upon his own consciousness rather than upon the appreciations of others. The poet who talks of high strains must not wait for results; "soaring in the high reason of his fancies, with his garland and singing-robes about him,"†

* Preface. † Milton.

he must not look too often on the world that he leaves beneath him. But diffidence is a good fault at any time.

This volume of poems has given us assurance against a misgiving that has occasionally insinuated itself into our minds—a fear that the great stream of English poetry may for a time be intermitted. Commencing at the close of the long interval which elapsed after Chaucer's time, the series of eminent poets may be regarded as continuous from the date of the revival of poetry with the Earl of Surrey down to the present day. Sir Philip Sydney followed soon after that early period: he was mourned by Spenser, whose career was a little earlier than Shakspeare's. The retired manhood of Shakspeare and the youth of Milton touched the same period of time. There is a tradition of an interview between Milton in his old age, and the youthful Dryden,—an interview, by-the-by, sought by the latter, for the purpose of making a request which gave but sorry promise of his subsequent power: he was seeking permission to turn "Paradise Lost" into a rhyming tragedy, called "The State of Innocence." In one of his letters Pope has recorded having once seen Dryden, with a lament that his acquaintance reached no further:—"*Virgilium tantum vidi.*" Gray and Cowper brought the series down towards the close of the last century, and Crabbe and Rogers may be looked on as the connecting links with the great contemporary poets. Of these, Coleridge, Walter Scott, and Byron, are in their graves; Southey seems to have taken up his abode "in the cool element of prose." The light is yet burning upon Rydal Mount,—with vigour enough, we fervently trust, to send forth its kindly influences upon human nature for years to come. But the course of nature is coming on; and, in his beautiful lines on the death of the Ettrick Shepherd, "the old man eloquent" has told of the warning he has felt in the death of his contemporaries:—

"Like clouds that rake the mountain summit
Or waves that own no curbing hand,
How fast has brother followed brother
From sunshine to the sunless land!

"Yet I, whose lids from infant slumbers
Were earlier raised, remain to hear
A timid voice, that asks in whispers,
'Who next will drop and disappear?'"

When Wordsworth, too, shall have passed to his rest,—well earned by a long life devoted, without reserve or intermission, to elevating the feelings and character of mankind,—where, we have sometimes asked ourselves, shall he be found who may prove equal to the inheritance? If there be no one worthy to transmit the trust which for three centuries has not been forfeited, it will tell that a sad change has come over the spirit of that race who speak the English tongue. Let not this be thought an exaggeration. It is only the vulgar in intellect, and the indiscriminating, who look upon poetry as a mere superfluity,—an ornament, perhaps, but still only an excrescence of the mind. Who half as much as the poets have given permanency to the thoughts and feelings of the world as it was long ago? What unaided human spirit in the wide universe of letters ever wrought half the influence of Shakspeare? What name suggests a tithe of his genius and power?

"No man," said the elder Coleridge, "was ever yet a great poet without being at the same time a profound philosopher; for poetry is the blossom and the fragrancy of all human knowledge, human thoughts, human passions, emotions, language." No poet, it may be added, entertaining an inadequate conception of his calling, can approach to eminence in it. We have no desire to wage a war for the poetasters,—the inspired of the annuals, whether of souvenirs or of the addresses of watchmen and newspaper-carriers: we are speaking of other gentry. The sublime notion of poetry which should always guide a critical taste has been upheld in a fine panegyric by Wordsworth, in one of his prose treatises, which are not known as they should be, and from which we are, therefore, the more induced to quote the passage:—

"The man of science seeks truth as a remote and unknown benefactor; he cherishes and loves it in his solitude: the poet, singing a song in which all human beings join with him, rejoices in the presence of truth as our visible friend and hourly companion. Poetry is the breath and finer spirit of all knowledge; it is the impassioned expression which is in the countenance of all science. Emphatically may it be said of the poet, as Shakspeare hath said of man, 'that he looks before and after.' He is the rock of defence of human nature,—an upholder and preserver, carrying everywhere with him relationship and love. In spite of difference of soil and climate, of language and manners, of laws and customs, in spite of things silently gone out of mind and things violently destroyed, the poet binds together by passion and knowledge the vast empire of human society, as it is spread over the whole earth and over all time. The objects of the poet's thoughts are everywhere; though the eyes and senses of man are, it is true, his favourite guides, yet he will follow wheresoever he can find an atmosphere of sensation in which to move his wings. Poetry is the first and last of all knowledge: it is immortal as the heart of man. If the labours of men of science should ever create any material revolution, direct or indirect, in our condition, and in the impressions which we habitually receive, the poet will sleep then no more than at present, but he will be ready to follow the steps of the man of science,—not only in those general indirect effects, but he will be at his side, carrying sensation into the midst of the objects of the science itself. The remotest discoveries of the chemist, the botanist or mineralogist, will be as proper objects of the poet's art as any upon which it can be employed,—if the time should ever come when these things shall be familiar to us, and the relations under which they are contemplated by the followers of these respective sciences shall be manifestly and palpably material to us as enjoying and suffering beings. If the time should ever come when what is now called science, thus familiarized to men, shall be ready to be put on, as it were, a form of flesh and blood, the poet will lend his divine spirit to aid the transfiguration, and will welcome the being thus produced as a dear and genuine inmate of the household of man."*

Now, with our minds filled with such conceptions

* Wordsworth's Poetical Works, Appendix II. Observations, &c.

of the divine art, let us look whether Hartley Coleridge gives promise of being worthy to continue the succession of English poets; let us see what is the character of his poetic aspirations, and how high they have carried him. We find a partial answer in two of his sonnets, which serve a double purpose of showing his conception of his calling, and his power over language and metre to give it utterance:—

"WHO IS THE POET?

"Who is the poet? Who the man whose lines
Live in the souls of men like household words?
Whose thought, spontaneous as the song of birds,
With eldest truth coeval, still combines
With each day's product, and like morning shines,
Exempt from age? 'Tis he, and only he,
Who knows that truth is free, and only free,—
That virtue, acting in the strict confines
Of positive law, instructs the infant spirit
In its best strength, and proves its mere demerit
Rooted in earth, yet tending to the sky,—
With patient hope surveys the narrow bound,
Culls every flower that loves the lowly ground,
And, fraught with sweetness, wings her way on high."

"THE USE OF A POET.

"A thousand thoughts were stirring in my mind,
That strove in vain to fashion utterance meet;
And each the other crossed,—swift as a fleet
Of April clouds perplexed by gusts of wind,
That veer, and veer around, before, behind.
Now History pointed to the customed beat;
Now Fancy's clue, unravelling, led their feet
Through mazes manifold, and quaintly twined.
So were they straying,—so had ever strayed,
Had not the wiser poets of the past

The vivid chart of human life displayed
And taught the laws that regulate the blast,
Wedding wide impulse to calm forms of beauty,
And making peace 'twixt liberty and duty."

The subject is also touched in some lines quaintly entitled "POIETES APOIETES," in which, after lamenting his own feebleness, he tells, with a very pleasing allusion to his nativity and infancy, and a dark intimation of some unhappiness, of his poetic longings:—

"Divinest Poesy! 'tis thine to make
Age young—youth old—to baffle tyrant Time,—
From antique strains the hoary dust to shake,
And with familiar grace to crown new rhyme

"Long have I loved thee,—long have loved in vain;
Yet large the debt my spirit owes to thee:
Thou wreathedst my first hours in a rosy chain,
Rocking the cradle of my infancy.

"The lovely images of earth and sky
From thee I learned within my soul to treasure;
And the strong magic of thy minstrelsy
Charms the world's tempest to a sweet, sad measure.

"Nor Fortune's spite, nor hopes that once have been,
Hopes which no power of Fate can give again,—
Not the sad sentence—that my life must wean
From dear domestic joys,—nor all the train

"Of pregnant ills and penitential harms
That dog the rear of youth unwisely wasted,—
Can dim the lustre of thy stainless charms,
Or sour the sweetness that in thee I tasted."

We are glad to find Hartley Coleridge expressing his sense also of the characteristic weakness of a great deal of contemporary verse. The danger to which the cause of poetry appears chiefly to be exposed is the process of evaporation or sublimation by which modern versifiers so frequently separate its more superficial properties of sound and diction from its deeper and more abiding qualities of thought and feeling; for, dealing out their light wares, they give a pretext to the prose-witted ground-walkers to sneer even at real poetry and turn away from it as if it too were milk for babes. These evils seem to lie beyond the reach of remedy, and, until the wit of criticism shall devise some artillery light enough for the warfare, the butterflies and the humming-birds must flutter with impunity. The manufacturers of the fantastic commodities of modern versification have become of late years so numerous, that they are setting up all the world over their little tabernacles of rhyme, which in solidity of structure mightily remind us of the fairy-palace described by old Michael Drayton :—

> "The walls of spiders' legs are made,
> Well mortiséd and finely laid;
> He was the master of his trade,
> It curiouslie that builded:
> The windows of the eyes of cats,
> And for the roof, instead of slats,
> Is covered with the skins of bats,
> With moonshine that are gilded."

The self-complacent tribe—no longer the "genus irritable"—are chided by Hartley Coleridge with great gentleness in a sonnet of exquisite beauty :—

> "Whither is gone the wisdom and the power
> That ancient sages scattered with the notes

Of thought-suggesting lyres? The music floats
In the void air; e'en at this breathing hour
In every cell and every blooming bower
The sweetness of old lays is hovering still:
But the strong soul, the self-constraining will,
The rugged root that bare the winsome flower,
Is weak and withered. Were we like the fays
That sweetly nestle in the foxglove-bells,
Or lurk and murmur in the rose-lipped shells
Which Neptune to the earth for quit-rent pays,
Then might our pretty modern Philomels
Sustain our spirits with their roundelays."

One of the best indications in this volume of poems is the power of reflection which pervades most of its pages. The sonnets (of which there are a considerable number) are of the first order of that difficult form of composition. It would not be easy to suggest three higher themes for the sonnet than are presented in those we are about to quote; and it would be extreme fastidiousness to desire an execution more faithful to their lofty conceptions:—

"HOMER.

"Far from all measured space, yet clear and plain
As sun at noon, 'a mighty orb of song'
Illumes extremest heaven. Beyond the throng
Of lesser stars, that rise, and wax, and wane,
The transient rulers of the fickle main,
One steadfast light gleams through the dark and long
And narrowing aisle of memory. How strong,
How fortified with all the numerous train
Of human truths, great poet of thy kind,
Wert thou, whose verse, capacious as the sea
And various as the voices of the wind,
Swelled with the gladness of the battle's glee,
And yet could glorify infirmity,
When Priam wept, or shame-struck Helen pined."

"SHAKSPEARE.

"The soul of man is larger than the sky,
Deeper than ocean or the abysmal dark
Of the unfathomed centre. Like the ark,
Which in its sacred hold uplifted high,
O'er the drowned hills, the human family,
And stock reserved of every living kind,
So, in the compass of the single mind,
The seeds and pregnant forms in essence lie
That make all worlds. Great poet! 'twas thy art
To know thyself, and in thyself to be
Whate'er love, hate, ambition, destiny,
Or the firm, fatal purpose of the heart,
Can make of man. Yet thou wert still the same,
Serene of thought, unhurt by thy own flame."

"TO WORDSWORTH.

"There have been poets that in verse display
The elemental forms of human passions:
Poets have been, to whom the fickle fashions
And all the wilful humours of the day
Have furnished matter for a polished lay:
And many are the smooth elaborate tribe
Who, emulous of thee, the shape describe
And fain would every shifting hue portray
Of restless nature. But thou, mighty seer!
'Tis thine to celebrate the thoughts that make
The life of souls, the truths for whose sweet sake
We to ourselves and to our God are dear.
Of nature's inner shrine thou art the priest,
Where most she works when we perceive her least."

The poet who succeeds in the sonnet enjoys at least this one great privilege:—that his name is associated with some of the most illustrious names in the history of English poetry, and for the obvious reason that comparatively very few have been successful in that form of metrical writing. The reader familiar with Shakspeare's sonnets—and who that loves his own language is not?—will not unfrequently find them recalled to his mind by the sonnets scattered through this volume; for, without the slightest appearance of imitation, there is a similarity in the vein of feeling,—in the expression of a desponding love, of self-reproach and regrets,—and in the play of fancy,—which redounds greatly to the honour of our contemporary. The following would not suffer by a direct comparison with Shakspeare's well-known and beautiful sonnet on the unchangeableness of love:—

"Is love a fancy or a feeling? No!
It is immortal as immaculate Truth.
'Tis not a blossom, shed as soon as youth
Drops from the stem of life; for it will grow
In barren regions, where no waters flow,
Nor ray of promise cheats the pensive gloom.
A darkling fire, faint hovering o'er the tomb,
That but itself and darkness naught doth show,
Is my love's being; yet it cannot die,
Nor will it change, though all be changed beside;
Though fairest beauty be no longer fair,
Though vows be false, and faith itself deny,
Though sharp enjoyment be a suicide,
And hope a spectre in a ruin bare."

Hartley Coleridge well knows that the sonnet may be used for other purposes than being charged with pensive regrets and the tender feelings. It was once the exclusive property of love and melancholy, who piped upon it by turns. Milton seized it and blew a blast that in a moment revealed its unknown tones, and it has since been sounded to animate the high and tumultuous passions,—to cheer a people in moments of virtuous exultation, and to shame them in the days of degeneracy and corruption. A thought in one of Milton's sonnets is finely amplified in the following:—

"LIBERTY.

"Say, what is Freedom? What the right of souls,
Which all who know are bound to keep or die,
And who knows not, is dead? In vain ye pry
In musty archives or retentive scrolls,
Charters and statutes, constitutions, rolls,
And remnants of the old world's history:—
These show what has been, not what ought to be,
Or teach at best how wiser Time controls
Man's futile purposes. As vain the search
Of restless factions, who, in lawless will,
Fix the foundations of a creedless church,—
A lawless rule,—an anarchy of ill.
But what is Freedom? Rightly understood,
A universal license to be good."

That is better doctrine than is brought to light by every class of politicians. We are not enthusiasts enough to fancy that a nation can be redeemed from political worthlessness by song; but it would be no difficult matter to show that the power of a popular poet may be a match against that of a demagogue. His influence may well be directed to control the feelings of a people,—to guide and to elevate them. The times are in need of writers to sustain a lofty tone of public sentiment; to depict, if it be only in fancy, a love of the common good, unqualified by private interest; to perpetuate, at least, the memory of the hardihood and simplicity of ancient patriotism. It may savour a little of satire, although we do not mean it as such, to say that this is a duty for the poets. Tyrtæus was blind of one eye, lame of a leg, something of a dwarf, and quite deformed: he could not have been what is called "a *pretty* poet," but he was, for all that, a good general. The vigour of a thousand swords was in his strains. Although we imagine it is more difficult to draw out votes, the modern weapons, than it was to draw out swords, yet, may not somewhat of the terror of Tyrtæus's lyre be revived? There is a power in poetry for him who knows how to wield it, that can awaken the sensibilities of a people not quite sunk into the last stages of forgetfulness and torpidity.

In order to enable the reader to form his opinion of the sonnets contained in this volume, we are induced to add two more to our quotations,—one on the vision of poets, conceived in a fine classical mood:—

"The vale of Tempe had in vain been fair,—
Green Ida never deemed the nurse of Jove,—
Each fabled stream, beneath its covert grove,
Had idly murmured to the idle air,—
The shaggy wolf had kept his horrid lair
In Delphi's cell and old Trophonius' cave,—
And the wild wailing of the Ionian wave
Had never blended with the sweet despair
Of Sappho's death-song,—if the sight inspired
Saw only what the visual organs show;
If heaven-born fantasy no more required
Than what within the sphere of sense may grow;
The beauty to perceive of earthly things,
The mounting soul must heavenward plume her wings."

The other is a charming instance of the strange thoughts that come into a poet's mind:—

"What was't awakened first the untried ear
Of that sole man who was all human kind?
Was it the gladsome welcome of the wind,
Stirring the leaves that never yet were sere?
The four mellifluous streams which flowed so near,
Their lulling murmurs all in one combined?
The note of bird unnamed? The startled hind
Bursting the brake,—in wonder, not in fear
Of her new lord? Or did the holy ground
Send forth mysterious melody to greet
The gracious pressure of immaculate feet?
Did viewless seraphs rustle all around,
Making sweet music out of air as sweet?
Or his own voice awake him with its sound?"

It is the meditative power of these poems that we have principally adverted to, not only because it is the property most favourably distinguishing them from the productions of many of the fraternity, but because it is that upon which the expectation of future success may be raised most securely. But this quality does not of itself constitute *poetry*, nor is it likely to form the most successful poetry, if it occur apart from the higher of the more properly poetical powers,—the imagination. It is the combined action of thought and imagination—of the reflective and creative powers—that indicates poetic genius; and, from observing traces of that action on many of his pages, we are led to believe that there is no poetic effort from which Hartley Coleridge need shrink, if the powers with which he is gifted are duly cultivated and actively exerted. We should be glad to see him adventuring an ode.

In every poetic mind—whether of the writer or the reader of poetry—there are certain subsidiary powers not to be overlooked. The poems in this volume, which, after the series of sonnets, are grouped under the title of "Thoughts and Fancies," contain, amid some of a high mood, several varieties of the lighter forms of poetry. In the songs there is something that reminds us of the gracefulness of Moore's Melodies,—his easy flow of versification, and the admirable art with which he gives wings to a sentiment. The piece entitled "A Medley" is an agreeable specimen of fancy disporting in its own nature,—revelling in its lawlessness,—darting away not quite out of sight, but far and wildly enough to occasion an amusing perplexity to readers who are sober-minded to an extreme,—straitened by a sort of intellectual over-righteousness. The following lines are of a more convenient length for quotation, and, though more regular in their conception, may illustrate the author's manner in what may be designated poems of fancy:—

"WHAT I HAVE HEARD.

"I've heard the merry voice of spring,
When thousand birds their wild notes fling
Here and there and everywhere,
Stirring the young and gladsome air:
I've heard the many-sounding seas,
And all their various harmonies,—
The tumbling tempest's dismal roar,
On the waste and wreck-strewed shore,—
The howl and the wail of the prisoned waves,
Clamouring in the ancient caves,
Like a stifled pain that asks for pity:
And I have heard the sea at peace,
When all its fearful noises cease,

Lost in one soft and multitudinous ditty,
Most like the murmur of a far-off city:
Nor less the blither notes I know,
To which the inland waters flow,—
The rush of rocky-bedded rivers,
That madly dash themselves to shivers;
But anon, more prudent growing,
O'er countless pebbles smoothly flowing,
With a dull, continuous roar,
Hie they onward, evermore:
To their everlasting tune
When the sun is high at noon,
The little billows, quick and quicker,
Weave their mazes, thick and thicker,
And beneath, in dazzling glances,
Labyrinthine lightning dances,
Snaky network intertwining,
With thousand molten colours shining,—
Mosaic rich with living light,
With rainbow-jewels gayly dight:
Such pavement never, well I ween,
  Was made, by monarch or magician,
For Arab or Egyptian queen;
  'Tis gorgeous as a prophet's vision:
And I ken the brook, how sweet it tinkles,
As 'cross the moonlight green it twinkles,
Or heard, not seen, mid tangled wood,
When the soft stockdove lulls her brood
With her one note of all most dear,—
More soothing to the heart than ear:
And well I know the smothered moan
  Of that low breeze, so soft and brief,
It seems a very sigh, whose tone
  Has much of love, but more of grief.
I know the sound of distant bells,
Their dying falls and lusty swells,—
That music which the wild gale seizes
And fashions howsoe'er it pleases.
And I love the shrill November blast,

That through the brown wood hurries fast
And strips its old limbs bare at last,
Then whirls the leaves in circling error,
As if instinct with life and terror;
Now bursting out enough to deafen
The very thunder in the heaven,
Now sinking dolefully and dreary,
Weak as a child with sport aweary.
And after a long night of rain,
When the warm sun comes out again,
I've heard the myriad-voicéd rills,—
The many tongues of many hills,—
All gushing forth in new-born glory,
Striving each to tell its story;
Yet every little brook is known
By a voice that is its own,
Each exulting in the glee
Of its new prosperity."

The longest poem in the volume is the tale of "Leonard and Susan,"—a narrative in which there is rather too much dallying with grief. It is one of those pieces of unmitigated tragedy in which the heart craves relief. The picture of their young loves, with which the poem opens, abounds with very delicate touches of nature and feeling:—

"They were a gentle pair, whose love began
They knew not when: they knew not of a time
When they loved not. In the mere sentient life
Of unremembered infancy, whose speech,
Like secret love's, is only smiles and tears,
The baby Leonard clapped his little hands,
Leaped in his nurse's arms, and crowed aloud,
When Susan was in sight, and uttered sounds
Most strange, and strangely sweet, that nothing meant
But merely joy, as in the greenwood tree
The merry merle awakes his thrilling song
Soon as the cool breath of the vernal dawn

Stirs the light leaflets on the motionless boughs.
Mute as the shadow of a passing bird
On glassy lake, the gentle Susan lay,
Hushed in her meek delight. A dimpled smile
Curled round her tiny, rosy mouth, and seemed
To sink, as light, into her soft full eyes,—
A quiet smile, that told of happiness
Her infant soul investing, as the bud
Enfolds the petals of the nascent rose.

"Born in one week, and in one font baptized
On the same festal day, they grew together;
And their first tottering steps were hand in hand,
While the two fathers, in half-earnest sport,
Betrothed them to each other. Then 'twas sweet
For mothers' ears to hear them lisp and try
At the same words, each imitating each;
But Leonard was the babe of nimbler tongue,
And 'Sister Susan' was the first plain phrase
His utterance mastered: by that dear kind name
He called the maid, supplying so a place
Which nature had left void. An only child
Of a proud mother and a high-born sire,
Full soon he learned to mount a palfrey small,
Of that dwarf race that prance unclaimed and free
O'er the bleak pastures of the Shetland Isles.
And who may tell his glory or his pride
When Susan, by her mother's arms upheld,
Sat, glad though fearful, on the courser's rear,
While he, exulting in his dauntless skill,
Reined its short testy neck and froward mouth,
Taming its wilful movement to the pace
That palfrey suits of wandering lady fair?
Bold were his looks; his speech was bold and shrill;
His smooth round cheeks glowed with a ruddy brown;
And dark the curls that clustered o'er his head,
Knotty and close. In every pliant limb
A noble boy's ambitious manliness
Elastic sprung. Yet child more loving, fond,
Ne'er sought the refuge of a parent's side.

But Susan was not one of many words,
Nor loud of laughter, and she moved as soft
As modest nymphs, in work of artist rare,
Seem moving ever. In her delicate eye
And damask cheek there dwelt a grace retired,
A prophecy of pensive womanhood.
And yet, in sooth, she was a happy child;
And, though the single treasure of her house,
She neither missed a brother's love, nor lacked
The blest emotions of a sister's soul.
She thought no sister loved a brother more
Than she her brother Leonard,—him who showed
The strawberry lurking in the mossy shade,
The nest in leafy thicket dark embowered,
The squirrel's airy bound. No bliss he knew,
No toy had he,—no pretty property,—
No dog,—no bird,—no fit of childish wrath,—
That was not hers. The wild and terrible tales
His garrulous old nurse o'er night had told,
He duly in the morning told to her,
With comments manifold; and when seven years
Made him a student of learned Lilly's page,
With simple, earnest, kindly vanity,
He filled her wondering ear with all his lore
Of tense and conjugation, noun and verb;
Searching the word-book for all pretty names—
All dainty, doating, dear diminutives—
Which the old Romans used to woo withal."

Imagination and fancy do not of themselves make up the poet's nature; they are elements which are to be animated by quick and natural feeling. Has Hartley Coleridge the heart as well as the intellect of a poet? The motto, from Chaucer, upon his title-page, conveys a sort of profession that the volume is a collection of love-poems; and on many of its pages there are indications of a deep susceptibility to the attractions of female character, under the impulse of which he has given some very finished delineations of true womanly nature. From a number of more passionate pieces the following may be selected as an exquisite portrait of female dignity and sorrow:—

"STANZAS.

"She was a queen of noble nature's crowning:
A smile of hers was like an act of grace;
She had no winsome looks, no pretty frowning,
Like daily beauties of the vulgar race:
But, if she smiled, a light was on her face,—
A clear, cool kindliness, a lunar beam
Of peaceful radiance, silvering o'er the stream
Of human thought with unabiding glory;
Not quite a waking truth, not quite a dream:—
A visitation, bright and transitory.

"But she is changed,—hath felt the touch of sorrow;
No love hath she, no understanding friend;
Oh, grief! when Heaven is forced of earth to borrow
What the poor niggard earth has not to lend;
But when the stalk is snapt the rose must bend.
The tallest flower that skyward rears its head,
Grows from the common ground, and there must shed
Its delicate petals. Cruel fate, too surely,
That they should find so base a bridal bed
Who lived in virgin pride so sweet and purely!

"She had a brother, and a tender father,
And she was loved, but not as others are
From whom we ask a return of love,—but rather
As one might love a dream; a phantom fair
Of something exquisitely strange and rare,
Which all were glad to look on, men and maids,
Yet no one claimed;—as oft in dewy glades
The peering primrose, like a sudden gladness,
Gleams on the soul, yet unregarded fades:
The joy is ours, but all its own the sadness.

"'Tis vain to say her worst of grief is only
The common lot, which all the world have known:
To her 'tis more, because her heart is lonely,
And yet she hath no strength to stand alone.
Once she had playmates, fancies of her own,
And she did love them. They are passed away,
As fairies vanish at the break of day;
And, like a spectre of an age departed,
Or unsphered angel woefully astray,
She glides along,—the solitary-hearted."

We have rarely met with any thing more felicitous than that closing line; the being described with such self-restraining power—never too much revealed from the cloud of mystery that envelops it—passes away an object of admiration more than of love,—too sacred for common human sympathy. The same pure feeling towards the sex pervades the volume, and finds expression in some elegiac pieces of a very touching character. There is evidence in the volume of a susceptibility to other emotions than the passion of love, and we are glad of it, for we have no great partiality for the poet amatory exclusively, whom we are tempted to fancy a sort of "Master Slender,"—"a softly-sprighted man, with a little yellow beard," who has but one thought, "Sweet Anne Page!" and no other recollections than "stewed prunes" and the bear-garden. Love-poets find their profit in the easy access they gain to the soft hearts that abound all the world over. But the true poet must deal with other feelings beside the one master-passion,—kindly affections, and calm and placid impulses As far as a writer's character may be conjectured from his writings, Hartley Coleridge must be a gentle and right-hearted being. Omitting those instances in which he speaks dramatically, there is an air of sincerity in his expressions of feeling which mightily wins his reader's good-will. We must except his expressions of mirth, which have not a real or healthy tone; and, although there are in the volume words which, as Jeremy Taylor says, are "as light as the skirt of a summer-garment," yet they seem to be rather the relief of a heavy heart than the ventings of a light one. Passing them by, the beauty of sincerity is not the least of the beauties of the following lines:—

"SENSE, IF YOU CAN FIND IT.

"Like one pale, flitting, lonely gleam
Of sunshine on a winter's day,
There came a thought upon my dream,
I know not whence, but fondly deem
It came from far away.

"Those sweet, sweet snatches of delight
That visit our bedarkened clay
Like passage-birds, with hasty flight:—
It cannot be they perish quite,
Although they pass away.

"They come and go, and come again;
They're ours, whatever time they stay:
Think not, my heart, they come in vain
If one brief while they soothe thy pain
Before they pass away.

"But whither go they? No one knows
Their home; but yet they seem to say
That far beyond this gulf of woes
There is a region of repose
For them that pass away!"

We feel as if we should be missing a rare opportunity for appropriate quotation, considering the approaching season, if we passed by the stanzas on "New Year's Day." We are pretty confident that the year will come to its close without producing any thing conceived in better feeling, and that many a New Year's sermon will be preached to duller ears. At all events, the stanzas will be less likely than the sermons to be applied by those to whom they are addressed, away from themselves, to their neighbours. We have ventured to call attention, by means of italics, to some of the lines which show the exuberance of the poet's fancy :—

"NEW YEAR'S DAY.

"While the bald trees stretch forth their long lank arms,
And starving birds peck nigh the reeky farms:
While houseless cattle paw the yellow field,
Or, coughing, shiver in the pervious bield,
And naught more gladsome in the hedge is seen
Than the dark holly's grimly-glistening green:
At such a time the ancient year goes by
To join its parent in eternity;
At such a time the merry year is born,
Like the bright berry from the naked thorn.

"The bell rings out; the hoary steeple rocks:
Hark! the long story of a score of clocks;
For once a year the village clocks agree,—
E'en clocks agree to sound the hour of glee;
And every cottage has a light awake,
Unusual stars long flicker o'er the lake;
The moon on high, if any moon be there,
May peep, or wink; no mortal now will care:
For 'tis the season when the nights are long.
There's time, ere morn, for each to sing his song.

"The year departs. A blessing on its head!
We mourn not for it, for it is not dead.

Dead? What is that? A word to joy unknown,
Which love abhors, and faith will never own.
A word whose meaning sense could never find,
That has no truth in matter, nor in mind.
The passing breezes gone as soon as felt,
The flakes of snow that in the soft air melt,
The wave that whitening curls its frothy crest
And falls to sleep upon its mother's breast,
The smile that sinks into a maiden's eye,—
They come, they go, they change; they do not die.
So the old year—that fond and formal name—
Is with us yet, another and the same.

"And are the thoughts that ever more are fleeing,
The moments that make up our being's being,
The silent workings of unconscious love,
Or the dull hate which clings, and will not move,
In the dark caverns of the gloomy heart,
The fancies wild and horrible, which start
Like loathsome reptiles from their crankling holes,
From foul, neglected corners of our souls:—
Are these less vital than the waves or wind,
Or snow that melts and leaves no trace behind?
Oh! let them perish all, or pass away,
And let our spirits feel a New Year's day.

"A New Year's day! 'tis but a term of art,—
An arbitrary line upon the chart
Of time's unbounded sea,—fond Fancy's creature,
To reason alien, and unknown to nature.
Nay: 'tis a joyful day,—a day of hope!
Bound, merry dancer, like an antelope;
And as that lovely creature, far from man,
Gleams through the spicy groves of Hindostan,
Flash through the labyrinth of the mazy dance
With foot as nimble, and as keen a glance.

"And we, whom many New Year's days have told
The sober truth that we are growing old,

For this one night—ay, and for many more—
Will be as jocund as we were of yore.
Kind hearts can make December blithe as May,
And in each morrow find a New Year's day."

Hartley Coleridge is an egotist; and gracefully does his egotism sit upon him. It is one of the poet's privileges. There are expressions throughout the volume calculated to excite commiseration and somewhat of curiosity in some breasts,—murmurings of self-reproach,—repinings after mis-spent time and neglected talent, together with intimations of domestic griefs. We know not what it may all mean, but certain are we that there is an air of sad reality about it: it is no fantastic woe,—none of the old *fashion* of melancholy that may be traced from the days of Ben Jonson's "Master Stephen" down to the times of Lord Byron. It is not possible to suspect Hartley Coleridge of playing any such small game,—of following the worn-out device of enacting "*Il Penseroso*" for effect. His allusions to his poverty do him honour, and we cannot believe that one who has learned to depict nature with the delicacy and fidelity which mark this volume has been idle, or unprofitably employed. At all events, he has before him the time and the power of self-recovery. Throwing aside all distrust of the poetic power of the English tongue, let him not waver or be drawn down by any despondency. Let him call to mind "the labour and intense study" which Milton looked upon as his portion in life, when he conceived the thought of "a work not to be raised from the heat of youth, nor to be obtained by the invocation of Dame Memory and her siren daughters, but by devout prayer to that eternal

Spirit who can enrich with all utterance and knowledge, and sends out his seraphim, with the hallowed fire of his altar, to touch and purify the lips of whom he pleases." Let him look to his favourite Wordsworth, and see what that career is which befits him who meditates the great achievements in verse, and we have no fear but that at some future day we shall behold him on higher ground than the beautiful effusions in the present volume. It has been our object to make our readers acquainted with a name that is well worth the knowing, and we have thus, we flatter ourselves, been helping Mr. Hartley Coleridge to gain some of his distant fame,—a commodity that loses none of its value because it comes from far away. We take our leave of him, for the present, by quoting a poem of exquisite finish and beauty, which we have reserved for a final impression :—

"THE SABBATH DAY'S CHILD.

TO ELIZABETH, INFANT-DAUGHTER OF THE REV. SIR RICHARD FLEMING, BART.

"Pure, precious drop of dear mortality,—
Untainted fount of life's meandering stream,
Whose innocence is like the dewy beam
Of morn, a visible reality,
Holy and quiet as a hermit's dream,—
Unconscious witness to the promised birth
Of perfect good, that may not grow on earth
Nor be computed by the worldly worth
And stated limits of morality,—
Fair type and pledge of full redemption given,
Through Him that saith, 'Of such is the kingdom of heaven.'

"Sweet infant, whom thy brooding parents love
For what thou art, and what they hope to see thee,

Unhallowed spirits and earth-born phantoms flee thee;
Thy soft simplicity—a hovering dove,
That still keeps watch, from blight and bane to free thee;
With its weak wings, in peaceful care outspread,
Fanning invisibly thy pillowed head—
Strikes evil powers with reverential dread
Beyond the sulphurous bolts of fabled Jove,
Or whatsoe'er of amulet or charm
Fond Ignorance devised to save poor souls from harm.

"To see thee sleeping on thy mother's breast,
It were indeed a lovely sight to see:
Who would believe that restless sin can be
In the same world that holds such sinless rest?
Happy art thou, sweet babe, and happy she
Whose voice alone can still thy baby-cries,
Now still itself; yet pensive smiles, and sighs,
And the mute meanings of a mother's eyes,
Declare her thinking, deep felicity,—
A bliss, my babe, how much unlike to thine,
Mingled with earthly fears, yet cheered with hope divine!

"Thou breathing image of the life of nature!
Say, rather, image of a happy death;
For the vicissitudes of vital breath,
Of all infirmity the slave and creature,
That by the act of being perisheth,
Are far unlike that slumber's perfect peace
Which seems too absolute and pure to cease,
Or suffer diminution or increase,
Or change of hue, proportion, shape, or feature;
A calm, it seems, that is not, shall not be,
Save in the silent depths of calm eternity.

"A star reflected in a dimpling rill
That moves so slow it hardly moves at all,—
The shadow of a white-robed waterfall,
Seen in the lake beneath when all is still,—
A wandering cloud that, with its fleecy pall,

Whitens the lustre of an autumn moon,—
A sudden breeze that cools the cheek of noon,
Not marked till missed, so soft it fades, and soon,—
Whatever else the fond inventive skill
Of Fancy may suggest,—cannot supply
Fit semblance of the sleeping life of infancy.

"Calm art thou as the blessed Sabbath eve,
The blessed Sabbath eve when thou wast born;
Yet sprightly as a summer Sabbath morn,
When, surely, 'twere a thing unmeet to grieve;
When ribbons gay the village-maids adorn,
And Sabbath music on the swelling gales
Floats to the farthest nooks of winding vales
And summons all the beauty of the dales.
Fit music this a stranger to receive;
And, lovely child, it rung to welcome thee,
Announcing thy approach with gladsome minstrelsy.

"So be thy life,—a gentle Sabbath, pure
From worthless strivings of the work-day earth!
May time make good the omen of thy birth,
Nor worldly care thy growing thoughts immure,
Nor hard-eyed thrift usurp the throne of mirth
On thy smooth brow. And, though fast-coming years
Must bring their fated dower of maiden fears,
Of timid blushes, sighs, and fertile tears,—
Soft sorrow's sweetest offspring, and her cure,—
May every day of thine be good and holy,
And thy worst woe a pensive Sabbath melancholy!"

THE END.

STEREOTYPED BY L. JOHNSON AND CO.
PHILADELPHIA.

www.ingramcontent.com/pod-product-compliance
Lightning Source LLC
LaVergne TN
LVHW020238110826
845151LV00003B/963

9781425529901